U.S. SECURITIES AND EXCHANGE COMMISSION

FISCAL YEAR 2013 AGENCY FINANCIAL REPORT

About This Report

The U.S. Securities and Exchange Commission's (SEC) fiscal year (FY) 2013 Agency Financial Report (AFR) provides financial and high-level performance results that enable the President, Congress and the public to assess the SEC's accomplishments and understand its financial picture. This report satisfies the reporting requirements contained in the following laws and regulations:

- Accountability of Tax Dollars Act of 2002
- Chief Financial Officers Act of 1990, as amended by the Reports Consolidation Act of 2000
- Dodd-Frank Wall Street Reform and Consumer Protection Act Section 922 Whistleblower Protection, and Section 963 Annual Financial Controls Audit
- Federal Financial Management Improvement Act of 1996
- Federal Managers Financial Integrity Act of 1982
- Government Management Reform Act of 1994
- GPRA Modernization Act of 2010
- Improper Payments Information Act of 2002, as amended by IPERA and IPERIA
- Office of Management and Budget Circular A-123, *Management's Responsibility for Internal Controls*
- Office of Management and Budget Circular A-136, *Financial Reporting Requirements*
- Recovery Auditing Act, Section 831, Defense Authorization Act, for 2002

For the second year in a row, the SEC is producing an AFR, with a primary focus on financial results, and an Annual Performance Report (APR), which focuses on strategic goals and performance results, in lieu of a combined Performance and Accountability Report. The FY 2013 APR will be included in the SEC FY 2015 Congressional Budget Justification in February 2014. Additionally, SEC will publish a Summary of Performance and Financial Information (SPFI), also to be released in February 2014. This AFR and prior year SEC AFRs are electronically available at *www.sec.gov/about/secreports.shtml*. To comment on this report, email SECAFR@sec.gov.

Pages 2 and 18 of this FY 2013 Agency Financial Report were updated on December 17, 2013 to correct the error in the amount of disgorgement and penalties ordered in FY 2012, which was $3.1 billion, not $2.8 billion.

Certificate of Excellence in Accountability Reporting

For the seventh year in a row, the SEC received a Certificate of Excellence in Accountability Reporting from the Association of Government Accountants. The award is presented to Federal Government agencies whose annual reports achieve the highest standards demonstrating accountability and communicating results.

U.S. GOVERNMENT ACCOUNTABILITY OFFICE

441 G St. N.W.
Washington, DC 20548

December 16, 2013

The Honorable Mary Jo White
Chair
United States Securities and Exchange Commission

Financial Audit: Securities and Exchange Commission's Fiscal Years 2013 and 2012 Financial Statements

Dear Ms. White:

This report transmits the GAO auditor's report on the results of our audits of the fiscal years 2013 and 2012 financial statements of the United States Securities and Exchange Commission (SEC) and its Investor Protection Fund (IPF),[1] which is incorporated in the enclosed *U.S. Securities and Exchange Commission Fiscal Year 2013 Agency Financial Report*.

As discussed more fully in the auditor's report that begins on page 54 of the enclosed agency financial report, we found

- the financial statements are presented fairly, in all material respects, in accordance with U.S. generally accepted accounting principles;
- SEC maintained, in all material respects, effective internal control over financial reporting as of September 30, 2013, although internal control deficiencies regarding information security exist that merit attention by those charged with governance; and
- no reportable noncompliance in fiscal year 2013 with provisions of applicable laws, regulations, contracts, and grant agreements we tested.

The Accountability of Tax Dollars Act of 2002 requires that SEC annually prepare and submit audited financial statements to Congress and the Office of Management and Budget.[2] The Securities Exchange Act of 1934, as amended in 2010 by the Dodd-Frank Wall Street Reform and Consumer Protection Act (Dodd-Frank Act), requires SEC to annually prepare and submit a complete set of audited financial statements for IPF to Congress.[3] We agreed, under our audit authority, to audit SEC's and IPF's financial statements. Section 963 of the Dodd-Frank Act further requires that (1) SEC annually submit a report to Congress describing management's responsibility for internal control over financial reporting and for assessing the effectiveness of

---

[1]IPF was established in 2010 by section 922 of the Dodd-Frank Wall Street Reform and Consumer Protection Act to fund the activities of SEC's whistleblower award program and the SEC Office of Inspector General suggestion program. IPF is a separate SEC fund and its financial statements present SEC's financial activity associated with its whistleblower and Inspector General suggestion programs. Accordingly, IPF's financial transactions are also included in SEC's overall financial statements.

[2]31 U.S.C. § 3515.

[3]Section 21F(g)(5) of the Securities Exchange Act of 1934, 15 U.S.C. § 78u-6(g)(5).

such internal control during the fiscal year, (2) the SEC Chairman and Chief Financial Officer attest to SEC's report, and (3) GAO attest to and report on the assessment made by SEC.[4] Accordingly, this report also includes our reporting in response to the requirement under the Dodd-Frank Act.

––––––––

We are sending copies of this report to the Chairmen and Ranking Members of the Senate Committee on Banking, Housing, and Urban Affairs; the Senate Committee on Homeland Security and Governmental Affairs; the House Committee on Financial Services; and the House Committee on Oversight and Government Reform. We are also sending copies to the Secretary of the Treasury, the Director of the Office of Management and Budget, and other interested parties. In addition, the report is available at no charge on the GAO website at http://www.gao.gov.

If you or your staff have questions about this report, please contact me at (202) 512-3133 or dalkinj@gao.gov. Contact points for our Offices of Congressional Relations and Public Affairs may be found on the last page of this report.

Sincerely yours,

James R. Dalkin
Director
Financial Management and Assurance

Enclosure

––––––––––––––––––––––––

[4]Dodd-Frank Act, Pub. L. No. 111-203, § 963(a), (b) (2), 124 Stat. 1376, 1910 (2010), *codified at* 15 U.S.C. § 78d-8(a), (b)(2).

Contents

Available on the Web at *www.sec.gov/about/secafr2013.shtml*

To contact the SEC, please see *www.sec.gov* or "Contact Us" at *www.sec.gov/contact.shtml*.
To comment on this report, email SECAFR@sec.gov.
For further information on selected terms and topics, please see "Fast Answers" at *www.sec.gov/answers.shtml*.

Message from the Chair

Over the past year, the men and women of the Securities and Exchange Commission continued to demonstrate an unyielding commitment to our core mission of protecting investors, promoting fair, orderly and efficient markets and facilitating capital formation.

Today, we can take pride in our many accomplishments in fiscal year 2013. We, among many other achievements: adopted significant rules to help reduce systematic risks in our financial system and rules intended to increase the flow of capital to smaller businesses while maintaining important safeguards for investors; successfully and aggressively pursued hundreds of enforcement actions covering a broad range of misconduct and market participants; and exploited new technology to bolster the integrity of our markets.

Through actions like these, and many others, the SEC is helping to ensure that the U.S. securities markets remain the envy of the world.

One of our major areas of activity was to implement the rules mandated by two landmark pieces of legislation—the Dodd-Frank Wall Street Reform and Consumer Protection Act (Dodd-Frank Act) and the Jumpstart Our Business Startups Act (JOBS Act).

Under the Dodd-Frank Act, the Commission moved closer toward finalizing an entirely new regulatory regime that will bring transparency to the multi-trillion dollar over-the-counter derivatives market and, for the first time, place major players in that market under regulatory supervision. The Commission also joined with several other federal agencies in proposing rules that would require sponsors of securitization transactions to retain a portion of the risk in the product being sold. The Commission acted as well to improve the supervision of clearing agencies; put in place a new regulatory regime for municipal advisors; and adopted the Volcker Rule, which will restrict banking entities from engaging in proprietary trading or from owning or sponsoring certain funds.

Under the JOBS Act, the Commission adopted new rules and advanced others intended to make it easier for small and emerging companies to raise funds, while also taking steps to ensure investors are protected in the process. We also provided guidance to companies, investors and other market participants navigating through the changes brought by the JOBS Act.

In addition to progressing towards implementation of Congressional rulemaking mandates, the Commission pursued other rules to protect investors and our financial system, including rules that would reform the way money market funds operate, as well as rules that would protect customers from the consequences of the financial failure of a broker-dealer.

Our enforcement program was very active in the past year, and we took steps to further enhance our robust program. We, for example, began to demand admissions of wrongdoing in certain cases where an added measure of public accountability was considered necessary. During the fiscal year, the agency also broadened our coverage of market participants, pursuing actions against a range of individuals and entities, including gatekeepers, like accountants and fund directors; exchanges and other trading platforms that lack required system controls; and municipal advisers, to name a few. By the end of the fiscal year, the agency obtained total penalties and disgorgements of $3.4 billion, an increase from the $3.1 billion awarded the year before.

There was also intensified focus on market structure issues, with the Commission taking a series of steps to further bolster the integrity of the markets. Among other things, the Commission proposed requirements for exchanges and other market platforms to develop reliable systems, to regularly test those systems and to correct and disclose irregularities that disrupt operations. Our market experts also continued to harvest and analyze millions of data inputs from the markets, using that data to inform further regulatory measures.

But our accomplishments were not confined to these areas. Our professionals across the entire agency worked to make our markets safer and more robust and efficient – from our information technology experts to our investor education staff; from our examiners and inspectors to our disclosure review teams who scour filings; and our administrative assistants to our financial experts who allow us to function effectively in so many areas.

I am pleased to report that the SEC's independent auditor, the Government Accountability Office, issued an unmodified audit opinion on the SEC's financial statements and has affirmed that the agency's financial statements are presented fairly in all material aspects, in conformity with the U.S. generally accepted accounting principles. The auditor report further indicated that we have remediated the two significant deficiencies identified in the prior year. A new significant deficiency was identified related to information security, for which we are implementing corrective actions. Based on our review, we can confirm that the financial and performance data presented in this report are complete, reliable and conform to the Office of Management and Budget guidance.

We continually look at our practices and processes in an effort to meet the ever-evolving challenges before us. Last year, as in prior years, the SEC rose to the occasion, and we must always strive to do more and do it better and more efficiently. I know that the staff of the SEC will continue to perform in an exemplary fashion in the coming year.

Mary Jo White
Chair
December 12, 2013

Introduction to the Agency Financial Report

The SEC Agency Financial Report (AFR) is organized in the following three major sections, and supplemental appendices.

Management's Discussion and Analysis

This section provides an overview of SEC's history, mission, organization, strategic goals and objectives, year in review, forward looking information, performance highlights and a summary of financial information. This section concludes with management's assurance on internal controls, financial systems and controls, and compliance with laws and regulations.

Financial Section

This section contains a message from the Chief Financial Officer followed by the independent auditor's report on our principal financial statements, management's response to the audit report, audited financial statements and accompanying notes, and required supplementary information. Concluding this section are stand-alone comparative financial statements and accompanying notes for the Investor Protection Fund as required by the Dodd-Frank Wall Street Reform and Consumer Protection Act.

Other Information

This section contains the statement prepared by the agency's Office of Inspector General (OIG) summarizing what the OIG considers to be the more serious management and performance challenges facing the agency followed by the SEC Chair's response outlining the agency's progress in addressing the challenges. Also included are a Summary of Financial Statement Audit and Management Assurances listing internal control material weaknesses and financial systems non-conformances; a schedule of spending showing how and where the SEC spends its funds; and a detailed explanation of any significant erroneous payments as required by the Improper Payments Information Act of 2002, as amended.

Appendices

This section includes biographies of the SEC Chair and Commissioners, a summary of the SEC's major enforcement cases, a listing of the SEC divisions and offices, a glossary of selected terms, and a list of acronyms used within the AFR.

MANAGEMENT'S DISCUSSION AND ANALYSIS

The U.S. Securities and Exchange Commission's (SEC) Management's Discussion and Analysis (MD&A) serves as a brief overview of this entire report. It provides a concise description of the agency's performance measures, financial statements, systems and controls, compliance with laws and regulations, and actions taken or planned. It also provides an assessment of the SEC's programs and financial performance, and the efficiency and effectiveness of the SEC's operations.

Information presented in this section satisfies the requirements for reporting on internal controls in Office of Management and Budget Circular A-123, *Management's Responsibility for Internal Control*.

Vision, Mission, Values and Goals

Vision

The SEC strives to promote a market environment that is worthy of the public's trust and characterized by transparency and integrity.

Mission

The mission of the SEC is to protect investors; maintain fair, orderly, and efficient markets; and facilitate capital formation.

Values

Integrity: As the Federal agency entrusted with regulating and conducting enforcement for the U.S. securities markets, each member of the SEC's workforce has a responsibility to demonstrate the highest ethical standards to inspire confidence and trust.

Accountability: The SEC embraces the responsibility with which it is charged. In carrying out its mission, SEC employees hold themselves accountable to the public and take responsibility for achieving the SEC's goals.

Effectiveness: The SEC strives to work creatively, proactively, and effectively in assessing and addressing risks to the securities markets, the public, and other market participants. The staff is committed to finding innovative and flexible approaches to the Commission's work and using independent judgment to explore new ways to fulfill the SEC's mission in the most efficient and effective manner possible.

Teamwork: The SEC recognizes that its success depends on a diverse, coordinated team committed to the highest standards of trust, hard work, cooperation, and communication. The staff is committed to working together and coordinating effectively with investors, businesses, governments, and other organizations in the U.S. and abroad.

Fairness: In exercising its regulatory and enforcement powers, the SEC treats investors, market participants, and others fairly and in accordance with the law. As an employer, the SEC seeks to hire and retain a skilled and diverse workforce, and to ensure that all decisions affecting employees and applicants are fair and ethical. As professionals, the staff treats all with respect and dignity.

Commitment to Excellence: The SEC is committed to the highest standards of excellence in pursuit of the agency's mission. The investing public and the U.S. securities markets deserve nothing less.

Strategic Goals and Outcomes

Strategic Goal 1: Foster and enforce compliance with the Federal securities laws

Outcome 1.1: The SEC fosters compliance with the Federal securities laws.

Outcome 1.2: The SEC promptly detects violations of the Federal securities laws.

Outcome 1.3: The SEC prosecutes violations of Federal securities laws and holds violators accountable.

Strategic Goal 2: Establish an effective regulatory environment

Outcome 2.1: The SEC establishes and maintains a regulatory environment that promotes high-quality disclosure, financial reporting, and governance, and that prevents abusive practices by registrants, financial intermediaries, and other market participants.

Outcome 2.2: The U.S. capital markets operate in a fair, efficient, transparent, and competitive manner, fostering capital formation and useful innovation.

Outcome 2.3: The SEC adopts and administers rules and regulations that enable market participants to understand clearly their obligations under the securities laws.

Strategic Goal 3: Facilitate access to the information investors need to make informed investment decisions

Outcome 3.1: Investors have access to high-quality disclosure materials that are useful to investment decision making.

Outcome 3.2: Agency rulemaking and investor education programs are informed by an understanding of the wide range of investor needs.

Strategic Goal 4: Enhance the Commission's performance through effective alignment and management of human, information, and financial capital

Outcome 4.1: The SEC maintains a work environment that attracts, engages, and retains a technically proficient and diverse workforce that can excel and meet the dynamic challenges of market oversight.

Outcome 4.2: The SEC retains a diverse team of world-class leaders who provide motivation and strategic direction to the SEC workforce.

Outcome 4.3: Information within and available to the SEC becomes a Commission-wide shared resource, appropriately protected, that enables a collaborative and knowledge-based working environment.

Outcome 4.4: Resource decisions and operations reflect sound financial and risk management principles.

History and Purpose

During the peak of the Depression, Congress passed the Securities Act of 1933[1] (Securities Act). This law, along with the Securities Exchange Act of 1934[2] (Exchange Act), which created the SEC, was designed to restore investor confidence in our capital markets by providing investors and the markets with more reliable information and clear rules of honest dealing. The main purposes of these laws were to ensure that:

- Companies publicly offering securities for investment dollars must tell the public the truth about their businesses, the securities they are selling, and the risks involved in investing.

- People who sell and trade securities – brokers, dealers and exchanges – must treat investors fairly and honestly, putting investors' interests first.

The SEC is responsible for overseeing the nation's securities markets and certain primary participants, including broker-dealers, investment companies, investment advisers, clearing agencies, transfer agents, credit rating agencies, and securities exchanges, as well as organizations such as the Financial Industry Regulatory Authority (FINRA), Municipal Securities Rulemaking Board (MSRB), and Public Company Accounting Oversight Board (PCAOB). Under the Dodd-Frank Wall Street Reform and Consumer Protection Act[3] (Dodd-Frank Act), the agency's jurisdiction was expanded to include certain participants in the derivatives markets, private fund advisers, and municipal advisers among other changes.

The SEC consists of five presidentially appointed Commissioners, with staggered five-year terms. One of them is designated by the President as Chair of the Commission (see *Appendix A: Chair and Commissioners*). President Franklin Delano Roosevelt appointed Joseph P. Kennedy to serve as the first Chairman of the SEC.

By law, no more than three of the Commissioners may belong to the same political party. The Commission convenes regularly at meetings that are open to the public and the news media unless the discussion pertains to confidential subjects, such as whether to begin an enforcement investigation.

Each year, the SEC brings hundreds of civil enforcement actions against individuals and companies for violation of securities laws. Examples of infractions include insider trading, accounting fraud, and providing false or misleading information about securities or the companies that issue them. One of the major sources of information that the SEC relies on to bring enforcement action is investors themselves – another reason that educated and careful investors are critical to the functioning of efficient markets. To help inform investors, the SEC offers the public a wealth of educational information on its website at *www.investor.gov*, as well as an online database of disclosure documents at *www.sec.gov/edgar/searchedgar/companysearch.html* that public companies and other market participants are required to file with the SEC.

---

[1] *Securities Act of 1933 www.sec.gov/about/laws/sa33.pdf*

[2] *Securities Exchange Act of 1934 www.sec.gov/about/laws/sea34.pdf*

[3] *Dodd-Frank Wall Street Reform and Consumer Protection Act www.sec.gov/about/laws/wallstreetreform-cpa.pdf*

Organizational Structure and Resources

SEC Office Locations

The SEC's headquarters are in Washington, DC, and the agency has 11 regional offices located throughout the country. The regional offices are responsible for investigating and litigating potential violations of the securities laws. The offices also have examination staff, who inspect regulated entities such as investment advisers, investment companies and broker-dealers. The map below shows the locations of the regional offices, and the states that are included in each region.

CHART 1.1

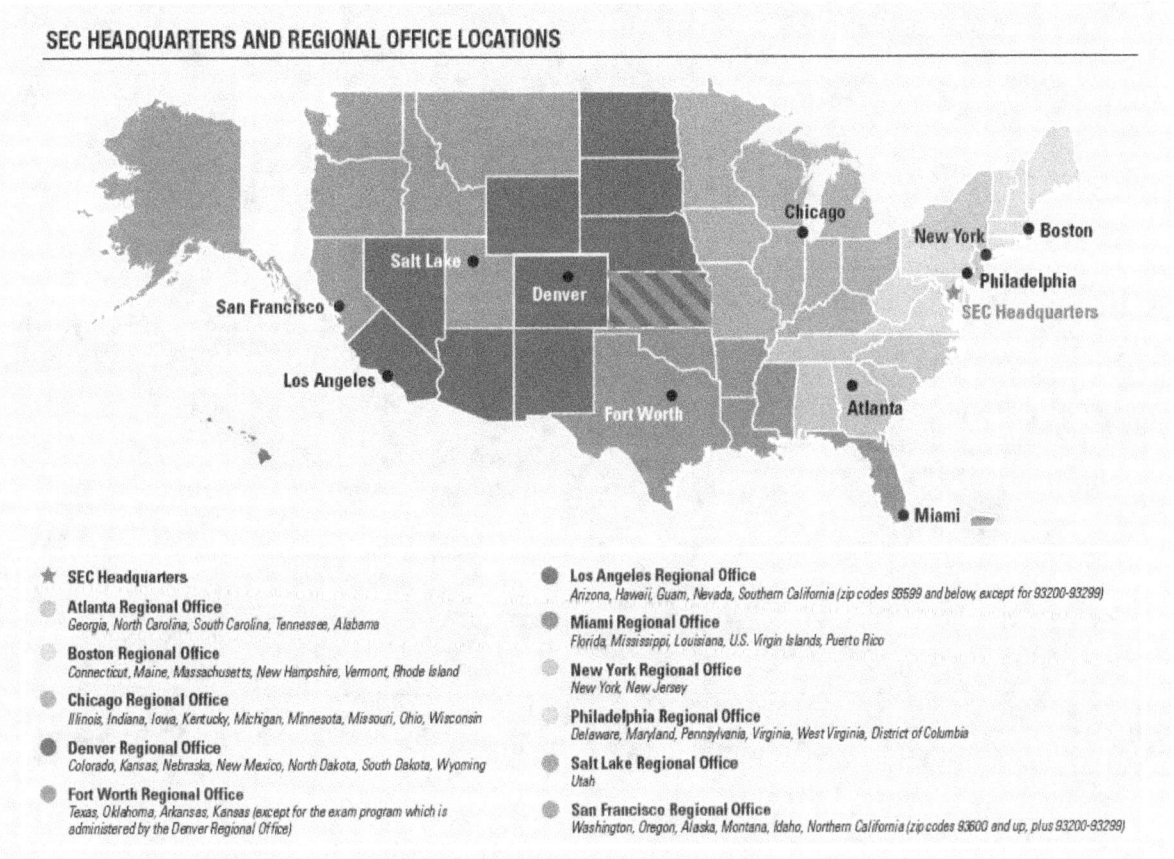

SEC HEADQUARTERS AND REGIONAL OFFICE LOCATIONS

★ **SEC Headquarters**

⬤ **Atlanta Regional Office**
Georgia, North Carolina, South Carolina, Tennessee, Alabama

⬤ **Boston Regional Office**
Connecticut, Maine, Massachusetts, New Hampshire, Vermont, Rhode Island

⬤ **Chicago Regional Office**
Illinois, Indiana, Iowa, Kentucky, Michigan, Minnesota, Missouri, Ohio, Wisconsin

⬤ **Denver Regional Office**
Colorado, Kansas, Nebraska, New Mexico, North Dakota, South Dakota, Wyoming

⬤ **Fort Worth Regional Office**
Texas, Oklahoma, Arkansas, Kansas (except for the exam program which is administered by the Denver Regional Office)

⬤ **Los Angeles Regional Office**
Arizona, Hawaii, Guam, Nevada, Southern California (zip codes 93599 and below, except for 93200-93299)

⬤ **Miami Regional Office**
Florida, Mississippi, Louisiana, U.S. Virgin Islands, Puerto Rico

⬤ **New York Regional Office**
New York, New Jersey

⬤ **Philadelphia Regional Office**
Delaware, Maryland, Pennsylvania, Virginia, West Virginia, District of Columbia

⬤ **Salt Lake Regional Office**
Utah

⬤ **San Francisco Regional Office**
Washington, Oregon, Alaska, Montana, Idaho, Northern California (zip codes 93600 and up, plus 93200-93299)

SEC Organization Structure

The SEC is an independent Federal agency established pursuant to the Exchange Act. It is headed by a bipartisan five-member Commission, comprised of the Chair and four Commissioners, who are appointed by the President and confirmed by the Senate (*see Appendix A: Chair and Commissioners*). The Chair serves as the chief executive. The agency's functional responsibilities are organized into five divisions and 23 offices, each of which is headquartered in Washington, DC. The SEC also has 11 regional offices which are comprised primarily of staff from the national enforcement and examination programs.

In fiscal year (FY) 2013, the agency employed 4,023 full-time equivalents (FTE), including 3,929 permanent and 94 temporary FTEs. The SEC organization chart below is as of September 30, 2013.

CHART 1.2

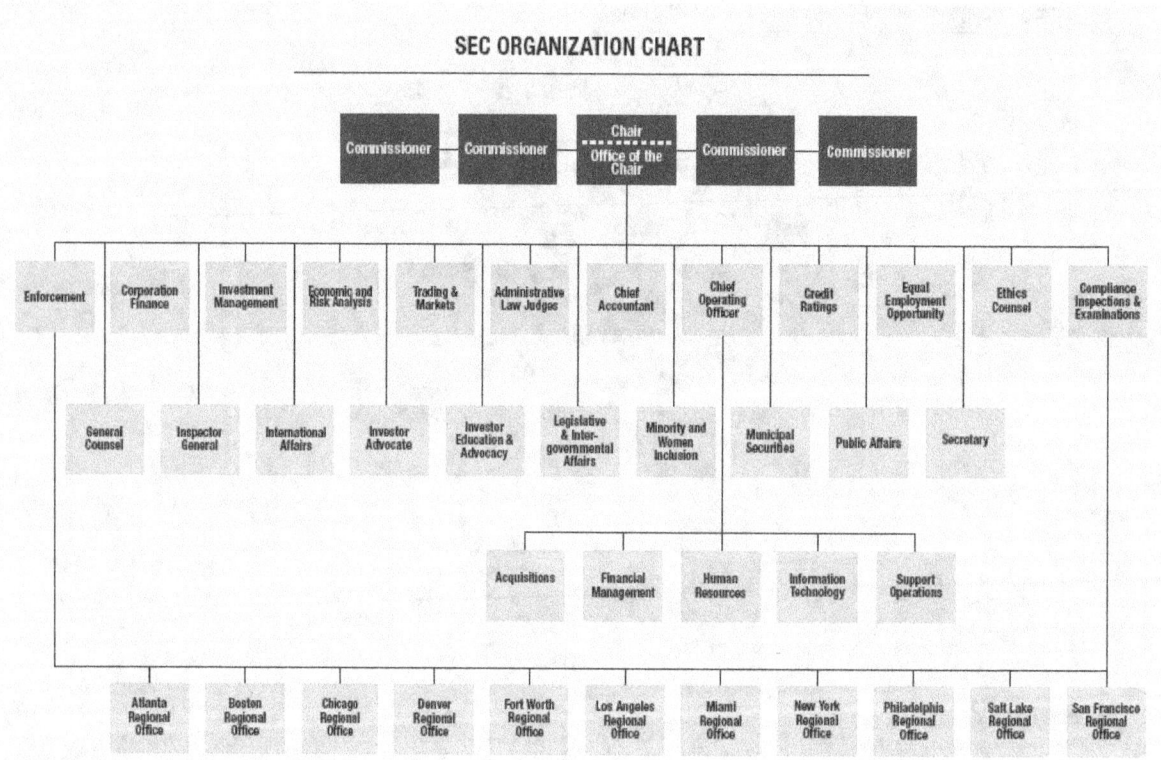

SEC Programs

The SEC organizes its divisions and offices under the 10 major programs outlined below in *Table 1.1, SEC Programs and Program Descriptions*.

TABLE 1.1
SEC PROGRAMS AND PROGRAM DESCRIPTIONS

Program	Divisions and Offices	Program Descriptions
Enforcement	Division of Enforcement and enforcement staff within the SEC's regional offices	This program investigates and brings civil charges in Federal district court or in administrative proceedings based on violations of the Federal securities laws. An integral part of the program's function is to seek penalties and the disgorgement of ill-gotten gains in order to return funds to harmed investors. Also organized within the Enforcement program is the Office of the Whistleblower, created under the Dodd-Frank Act to administer the SEC's Whistleblower Program that rewards individuals who provide the agency with tips that lead to successful enforcement actions.
Compliance Inspections and Examinations	Office of Compliance Inspections and Examinations and examinations staff within the SEC's regional offices	This program conducts the SEC's examinations of registrants such as investment advisers, investment companies, broker-dealers, self-regulatory organizations (SROs), credit rating agencies, transfer agents, and clearing agencies.
Corporation Finance	Division of Corporation Finance	This program performs functions to help investors gain access to materially complete and accurate information about securities, and to deter fraud and misrepresentation in the public offering, trading, voting, and tendering of securities.
Trading and Markets	Division of Trading and Markets	This program conducts activities to establish and maintain standards for fair, orderly and efficient markets, while fostering investor protection and confidence in the markets.
Investment Management	Division of Investment Management	This program seeks to minimize the financial risks to investors from fraud, mismanagement, self-dealing, and misleading or incomplete disclosure in the investment company and investment adviser segments of the financial services industry.
Economic and Risk Analysis	Division of Economic and Risk Analysis	The division provides economic analyses as part of the Commission's rulemaking process; supports its rule review, examination and enforcement programs with data-driven, risk-based analytical methods; and oversees its Tips, Complaints and Referrals (TCR) and interactive data programs.
General Counsel	Office of the General Counsel	The Office of the General Counsel (OGC) serves as the chief legal officer of the Commission and provides independent legal analysis and advice to the Chairman, Commissioners, and operating divisions on all aspects of the Commission's activities. The General Counsel also defends the Commission in Federal district courts, represents the Commission in all appellate matters and *amicus curiae* filings, and oversees the SEC's bankruptcy program.

(Continued on next page)

TABLE 1.1 *Continued from previous page*

Program	Divisions and Offices	Program Descriptions
Other Program Offices	• Office of the Chief Accountant; • Office of Investor Education and Advocacy; • Office of International Affairs; • Office of Administrative Law Judges; • Office of the Investor Advocate • Office of Credit Ratings; and • Office of Municipal Securities	These offices are responsible for: • Serving as the chief advisor to the Commission on all accounting and auditing policy and overseeing private sector standards setting; • Serving investors who contact the SEC, ensuring that retail investors' perspectives inform the Commission's regulatory policies and disclosure program, and improving investors' financial literacy; • Administering the rules of the Commission with respect to the practices of municipal securities brokers and dealers, municipal advisors, and investors in municipal securities, and the practices of nationally recognized statistical rating organizations (NRSROs), including examinations of NRSROs; • Advancing international regulatory and enforcement cooperation, promoting converged high regulatory standards worldwide, and facilitating technical assistance programs in foreign countries; and • Adjudicating allegations of securities law violations.
Agency Direction and Administrative Support	• The Chair and Commission; • Office of Legislative and Intergovernmental Affairs; • Office of Public Affairs; • Office of the Secretary; • Office of the Chief Operating Officer; • Office of Financial Management; • Office of Information Technology; • Office of Human Resources; • Office of Acquisitions; • Office of Support Operations; • Office of the Ethics Counsel; • Office of Minority and Women Inclusion; and • Office of Equal Employment Opportunity	The Chair is responsible for overseeing all aspects of agency operations, and the Chair and Commissioners are responsible for the review and approval of enforcement cases and formal orders of investigation and the development, consideration, and execution of policies and rules. The other offices in Agency Direction and Administrative Support are responsible for: • Working with Members of Congress on issues that affect the Commission; • Coordinating the SEC's communications with the media, the general public, and foreign visitors; • Reviewing all documents issued by the Commission, and preparing and maintaining records of Commission actions; • Maximizing the use of SEC resources by overseeing the strategic planning, information technology, procurement, financial management, records management, human resources, and administrative functions of the agency; • Ensuring that the SEC is an equal opportunity employer in full compliance with all Federal equal employment opportunity laws; and • Enhancing the diversity of the SEC's workforce, contractors, and regulated entities in accordance with existing Federal laws and regulations.
Inspector General	Office of Inspector General	The Office of Inspector General (OIG) is an independent office that conducts audits of programs and operations of the SEC and investigations into allegations of misconduct by staff or contractors. The mission of OIG is to detect fraud, waste, and abuse and to promote integrity, economy, efficiency, and effectiveness in the SEC's programs and operations.

As shown in the *Statements of Net Cost* on page 65, the SEC presents its net costs of operations by the programs outlined above, consistent with the presentation used by the agency in submitting its budget requests.

Fiscal Year 2013 in Review

Continuing the Commitment to Excellence

In fiscal year (FY) 2013, under the leadership of three separate Chairs, the SEC continued to pursue an aggressive rulemaking agenda, strengthen its enforcement and examination programs, and enhance its technological capabilities to better oversee the increasingly complex and rapidly changing securities markets.

At the same time, the SEC continued to carry out the many day-to-day responsibilities that often go unnoticed but, nevertheless, are a critical part of its ability to fulfill its mission to protect investors, ensure that markets operate fairly and efficiently, and facilitate capital formation.

Throughout the fiscal year, and with renewed intensity following the appointment of Mary Jo White as the 31st Chair of the SEC, one of the agency's top priorities has been the completion of the many rulemaking mandates stemming from the Dodd-Frank Wall Street Reform and Consumer Protection Act of 2010 (Dodd-Frank Act) and the Jumpstart Our Business Startups Act (JOBS Act). This legislation brought sweeping changes to the financial markets and charged the SEC with implementing a myriad of rules to address a diverse set of challenges.

Over the past fiscal year alone, the SEC moved forward with rules designed to, among other things, address the application of U.S. regulation of security-based swaps to the cross-border activities of U.S. and non-U.S. market participants, ease capital access for companies without putting investors at risk, regulate for the first time municipal financial advisors, and provide disclosure about the ratio of a Chief Executive Officer's (CEO's) compensation to the median compensation of the company's workforce.

The SEC's major rulemaking efforts, however, extended beyond the Congressional mandates. Most notably, the agency also advanced rules that would reform the money market fund industry to make funds less susceptible to runs and enhance the financial responsibility of broker-dealers through improved capital requirements and protections for customer assets.

In FY 2013, the SEC also implemented new policies and practices designed to ensure that its enforcement and examination programs continue to be as vigorous and aggressive as possible. For example, the agency began to insist on admissions in certain cases and employ cutting-edge analytics created in-house to identify potentially fraudulent conduct. The SEC also pursued violations of all shapes and

sizes, including complex cases stemming from the financial crisis, to send a strong message of deterrence.

In addition, the SEC took steps during the past fiscal year to bolster the integrity of the securities markets. Among other things, the agency continued to implement a variety of controls intended to reduce extraordinary volatility and proposed new rules to increase the operational integrity of the technology and systems that are at the core of today's securities markets. The SEC also developed a new website designed to promote a better understanding of equity market structure and help inform future regulatory activity by providing wide-ranging market data and analyses to investors and other market participants.

The SEC continued to employ robust data analytics that have reaped benefits across the agency in the areas of rulemakings, enforcement actions, examinations, and many other responsibilities central to the SEC's mission.

Finally, the SEC continued to educate investors about risky investments, coordinate with foreign counterparts, modernize agency technology, and scrutinize disclosures to ensure that investors are getting appropriate information.

Building on the many achievements and internal reforms of the recent past, the SEC has established a broader and more effective presence through the use of innovative strategies, new technology, and the work of experienced, talented experts throughout the agency.

An Intensified Rulemaking Program

In FY 2013, the SEC intensified its efforts to advance a broad rulemaking agenda. This included continuing its commitment to executing the mandates of the Dodd-Frank Act and JOBS Act, the most significant changes to the regulation of financial markets in decades. At the same time, the agency pursued important new rules addressing other issues critical to its mission, including money market funds, the financial responsibility of broker-dealers and the operational integrity of the financial markets.

These rulemaking efforts have been supported by comprehensive implementation of the SEC staff guidance on economic analysis. The guidance supports a determined, agency-wide effort to craft regulations that create strong and effective safeguards for investors, while maintaining efficiency and avoiding undue burdens on market participants.

The Dodd-Frank Act

The Dodd-Frank Act contains more than 90 provisions that require SEC rulemaking. Over the past fiscal year, the SEC has continued to build on its implementation effort with rules addressing the over-the-counter derivatives market, clearing agencies, the municipal markets, securitization, and other areas.

Derivatives

The SEC continued to advance a broad-based rulemaking program to implement Title VII of the Dodd-Frank Act, which requires the creation of an entirely new regulatory framework for over-the-counter derivatives. To date, the SEC has proposed substantially all the core rules required by Title VII, adopted a number of final rules and interpretations, provided a "roadmap" to implementation of Title VII, and taken other actions to provide legal certainty to market participants during the implementation process.

In the past fiscal year, the SEC took a major step forward by proposing rules and interpretive guidance regarding the application of Title VII to cross-border security-based swap transactions. These rules are designed to clarify the governing regulatory requirements for parties to a transaction that occurs in part outside the United States. The proposal also would provide guidance regarding the requirements for trading platforms and clearing agencies to register with the Commission.

As part of its effort to create the new regulatory framework, the SEC also proposed financial responsibility requirements for security-based swap dealers and major security-based swap participants. If adopted, these rules would determine the amount of capital that dealers in security-based swaps need to hold; when and how these dealers need to collect collateral or margin to protect against losses from counterparties; and how these dealers segregate and protect funds and securities held for customers.

Clearing Agencies

In FY 2013, the SEC took a number of steps to improve the supervision of clearing agencies, with particular focus on those designated by the Financial Stability Oversight Council as systemically important. These steps included the adoption of new standards focused on the risk management practices of all registered clearing agencies, expansion of the agency's resources focused on clearing agency supervision, and the implementation of new consultation practices with the Federal Reserve Board in connection with planning annual compliance examinations and reviewing certain rule filings by clearing agencies.

Municipal Markets

In the municipal markets area, the SEC adopted rules implementing a new regulatory regime for municipal advisors. These rules require individuals who provide advice to municipal entities and obligated persons regarding municipal financial products and bond issuances to register with the Commission and be subject to a fiduciary duty. Before the Dodd-Frank Act, these individuals were largely unregulated in their capacity as municipal advisors.

Securitization

The SEC, along with five other Federal agencies, revised a proposed rule from 2011 requiring sponsors of securitization transactions to retain risk in those transactions. The re-proposed rule would provide sponsors of asset-backed securities with several options to satisfy the risk retention requirements. To inform the development of the re-proposed rule, agency staff prepared a white paper analyzing the effect of loan and borrower characteristics on serious delinquencies among securitized private label mortgages.

Investor Advisory Committee

The SEC's Investor Advisory Committee (IAC), established by the Dodd-Frank Act, advises the Commission on regulatory priorities, the regulation of securities products, trading strategies, fee structures, the effectiveness of disclosure, and on initiatives to protect investor interests and promote investor confidence and the integrity of the securities marketplace. In FY 2013, the IAC submitted its initial recommendations for review and consideration by the Commission. These recommendations addressed universal proxy ballots, data tagging, target date mutual funds and implementation of the JOBS Act rulemaking mandate to remove the ban on general solicitation in private offerings.

Additional Dodd-Frank Act Activities

In FY 2013, the SEC engaged in a number of additional rulemaking and other activities under the Dodd-Frank Act:

- The SEC proposed a rule that would require public companies to disclose the ratio of the compensation of its CEO to the median compensation of its employees. The rule would not prescribe a specific methodology for companies to use in calculating this ratio, but would provide a company with the flexibility to determine the median annual total compensation of its employees in a manner that suits its individual circumstances.

- The SEC adopted rules required by the Dodd-Frank Act disqualifying convicted felons and other "bad actors" from participating in securities offerings under Rule 506 of Regulation D including offerings that use general solicitation and advertising under new rules adopted by the Commission as required by the JOBS Act.

- The SEC adopted rules allowing broker-dealers to continue to engage in retail foreign exchange transactions while the Commission studies the practices of broker-dealers and investors in the foreign exchange market.

- The SEC adopted rules requiring broker-dealers to conduct searches for holders of securities with whom they have lost contact. Previously, these types of searches were required only of recordkeeping transfer agents, who are the intermediaries between clearing agencies and broker-dealers.

- The SEC and the Commodity Futures Trading Commission (CFTC) adopted rules designed to improve the integrity and privacy of investors' personal information by requiring broker-dealers, mutual funds and investment advisers, among others, to adopt and administer programs to identify and respond to "red flags" that may indicate potential identity theft.

- The SEC staff completed a report to Congress regarding matters related to assigning credit ratings for structured finance products, including a discussion of potential regulatory or statutory changes that the Commission could consider if it determines to implement such assignments or an alternative.

- The SEC issued a public request for data and other information seeking input from all interested parties concerning the benefits and costs of the current standards of conduct for broker-dealers and investment advisers. The request was a follow-up to a 2011 staff study making two principal recommendations: that the Commission develop rules to implement a uniform fiduciary standard of conduct for investment advisers and brokers-dealers when they provide personalized investment advice about securities to retail investors; and that the Commission consider harmonization of regulatory requirements for broker-dealers and investment advisers when it would add meaningfully to investor protection.

The JOBS Act

The JOBS Act requires the SEC to implement rules and issue studies in a number of areas designed to promote initial public offerings (IPOs) of smaller companies and small business capital formation. The SEC worked diligently throughout the year to complete these mandates.

General Solicitation

The SEC adopted JOBS Act-mandated rules eliminating the prohibition against general solicitation and general advertising in securities offerings under Rule 506 of Regulation D and Rule 144A. This market continues to be a significant source of capital, with more than $900 billion of unregistered offerings reported in 2012.

In conjunction with these new rules, the SEC also proposed additional amendments to Regulation D and certain other rules to enhance its ability to evaluate the development of market practices following the elimination of the ban on general solicitation and general advertising. The rule proposal would require issuers to provide additional information about these offerings, implement a new mechanism for enforcing compliance with certain filing requirements and mandate certain legending requirements.

Additional JOBS Act Activities

Beyond rulemaking, the SEC's Division of Corporation Finance (Corporation Finance) continued to simplify the process for submitting draft registration statements for confidential non-public review, as permitted by the JOBS Act. Corporation Finance also provided interpretive guidance to issuers and their advisors on the implementation and application of the JOBS Act.

In addition, the SEC staff issued a required report on the authority to enforce certain Exchange Act rules that require certain issuers to file periodic and current reports with the Commission. The staff concluded that the enforcement tools currently available to the Commission are sufficient to enforce the anti-evasion provision of Rule 12g5-1, and that legislative recommendations regarding enforcement tools were unnecessary.

Other Major Rulemaking Initiatives

Beyond the many Dodd-Frank Act and the JOBS Act rulemaking mandates, the SEC continued to advance significant rulemaking efforts to better protect investors and maintain market integrity.

Money Market Funds

Drawing on legal expertise, economic analysis, and regulatory experience from across the agency, the SEC proposed measures to reduce the risk of contagion from rapid, heavy money market fund redemptions. The Commission's proposal included two principal alternative reforms that could be adopted alone or in combination: requiring a floating net asset value for prime institutional money market funds; and facilitating the use of liquidity fees and redemption gates in times of redemption stress. The Commission's proposed rulemaking was informed by a comprehensive staff study addressing three major issues: the determinants of investor behavior and its effect on money market fund performance during the 2008 financial crisis; the effect of the SEC's 2010 money market fund reform rulemaking; and how potential future reforms could affect the demand for investments in money market funds and their substitutes across different markets.

Broker-Dealer Financial Responsibility

The SEC also took significant steps to enhance the financial responsibility framework for broker-dealers. This framework helps to protect customers from the consequences of the financial failure of a broker-dealer by, among other things, requiring the safeguarding of customer securities and funds held by the broker-dealer.

- The SEC adopted amendments to the net capital, customer protection, books and records, and notification rules for broker-dealers. The amendments are designed to better protect a broker-dealer's customers and enhance the SEC's ability to monitor and prevent unsound business practices.

- The SEC adopted amendments to certain broker-dealer annual reporting, audit and notification requirements to better facilitate audits of broker-dealers conducted in accordance with Public Company Accounting Oversight Board (PCAOB) standards, as required by the Dodd-Frank Act. The PCAOB subsequently approved two new attestation standards tailored to the SEC's amendments that substantially strengthen the audit requirements for broker-dealers.

Further, the SEC proposed amendments to the financial responsibility rules that would raise current capital requirements for certain larger broker-dealers and subject such broker-dealers to new liquidity standards.

A More Aggressive Enforcement Effort

The SEC's strong performance in financial crisis-related enforcement actions carried over into the post-financial crisis environment. While continuing to bring important cases related to the financial crisis, the agency also dedicated resources to pursuing cases involving other ongoing threats to investors and the markets. In building an impressive record of successful actions on a number of these fronts, the SEC sent notice to institutions, investors, and would-be violators that the SEC is a strong and sophisticated enforcer, ready to take swift and forceful action against violators of the securities laws. The message conveyed to the market was clear: no institution is too large to be held to account and no violation is too small to escape scrutiny.

The SEC ended the fiscal year with 686 enforcement actions, including 402 in the last six months of the year. These numbers do not, however, reflect the outstanding quality of the enforcement actions brought during the year. In FY 2013, the Division of Enforcement (Enforcement) brought groundbreaking cases across the range of substantive priority areas, uncovered and pursued sophisticated wrongdoing, obtained meaningful and targeted remedies, including industry and officer and director bars, and recovered billions of dollars for investors.

Enforcement's breadth consistently spans the entire industry spectrum and FY 2013 was no exception. The fiscal year was marked by the pursuit of institutions and individuals whose misconduct led to or exacerbated the financial crisis, strategic prosecution of "smaller" violations in an effort to send a broader deterrent message, novel investigation of market structure issues and improper conduct by exchanges, relentless focus on those who trade illegally based on material non-public information, and enhanced attention to gatekeepers, misconduct in the municipal securities market, investment advisors, and activities occurring beyond U.S. borders that have an impact in the United States.

Of course, deterrence remains the most effective enforcement strategy. Therefore, in addition to pursuing creative, aggressive strategies for conducting investigations and bringing actions, Enforcement increased the deterrent value of its actions in a number of ways: developing new tools that expanded the agency's reach; seeking stronger penalties, which raised the opportunity cost of malfeasance; crafting more focused remedies, including conduct-based injunctions and requiring admissions in certain cases; and coordinating more closely with other SEC divisions and offices, as well as with other regulatory and law enforcement agencies, to identify suspicious activity more rapidly and investigate it more effectively.

The SEC's enforcement presence has helped to foster a market environment that bolsters investor confidence and enhances market integrity.

Increased Deterrence

Enforcement sent a strong deterrent message through its aggressive pursuit of monetary penalties and other remedies. In the fiscal year, total penalties and disgorgement ordered increased to $3.4 billion, up from $3.1 billion in the prior fiscal year. Notable matters included:

- Hedge fund advisory firm CR Intrinsic Investors LLC, an affiliate of S.A.C. Capital, agreed to the largest insider trading settlement in SEC history, settling charges that it participated in an insider trading scheme involving a clinical trial for an Alzheimer's drug. Under the terms of this historic settlement, CR Intrinsic was required to pay more than $600 million, including disgorgement of almost $275 million, $52 million in prejudgment interest, and a $275 million penalty.

- The SEC charged J.P. Morgan Chase & Co. with misstatements of its financial results and a lack of effective controls to prevent or detect a scheme to conceal the extent of massive trading losses. J.P. Morgan settled the charges, admitting publicly that it had violated Federal securities laws and paying a $200 million penalty.

- Total S.A. disgorged $153 million in illicit profits obtained through bribes paid to intermediaries of an Iranian government official in exchange for his assistance in obtaining valuable contracts with the National Iranian Oil Company.

- Nasdaq Stock Market, LLC paid a $10 million penalty, the largest ever against a stock exchange, after being charged with securities laws violations resulting from its poor systems and decision-making during the IPO and secondary market trading of Facebook shares.

In FY 2013, in a significant departure from past practice, the SEC announced that it would require admissions of facts and misconduct in cases where there is a heightened need for public accountability, particularly where the misconduct is egregious, involves large numbers of investors, or poses serious risks to the markets. The SEC made clear that it would be prepared to proceed to trial if alleged violators refuse to admit or acknowledge what they did.

- In the SEC's first settlement implementing this policy shift, New York-based hedge fund adviser Phillip A. Falcone and his advisory firm, Harbinger Capital Partners, admitted to multiple acts of misconduct that harmed investors and interfered with the normal functioning of the securities markets. The defendants also agreed to settle the SEC enforcement action by paying more than $18 million in disgorgement, interest and fines, and Falcone agreed to be barred from the securities industry for five years.

- In the settlement with J.P. Morgan Chase & Co. referenced above, the SEC required J.P. Morgan to admit to a 15-page statement of detailed facts and that its conduct violated Federal securities laws.

Financial Crisis Cases

In FY 2013, the SEC continued to hold accountable individuals and entities whose misconduct contributed to the worst financial crisis since the Great Depression. Through the end of the fiscal year, the SEC has filed 96 separate enforcement actions against 161 individuals and corporate entities relating to the financial crisis. These cases resulted in $2.73 billion in disgorgement, penalties, and other monetary relief. Most of this money has been or will be distributed to harmed investors.

Of the individuals charged in the financial crisis cases, 66 were CEOs, CFOs or other senior corporate executives, and 70 percent of the 105 individuals in these actions were charged in litigated complaints or administrative proceedings, demonstrating that the SEC is ready and willing to litigate. Of these individuals, 36 have been barred from the securities industry or from serving as officers or directors of public companies.

- The SEC won its jury trial against Fabrice Tourre, a former Goldman, Sachs & Co. employee charged with fraud for his role in assembling a complicated financial product without proper disclosure of the risks involved. In July 2010, Goldman settled charges in the same case by paying $550 million and undertaking to reform its business practices. Tourre, however, did not settle. Consequently, with significant support from its Office of International Affairs (OIA), the SEC pursued this complex case through three years of pretrial proceedings before proceeding to trial and winning a multi-week jury trial, highlighting the strength of the agency's trial unit.

- The SEC continued to pursue cases against the largest and most powerful financial institutions for their role in the financial crisis, including cases against Bank of America,

Capital One Financial, Credit Suisse Securities, J.P. Morgan Securities and UBS Securities. Together, these matters resulted in penalties and disgorgement of more than $468 million.

Pursuing Smaller Violations

Even with a number of headline-making actions, Enforcement maintained an eye on smaller technical and compliance-related violations. When minor violations are overlooked or ignored, they can feed bigger violations and foster a culture where laws are treated as mere guidelines. Accordingly, the SEC moved to pursue smaller infractions through streamlined investigative and settlement approaches. For example, the SEC obtained disgorgement – ranging from $4,000 to more than $2.5 million – from nearly two dozen firms for violations of Rule 105, an anti-manipulative rule that prohibits firms from improperly participating in public offerings soon after short-selling those same stocks. Other noteworthy examples are the cases arising from an initiative spearheaded by Enforcement's Asset Management Unit in coordination with the SEC's Office of Compliance, Inspections and Examination's (OCIE) examination program. The initiative is designed to address repeated compliance failures at registered investment advisers that may lead to bigger problems, by having Enforcement's Asset Management Unit work proactively with OCIE examiners to ensure that firms have viable compliance programs in place, as required by law, and by pursuing appropriate enforcement actions when they do not.

Market Structure and Exchanges

As the technologies on which the financial system relies grow increasingly complex and intertwined, Enforcement must be focused on engaging with exchanges and alternative trading systems that do not have the required controls over their trading functions, do not treat all investors fairly or do not provide equal access to critical market information. Enforcement actions in this area, which are critical to ensuring public confidence in our securities markets, included the following:

- The SEC charged Boston-based dark pool operator eBX LLC with failing to protect its subscribers' confidential trading information and failing to disclose to all of its subscribers that eBX LLC allowed an outside firm to use the subscribers' confidential trading information. eBX had informed its subscribers that their flow of orders

to buy or sell securities would be kept confidential and not shared outside of its alternative trading system. eBX agreed to pay an $800,000 penalty to settle the charges.

- The SEC obtained its first-ever financial penalty for violations related to an exchange's failure to discharge its regulatory oversight obligations. The penalty resulted from an action against the Chicago Board Options Exchange and its affiliate, C2 Options Exchange, in which the SEC alleged that there were various systemic breakdowns in their regulatory and compliance functions as a self-regulatory organization, including a failure to enforce or even fully comprehend rules to prevent abusive short selling.

Insider Trading

The SEC continued its relentless pursuit of individuals who trade unlawfully on material, nonpublic information, which undermines investor confidence and threatens the level playing field that is fundamental to the integrity of the markets. During the fiscal year, the SEC brought 44 insider trading actions against a wide range of entities and individuals sending a resounding message of deterrence.

- The SEC charged Scott London, the former partner in charge of KPMG's Pacific Southwest audit practice, and his friend, Bryan Shaw, with insider trading on nonpublic information about KPMG clients. London allegedly tipped confidential details about five KPMG audit clients and enabled Shaw to make more than $1.2 million in illicit profits by trading ahead of earnings or merger announcements. London allegedly provided the tips in exchange for cash, jewelry, meals and tickets to entertainment events. Shaw allegedly traded on this information at least a dozen times and grossed more than $714,000 in illicit profits.

- In a matter related to the CR Intrinsic case, the SEC charged hedge fund manager Steven A. Cohen, who managed S.A.C. Capital, for failing to supervise former portfolio managers Matthew Martoma and Michael Steinberg to prevent them from engaging in insider trading. The SEC alleged that Cohen received information that should have caused any reasonable hedge fund manager to investigate the basis for the trades. Cohen's hedge funds earned profits and avoided losses of more than $275 million as a result of the illegal trades.

Gatekeepers

As part of the effort to enlarge its footprint, Enforcement focused on potential violations by gatekeepers, such as attorneys, accountants and fund directors. Gatekeepers play a critical role in the securities industry and have special duties and responsibilities to ensure that investor interests are safeguarded. The risks posed to investors by fraud, compliance breakdowns or other regulatory failure increases significantly when gatekeepers fail to perform their duties and responsibilities.

- Eight former regional directors of certain Morgan Keegan mutual funds, which were invested heavily in securities backed by subprime mortgages, were charged for failing to ensure that those assets were appropriately valued.

- The SEC filed an action against KPMG – the auditor of TierOne Bank – alleging that KPMG failed to scrutinize appropriately management's allowance for loans and lease losses. Even though the allowance related to one of the highest-risk areas of the audit, KPMG's auditors allegedly failed to act on numerous red flags or obtain sufficient support for management estimates of the fair value of the collateral underlying the bank's troubled loans, relying instead on stale appraisals and management's uncorroborated representations.

Municipal Securities

In FY 2013, the SEC's enforcement actions relating to the municipal securities market garnered significant attention as the agency remained focused on violations in this multi-trillion dollar marketplace. The SEC charged the full panoply of market participants, including municipalities, government officials, financial advisors and underwriters.

- The SEC charged the State of Illinois with securities fraud for misleading investors by failing to inform them of the impact of problems with a pension funding schedule prior to offering and selling more than $2.2 billion in municipal bonds.

- The SEC charged the City of Harrisburg (Pennsylvania) with securities fraud for making misleading public statements at a time when its financial condition was deteriorating, and for providing financial information to investors in its municipal bonds that was either incomplete or outdated. This action marked the first time the SEC charged a municipality for misleading statements made outside of its securities disclosure documents.

- The SEC charged the City of Miami (Florida) and its former budget director with securities fraud for making materially false and misleading statements and omissions about certain interfund transfers in three 2009 bond offerings totaling $153.5 million. They also allegedly made false and misleading statements in the city's fiscal year 2007 and 2008 annual financial reports. The budget director allegedly orchestrated the transfers from the city's capital improvement fund to its general fund to mask increasing deficits in the general fund, a key indicator of financial health.

Investment Advisers

A large number of individuals and institutions invest a significant amount of assets with investment advisers, making oversight of these financial professionals critical to the securities markets. The SEC continued to pursue actions against investment advisers who engage in fraudulent conduct, who lack effective compliance programs, who misrepresent their investment returns and who breach their fiduciary duties to their clients.

- The SEC charged former hedge fund advisory firm Yorkville Advisors LLC, its founder and President Mark Angelo, and CFO Edward Schinik with scheming to overvalue assets under management and exaggerate the reported returns of hedge funds they managed in order to hide losses and increase the fees collected from investors, which included pension funds. The defendants also allegedly misrepresented the safety and liquidity of the investments made by the hedge funds, and charged at least $10 million in excessive fees to the funds based on fraudulently inflated values of Yorkville's assets under management.

- The SEC charged Oppenheimer & Co. and former Oppenheimer portfolio manager Brian Williamson in separate actions with misleading investors about the valuation and performance of a fund consisting of private equity funds. Oppenheimer agreed to pay more than $2.8 million to settle the charges.

- The SEC charged Charles Dushek, Sr., his son, Charles Dushek, Jr., and their Illinois-based investment advisory firm, Capital Management Associates, Inc., with violations of the Federal securities laws for defrauding its clients in a "cherry picking" scheme that garnered the Dusheks nearly $2 million in illicit profits. The SEC alleged that the Dusheks placed securities trades without designating in advance whether they were trading their personal funds or the funds of the firm's clients, and delayed allocating the trades until they knew whether the trades would be profitable. The Dusheks then allegedly allocated winning trades to their personal accounts and dumped losing trades on the firm's unwitting clients.

- The SEC charged the CEO of Chicago-based investment advisory firm Simran Capital Management with lying to clients, including the California Public Employees' Retirement System, and potential clients about the amount of assets under management.

International Enforcement

In today's global financial markets, where securities fraud crosses borders, international cooperation, particularly as it relates to enforcement matters, is paramount to ensuring transparency and public confidence in the markets. In FY 2013, Enforcement continued to improve its international enforcement efforts on several fronts.

- The SEC charged Eli Lilly and Company for violations of the Foreign Corrupt Practices Act (FCPA) for improper payments its subsidiaries made to foreign government officials to obtain millions of dollars of business in Russia, Brazil, China and Poland. The SEC alleged that the pharmaceutical company's subsidiary in Russia used offshore "marketing agreements" to pay millions of dollars to third parties chosen by government customers or distributors. These offshore entities rarely provided any services and, in some instances, were used to funnel money to government officials in order to obtain business for the subsidiary. The SEC further alleged that after the company became aware of possible FCPA violations in Russia, it failed to curtail the subsidiary's use of the marketing agreements for more than five years. Eli Lilly subsidiaries in Brazil, China, and Poland also made improper payments to government officials or third-party entities associated with government officials. Eli Lilly agreed to pay more than $29 million to settle the SEC's charges.

- As noted above, the SEC charged France-based oil and gas company Total S.A. with violating the FCPA by paying $60 million in bribes to intermediaries of an Iranian government official in exchange for his assistance in obtaining valuable contracts with the National Iranian Oil Company for Iran. Total S.A. agreed to pay disgorgement of more than $153 million in illicit profits and to retain an independent compliance consultant to review and consult on its compliance with the FCPA.

In addition, the SEC's Cross-Border Working Group continued to focus on companies with substantial foreign operations that are publicly traded in the United States. The working group's efforts have contributed significantly to the filing of fraud cases against more than 65 foreign issuers or executives, and the deregistering of securities of more than 50 companies.

- The SEC alleged that China-based China MediaExpress and its CEO fraudulently misled investors about the company's financial condition by touting cash balances that were millions of dollars higher than the actual amounts. China MediaExpress was charged with violations of reporting, books and records and internal control provisions, and its CEO was charged with a violation of the SEC's rules prohibiting lying to auditors and with making false certifications in filings required by the Sarbanes-Oxley Act. The agency sought financial penalties, permanent injunctions, disgorgement, and an officer and director bar against the CEO.

OIA also continued to improve coordination and cooperation with foreign securities regulators and other overseas regulators and law enforcement agencies. During the fiscal year, OIA made 717 outgoing requests for assistance and responded to 508 incoming requests.

- OIA obtained documents, bank account and brokerage records, and Internet service provider information in a variety of cases, and advised SEC litigators on international service of process and cross border discovery mechanisms.

- OIA experts helped trace, freeze and repatriate proceeds of securities fraud that were transferred offshore, coordinating with receivers in foreign litigation, foreign criminal authorities and financial intelligence units. In FY 2013, OIA assisted in freezing approximately $72 million and repatriating approximately $36 million.

Supporting Enforcement Efforts

In FY 2013, the SEC expanded its use of technology and analytical tools to produce an unprecedented quantity of high-quality cases – using data to determine ill-gotten gains, harm to investors, materiality, valuation and market manipulation.

- The SEC's Division of Economic and Risk Analysis (DERA) provided expert testimony in support of Enforcement's successful request to freeze assets and protect investor funds in a $150 million scheme allegedly orchestrated by Anshoo R. Sethi to defraud foreign investors seeking profitable returns and a legal path to U.S. residency through a Federal visa program.

- Economists provided valuable assistance in several market manipulation investigations by creating algorithms to analyze the order and transaction files of high-speed traders and quantify the extent of abusive trading. In one action, the founders of a Canadian broker-dealer, Biremus, were barred and the broker-dealer's registration revoked after analysis revealed that brokers repeatedly engaged in a manipulative practice called "layering."

- DERA staff also assisted the Federal prosecutors who charged Level One Global Investors co-founder Anthony Chiasson and former Diamondback Capital Management

portfolio manager Todd Newman with insider trading, by analyzing evidence of materiality, and by supporting the cross-examination of expert witnesses retained by the defendants. The testimony proffered by defendants' experts was largely excluded and ultimately both defendants were found guilty.

- The recently formed Center for Risk and Quantitative Analytics (CRQA) supports and coordinates Enforcement's risk identification, risk assessment and data analytic activities by identifying risks and threats that could harm investors, and by assisting staff nationwide in conducting risk-based investigations and developing methods of monitoring possible wrongdoing. CRQA works with other SEC divisions and offices to provide strategic guidance on resource allocation in light of identified risks, and serves as an analytical hub during searches for patterns indicative of possible fraud or other illegality.

- The SEC developed the Advanced Bluesheet Analysis Program, an initiative to analyze data on specific securities transactions provided to the SEC by market participants and identify suspicious trading in advance of market-moving events. This analysis can aid in identifying relationships among different parties involved in a suspicious trade or series of trades, which might not otherwise be apparent.

A More Effective Examination Program

OCIE's National Examination Program (NEP) is an integral part of the SEC's multi-faceted approach to protect investors and safeguard the integrity of our markets. Every year, under the auspices of the NEP, OCIE conducts risk-based examinations of a vast array of registered entities, such as broker-dealers, investment advisers, investment companies, the national securities exchanges, self-regulatory organizations, transfer agents and clearing agencies, to assess their compliance with the applicable regulatory requirements. OCIE makes strategic use of the findings from these examinations, not only to address deficiencies at the registrant level, but also more broadly, to foster its mission to improve industry compliance, detect and prevent fraud, monitor risk and inform policy. In FY 2013, OCIE conducted 1,615 formal examinations of registrants, which is a slight increase over the prior two fiscal years. OCIE also monitored the activities of thousands of other registrants through non-examination surveillance and filing reviews.

Promoting and Improving Industry Compliance

OCIE's mission and robust compliance programs go hand-in-hand. Guided by this principle, OCIE instituted a nationwide outreach effort to support and improve industry compliance through better communication and transparency concerning OCIE's priorities, higher profiles for registrants' compliance programs and ensuring that registrants have the proper "tone at the top."

- OCIE published its first-ever annual public statement of examination priorities, which were determined by OCIE senior management and staff in consultation with senior representatives from SEC divisions and offices. The priorities were determined through careful analysis and risk-assessment of a wealth of information, including information reported by registrants on required filings, information gathered through examinations, communications with other Federal, state and foreign regulators, and industry and media publications.

- OCIE issued public "Risk Alerts," setting forth findings and observations from examinations, including areas of non-compliance that were common among registrants.

- OCIE conducted regional and national industry outreach conferences, providing effective forums for industry participants to gain a better understanding of examination priorities and common observations of deficiencies, and to discuss best practices for compliance programs.

- OCIE conducted enterprise risk management meetings with CEOs, boards of directors and senior management of certain large registrants, including seven of the country's largest financial service firms. OCIE used these meetings to, among other things, reiterate the critical role of compliance in enterprise risk management and assess "tone at the top" and commitment to effective compliance programs.

- OCIE conducted nearly 50 Corrective Action Review examinations to determine whether registrants had implemented agreed-upon corrective actions that adequately addressed deficiencies noted in prior examinations.

- OCIE launched a nationwide Presence Exam Initiative, which uses risk-based examinations of recently registered private fund investment advisers to educate them on their regulatory obligations.

Identifying and Preventing Fraud

The vast majority of deficiencies that OCIE identifies during examinations are resolved through the examination process itself. In addition to its important role in ensuring that registrants address deficiencies noted in examinations, OCIE plays an equally important role in identifying fraud and other serious misconduct. When OCIE uncovers information in an examination indicating or suggesting such misconduct, it refers the matter to Enforcement for investigation and appropriate action. In FY 2013, OCIE made more than 200 such referrals, many of which resulted in enforcement actions. Some notable examples are described below:

- In a matter involving J.S. Oliver Capital Management, L.P., an OCIE examination uncovered evidence of numerous violations by the investment advisory firm and its President, Ian O. Mausner, ultimately resulting in charges against both. The SEC alleged that the firm awarded more profitable trades to hedge funds in which Mausner and his family had invested and treated other clients improperly by allocating less profitable trades to them, resulting in approximately $10.7 million in client losses. The SEC also alleged that Mausner misused soft dollar credits and rebates from brokerage firms, misappropriating more than $1.1 million of client funds that he used for his personal benefit.

- In a matter involving City Securities Corporation, a municipal bond underwriter, an OCIE examination uncovered evidence that led to charges against the firm and its client, a school district in Indiana, for false statements to investors that the school district had

properly provided annual financial information and notices that were required as part of its prior bond offerings.

- An OCIE examination uncovered evidence that led to a Commission action involving the brokerage firm Direct Access Partners, alleging a scheme involving millions of dollars in bribes to a high-ranking Venezuelan finance official to obtain the bond-trading business of a state-owned Venezuelan bank. Based on Enforcement's ensuing investigation, the SEC charged four individuals of the firm, two of whom were also indicted by the Department of Justice.

- An OCIE examination of a hedge fund adviser led to charges that the adviser breached his fiduciary duty in connection with an undisclosed principal transaction of $7.5 million, which constituted a conflict of interest. The adviser was also prosecuted criminally, pleading guilty to several charges, including making false statements to the OCIE staff.

- OCIE examinations also uncovered evidence of violations by three investment advisory firms of requirements related to custody of clients' assets, which ultimately resulted in charges against all three firms.

OCIE continues to employ innovative approaches to improve and refine its examination process, and enhance its approach to identifying and preventing fraud. For instance, OCIE created specialized working groups in a number of key areas, such as Equity Market Structure and Trading Practices, Microcap Fraud, and Valuation. These working groups bring a wealth of subject matter expertise to complex areas and coordinate closely with the examination teams, providing "real time" advice on novel and complex issues. OCIE also developed a risk analysis examination team, which uses sophisticated data analytics to collect and distill voluminous amounts of data from registrants, and cull patterns that suggest problematic conduct warranting further scrutiny.

In addition, OCIE collaborates with other areas in the agency and with other regulatory and law enforcement agencies in its continuing effort to identify and prevent serious misconduct. For example, OCIE teamed up with the SEC's Division of Trading and Markets (Trading and Markets), the Federal Reserve, the Internal Revenue Service and the Department of Justice on an anti-money laundering task force established to evaluate and recommend measures to enhance the

protections afforded by the Bank Secrecy Act, its implementing regulations and guidance, and the accompanying civil and criminal enforcement mechanisms.

Informing Policy

As the SEC's "eyes and ears" on the ground, OCIE is often called upon to assist in the rulemaking process and other policy guidance issued by the SEC and it divisions and offices.

- OCIE examined investment companies, in close coordination with other SEC divisions and offices, focusing on payments to fund distributors, undisclosed compensation for sales of fund products, and the various forms of payments to distributors for access to their platforms and/or sales force. OCIE's findings and information from these examinations will aid the SEC's evaluation of the impact of Rule 12b-1 and other rules related to fund distribution.

- The SEC's Division of Investment Management (Investment Management), aided by findings from OCIE examinations, issued guidance to address circumstances in which application of the Investment Adviser Act Custody Rule to non-tradeable, uncertificated securities resulted in increased costs to investors with little corresponding benefit.

- OCIE's Presence Exam Initiative revealed that certain advisers to private equity funds were engaging in activities that raised questions as to whether they were acting as unregistered broker-dealers. Trading and Markets, aided by OCIE's observations, issued guidance concerning the implications to broker-dealer registration that could arise from such activities.

- OCIE's Office of Large Firm Monitoring, which has staff dedicated to the ongoing monitoring of select large firms, coordinated with the Federal Reserve Bank of New York and Investment Management, which issued guidance on fund counterparty risk management practices with respect to tri-party repurchase agreements.

- OCIE also focused on compliance with previously granted exemptive orders, including orders related to closed-end funds and managed distribution plans, exchange traded funds and the use of custom baskets, and orders permitting fund advisers and their affiliates to engage in co-investment opportunities with the funds. OCIE's findings and observations in these areas have, for example, helped Investment Management better assess the extent to which the conditions of an exemptive order for managed distribution plans by closed-end funds is functioning as intended.

Identifying New and Emerging Risks

OCIE continues to improve its ability to assess and monitor risk, which enables the SEC to allocate limited resources more effectively and focus them on areas and entities that pose the greatest risk to investors and market stability.

- OCIE's Quantitative Analytics Unit (QAU) employs quantitative techniques and modeling to hone in on areas that pose substantial risk, such as potential fraud and market abuse. The QAU was formed in 2012 and, during FY 2013, increased its resources, adding a number of experts in quantitative analysis, such as mathematics and financial engineering. The QAU's expertise provides valuable support to OCIE's examinations of investment advisers and investment companies by creating and deploying customized data analytic tools. The QAU also works closely with the OCIE's Office of Risk Assessment and Surveillance (RAS) and DERA on quantitative system architecture and software tool projects designed to improve the collection and analysis of data from registrants.

- OCIE's RAS devotes significant resources to guiding risk-focused exam strategy across each of OCIE's examination program areas through data and risk analysis, as well as surveillance activities of the registrant population, seeking to identify firms, individuals and business practices that pose the greatest risk to market integrity and investor protection.

- OCIE coordinates an inter-disciplinary and cross-divisional task force called the Market Event Response Team, a mechanism through which OCIE, Enforcement, Trading and Markets, other SEC divisions and offices, and self-regulatory organizations work collaboratively to respond real-time to rapidly evolving market events.

- OCIE participated in a number of collaborative efforts within the SEC and with other state and Federal regulators to increase examination coverage of important areas,

such as automated trading systems and controls, cyber-security protocols and compliance with the Market Access Rule, and to reduce duplication of effort across regulators.

- OCIE developed and implemented a risk-assessment program for the securities exchanges and FINRA, enabling a comprehensive, risk-based approach to self-regulatory organization oversight. OCIE effectively utilized this risk-assessment program to develop its 2014 examination plan for self-regulatory organizations.

Strengthening Market Structure

The SEC is focused on improving the robustness and resilience of our market structure, both through advanced regulatory initiatives and enhanced data capabilities that can help the agency and market participants better understand the benefits and challenges of trading in the current market structure.

In FY 2013, the SEC proposed Regulation Systems Compliance and Integrity, which would require exchanges, certain alternative trading systems and other key market participants to design, develop, test, maintain and surveil systems that are integral to their operations, ensure that their core technology meets certain standards, conduct business continuity testing, and provide notifications in the event of systems disruptions and other events.

The SEC also coordinated with the equity exchanges and FINRA to extend the "limit up-limit down mechanism" to all stocks. That mechanism is designed to reduce excess market volatility by limiting trades of individual stocks outside of certain price bands.

In addition, the SEC continued to work with exchanges and FINRA as they developed the market-wide consolidated audit trail required by Commission rules, which will significantly enhance their collective ability to monitor and analyze trading activity. Separately, the Commission brought the Market Information Data and Analytics System (MIDAS) on line, providing the SEC with immediate new capabilities based on access to all of the real-time data feeds made available to market participants by the exchanges. Using MIDAS, the SEC has developed an initial set of data analysis that directly informs on market structure policy questions. A number of investigations, exams and analyses, based on MIDAS-generated data, also have been launched.

The initial MIDAS analyses, together with other SEC staff research on market structure, were collected on a single website that was made available to the public. Among the staff research was a summary of the economic literature on market fragmentation and a white paper on alternative trading systems.

Ensuring High-Quality Disclosures and Information Sharing

Quality information is the linchpin of informed investment decision-making. In FY 2013, Corporation Finance and Investment Management continued to work to ensure that companies disclose material information appropriately.

- Corporation Finance continued to enhance investor protection through focused comments on offering documents, including the registration statements for several high-profile IPOs.

- Each disclosure office in Corporation Finance continued to improve the effectiveness of its comments by focusing on industry trends and disclosures, and encouraging companies to improve the quality of reported information. Corporation Finance also published interpretative guidance covering a number of topics, including disclosure guidance regarding non-traded REITS.

- Corporation Finance reviewed a number of structured note offering documents, producing product-focused evaluations of offering documents by issuing letters to the largest issuers of structured notes that called for improved disclosure in future offerings.

- Investment Management sharpened its focus on the adequacy of derivative-related disclosures in the fund industry, including actively-managed exchange traded funds. Investment Management also published updated guidance regarding fund investment in commodities.

- The SEC oversaw the work of the PCAOB, including the advancement of its standard-setting agenda and its inspections of registered public accounting firms. Significantly, the PCAOB adopted, and the SEC approved, a new auditing standard intended to enhance the relevance and timeliness of communications between auditors and audit committees.

The PCAOB also issued for public comment proposed auditing standards to update the auditor's reporting model as well as the auditor's responsibilities for, and reporting on, other information in annual reports filed with the SEC.

Educating Investors

Investors are the first line of defense against fraud and other misconduct. In FY 2013, the SEC continued to make it a priority to educate investors about possible risks to their investment portfolios, publishing 26 investor alerts and bulletins, the most ever in a year. These alerts and bulletins warned investors of possible fraudulent scams and educated them on a variety of investment-related topics, including:

- Ponzi schemes using Bitcoin and other virtual currencies.

- The effect of market interest rates on bond prices and yield.

- JOBS Act rulemaking, including information concerning advertising for unregistered offerings.

The SEC also worked with other regulators to issue joint alerts and bulletins, including an SEC-CFTC investor alert on binary options, an SEC-FINRA alert on pump-and-dump stock schemes and an SEC-FINRA bulletin on pension and settlement income streams.

Increased International Collaboration

In today's global securities markets, multi-jurisdictional registrants and cross-border transactions are commonplace. As a result, the SEC continues to focus on international consistency in key regulatory areas, working with foreign counterparts to supervise globally active, cross-border regulated entities. For example, the SEC engaged in a number of joint supervisory exercises and deployment of information exchange mechanisms in connection with dually registered hedge fund advisers and globally active credit rating agencies.

The SEC, through its work with the International Organization of Securities Commissions (IOSCO) and the Financial Stability Board (FSB), also continued to promote international regulatory convergence toward high-quality standards and practices. The SEC focused on assisting IOSCO and the FSB in appropriately addressing the role of non-bank financing in global markets, developing and deploying tool kits for cross-border regulation of globally active entities, and bringing securities market regulator expertise to bear in ongoing assessments of financial regulatory reforms by IOSCO, the FSB and other international organizations.

Enhanced Internal Controls and Efficiencies

In today's time of budgets constraints, it is incumbent on the SEC to increase efficiency and productivity. The agency continues to find new and more efficient ways to stretch resources and deliver more services to taxpayers and investors.

A More Effective Support Structure

- To bolster the internal controls environment and improve the management and reporting of agency-wide operational risks, the SEC's Office of the Chief Operating Officer established the Operational Risk Management Oversight Committee and updated the agency's policy on operational risks and internal controls.

- The SEC continues to modernize its technology systems, enhancing agency effectiveness, public responsiveness and oversight of the financial markets.

- Significant investments in business process redesign during the fiscal year, such as the replacement of outdated manual and paper-based processes with modernized technology-based workflows, will yield control improvements and cost efficiencies.

Improved Financial Performance

Since migrating to a Federal Shared Service Provider in 2012, the SEC continues to stabilize its financial processes and procedures, and has reorganized the Office of Financial Management (OFM) to better align functions and systems.

- OFM further enhanced the agency's internal controls processes, financial systems, and operational effectiveness and efficiencies by eliminating certain manual processes in the areas of filing fees, disgorgements and penalties, while improving the processes for recording obligations, supporting the Office of Acquisition's efforts to deobligate unused funds, and recording and tracking property and equipment.

- The Office of Acquisitions achieved significant cost savings in a number of ways, including improving competition among vendors and suppliers, strategic sourcing, employing longer performance periods to foster partnerships with the agency's private sector vendors, and improving performance in key areas, such as closing contracts more effectively, improving the content and administration of service contracts, implementing an oversight program, stabilizing the agency's contract writing and financial systems, and fostering standardization across the organization. Finally, more than half of the SEC's contracts were awarded to small businesses.

Conclusion

In FY 2013, an increasingly complex and global marketplace, coupled with ever-increasing responsibilities, posed great challenges to the SEC. Embracing those challenges, the SEC achieved remarkable success, resulting in increased safeguards for investors, enhanced stability of the securities markets and greater opportunities for capital formation.

Looking Forward

In FY 2014, the SEC will continue its unwavering commitment to excellence, employing innovative strategies to manage ever-expanding responsibilities, and enhance the agency's ability to protect investors, maintain fair, orderly, and efficient markets, and facilitate capital formation.

The year will be marked by a continued aggressive push to advance an expansive rulemaking agenda that encompasses both mandated efforts and other mission-critical initiatives important to investors, entrepreneurs and markets; a broad and aggressive focus in pursuit of violators of the Federal securities laws; further refined and sophisticated oversight of registrants; increased deployment of cutting-edge technology as an analytic, investigative and management tool; and enhanced operational efficiency.

Continuing to Advance an Expansive Regulatory Agenda

The Dodd-Frank Act

The Dodd-Frank Act rulemaking process – informed by stronger analytics and feedback from a wide range of stakeholders – continues to progress and build toward a financial system that is more transparent, stable, and responsive to investors and other market participants. In FY 2014, the SEC will:

- Continue to implement the comprehensive regulatory framework for over-the-counter derivatives required by the Dodd-Frank Act, advancing significant new rules for clearing and reporting transactions in such instruments.

- Continue to work with other financial regulators toward adoption of the Volcker Rule, which will restrict federally insured banking institutions and their affiliates from engaging in proprietary trading and making certain fund investments.

- Strive to finalize rules regarding improvements to the regulation of credit ratings and nationally recognized statistical rating organizations, and the removal of certain credit rating references in SEC rules, and determine the appropriate measures in response to the staff study on assigning credit ratings for certain structured transactions.

- Move forward with rules intended to improve the disclosure and offering process for asset-backed securities, including rules regarding risk retention, the disclosure of asset-level information and revised criteria for shelf registration eligibility.

- Continue to implement the provisions of the Dodd-Frank Act related to executive compensation, including the disclosure requirements regarding the ratio of CEO compensation to median employee pay, pay for performance, employee and director hedging, and compensation clawbacks.

- Evaluate and determine whether any changes to the definition of the term "accredited investor" are necessary in light of market and regulatory developments.

- Drawing on the request for data and other information published in FY 2013, move forward with recommendations from a staff report regarding a uniform fiduciary standard of conduct for investment advisers and broker-dealers when providing personalized investment advice to retail investors about securities. The agency will also continue to assess ways to better harmonize the regulatory requirements of investment advisers and broker-dealers when they are providing the same or substantially similar services to retail investors.

The JOBS Act

The SEC is also working to complete the rulemakings and studies required by the JOBS Act, encouraging greater capital formation for small businesses while preserving strong investor protections. In FY 2014, the SEC will:

- Continue to advance rules to implement the exemptions under the Securities Act for "crowdfunding" offerings and unregistered public offerings of up to $50 million, commonly referred to as "Regulation A+" offerings.

- Finalize the review of Regulation S-K's requirements to help inform how such requirements may be updated to modernize and simplify the registration process, and reduce costs for emerging growth companies.

- Continue to work toward amendments to enhance the Commission's ability to evaluate the development of market practices in Rule 506 offerings and to address concerns that may arise in connection with permitting issuers to engage in general solicitation and general advertising in such offerings.

- Continue to provide interpretive guidance to issuers and their advisers on the implementation and application of the JOBS Act, and review emerging practices in the securities market following the implementation of JOBS Act rules, including practices related to the offering and sale of private fund interests.

- Continue to work with the self-regulatory organizations to develop a potential pilot program for issuer stocks to trade at increments other than a penny, building on a staff study on decimalization required by the JOBS Act.

Other Major Regulatory Initiatives

The SEC will also continue to pursue rulemaking in areas that, while not mandated by statute, are critical to strengthening the securities markets and protecting investors.

In FY 2014, the SEC will:

- Continue to advance toward final rules on money market funds that are intended to reduce the risk of contagion from rapid, heavy redemptions in such funds.

- Continue to work toward a stronger financial responsibility framework for broker-dealers, including through new capital and liquidity requirements.

- Advance improvements to the quality of reports and other information provided to investors in mutual funds and variable annuities.

- Review potential updates and improvements to core agency programs, including the disclosure framework for public companies, the regulatory framework for transfer agents, and the regulatory treatment of exchange-traded funds and target date funds.

Building on Success in Enforcement and Examinations

Enforcement and OCIE will build on their great results in 2013, focusing on high priority and emerging high-risk areas, and on enhancing their use of cutting-edge technology and analytics. The priorities include a focus on the identification of misconduct in its early stages, which will allow for corrective action before wrongdoing escalates and causes significant and widespread investor harm. OCIE's outreach efforts, including its enterprise risk management program, which seek to ensure that strong compliance cultures are interwoven in the fabric of registrants' firms, also remains a key focus.

- Enforcement will investigate and bring actions in high priority areas, including complex financial products, gatekeepers, insider trading, market structure, investment advisers and private funds, and municipal securities. Enforcement's Financial Reporting and Audit Task Force will focus on violations relating to the preparation of financial statements, issuer reporting and disclosure, and audit failures. The Microcap Fraud Task Force will continue to investigate fraud in the issuance, marketing, and trading of microcap securities and long-term strategies for combating fraud in that market.

- Enforcement will focus also on current issues and practices within the broker-dealer community and develop national initiatives for potential investigations. Enforcement will coordinate these broker-dealer related initiatives across the agency, and centralize information and expertise regarding ongoing investigations and examinations, and industry practices and trends, to generate quality referrals and investigations.

- Enforcement will monitor the evolving legal landscape and address any securities laws violations or issues relating to the SEC's new JOBS Act rules.

- OCIE will focus on potential conflicts of interest, an indicator of significant regulatory issues, and the risk governance frameworks that firms may have in place to identify and address conflicts.

- OCIE will make governance and supervision of information technology systems a priority, including operational capability, business continuity planning, market access and information security.

- OCIE will review the practices of broker-dealers and other advisers that develop in connection with the elimination of the ban on general solicitation and advertising, including the types of solicitation and advertising practices that develop with respect to the verification of accredited investor status.

- OCIE will examine intermediary activities in connection with the implementation and effectiveness of the new rules relating to crowdfunding.

- OCIE will conduct reviews to assess implementation of compliance frameworks at municipal advisors in light of rules finalizing registration requirements adopted in FY 2013.

Enhancing Market Stability

The SEC will continue to advance a broad-based program for improving the operational integrity and operation of our securities markets, seeking improvements in critical market infrastructure and enhancing data and analytical capabilities. The SEC also will work with investors, issuers and other market participants to assess whether additional changes are required to foster a robust, efficient market structure.

In FY 2014, the SEC will:

- Continue to work toward finalizing rules to improve the design, deployment, integrity and operation of automated systems controlled by exchanges and other key market participants to help ensure that they are prepared to respond quickly and effectively to system errors and malfunctions.

- Continue to coordinate closely with the exchanges and FINRA on their development of concrete measures to improve critical market infrastructures, such as securities information processors, and enhance procedures market-wide for halting trading and, where necessary, breaking trades.

- Leverage the new data capabilities of MIDAS and other sources to further expand the SEC website launched in October 2013 to consolidate the agency's public analyses of market structure. The website will become an increasingly important tool for investors and others wishing to examine interactively a range of market metrics and access empirical research and analyses, and will further inform the broader public debate on market structure.

- Continue to support the development of a consolidated audit trail by the exchanges and FINRA.

Continuing to Refine and Enhance the Use of Data Analytics

The SEC will continue to develop and use sophisticated models and data analytics to support the risk assessment activities across the agency.

- DERA, working with other divisions and offices, will continue to develop the Accounting Quality Model, which is designed to provide a set of quantitative analytics that can be used by staff across the SEC to assess the degree to which registrants' financial statements appear anomalous.

- Corporation Finance, working with DERA, will continue to explore ways to incorporate the Accounting Quality Model into its disclosure review program to increase the effectiveness and efficiency of its reviews.

- Corporation Finance, working with DERA, will also use information collected from Form D to track the use of general solicitation and general advertising in Rule 506 offerings to assess the impact of its use on capital raising in private markets, including the impact on the size of offerings, number of participating investors, and the use of placement agents and other intermediaries.

- Investment Management, in collaboration with DERA, will use Form PF data to develop risk-monitoring analytics, as well as to provide internal periodic reports regarding the private fund industry and particular market segments. DERA has successfully incorporated Form PF data into its proprietary analytical tools, and OCIE anticipates using the information collected on Form PF in conducting pre-examination research and due diligence.

- Trading and Markets will continue to analyze data on broker-dealers' balance sheets, income statements and inventory positions, using a variety of cross-sectional and time series metrics. The metrics are used to investigate data anomalies and material changes for specific broker-dealers, as well as to understand larger industry trends.

- Trading and Markets, with support from DERA, will also continue to analyze the use of security-based swaps in the over-the-counter derivatives market to assess the impact of developing practices on the clearing of transactions, participation by end users, including special entities, and cross border activity. This analysis will be used to help advance the implementation of the Dodd-Frank Act Title VII rulemakings.

The SEC also will build on the use of risk-based analytics and other technologies to identify threats to the markets and investors at an earlier stage and to act quickly to halt misconduct. Performance metrics will be refined in support of case and resource allocation and prioritization, as well as the quality of information provided to the public.

- Enforcement's recently-created CRQA will help identify high-risk areas and threats that could harm investors, markets or regulated entities. CRQA will support and coordinate risk identification, risk assessment and data analytic activities, and assist staff nationwide in conducting risk-based investigations and developing methods of monitoring for signs of possible wrongdoing.

- Enforcement will continue to invest in technology, allowing it to better process the tremendous amount of electronic evidence it gathers and to operate more effectively by applying knowledge management and document management tools to support mission-critical functions.

- OCIE will continue to employ advanced technology through its risk analysis and quantitative teams to review large volumes of trade data sets from a wide range of brokerage and clearing firms, seeking to identify illegal and fraudulent trading activity by registrants.

Continuing to Educate Investors

The SEC will promote investor education campaigns to continue to help investors make informed decisions by:

- Posting online resources for researching investment professionals and investments, understanding fees and identifying fraud.

- Conducting further research on investment decision-making behavior, which will inform the agency's investor education initiatives and materials.

Finance and Operations

The SEC's commitment to a more responsive, effective and efficient agency will continue to drive improvements in finance, management and operational infrastructure.

Finance

- The SEC will participate in the Federal Government-wide effort to deploy a new travel system, work to replace the system supporting budget execution and formulation, and focus on reforming the systems related to filing fees and registrant deposits.

- As part of its enterprise data warehouse initiative, the SEC will begin to integrate data from various systems to provide more comprehensive management and financial reporting on a regular basis and facilitate better decision-making.

- The agency expects to achieve further cost savings through reductions in its lease-space inventory. Moving personnel and assets from an operations center in Virginia to SEC headquarters in Washington, DC, will result in annual savings in the range of $6 million. The SEC's work with the General Services Administration to move four regional offices to smaller leased spaces will also yield benefits.

Workforce

- The SEC will continue to pursue high-quality, talented professionals, and provide the necessary development opportunities to ensure that its employees' skills and expertise remain competitive in an increasingly complex financial world, and support the agency's mission effectively.

- In collaboration with the National Treasury Employees Union, the SEC will continue to implement programs to improve agency-wide internal communications and cooperation, engagement and culture, and employee work-life balance.

- The SEC will work to enhance its performance by actively recruiting diverse candidates for employment with the Commission and making the SEC a desirable workplace for candidates of all backgrounds, thereby ensuring access to the largest possible pool of professional talent. Outreach efforts will include participating in meetings and developing collaborative relationships with diverse educational institutions and professional associations, and placing targeted advertisements for positions at all levels.

- Similarly, the SEC will use expanded outreach to minority-owned and women-owned businesses, along with its market research, to identify a large and diverse pool of companies with capabilities that meet the agency's contracting needs, which will help the agency meet management and finance goals.

Technology

In FY 2013, the SEC introduced "Working Smarter," a multi-year technology transformation plan designed to improve core operations and implement the new responsibilities assigned the agency by recent financial reform legislation. The SEC will carry Working Smarter forward throughout FY 2014, including initiatives to standardize enterprise-wide platforms, modernize SEC.gov and the EDGAR filer system, develop advanced search and discovery capabilities, and build complex, predictive analytical capabilities.

Other upgrades to the SEC's technological infrastructure to be advanced in 2014 include:

- A new electronic data warehouse that will enhance business intelligence, augment data quality and consistency, and generate a high return on investment by allowing users to quickly search and access critical data from a single location and obtain historical intelligence to analyze different time periods and performance trends in order to make future predictions.

- Data integration and enhanced analytical tools to allow seamless searches of data sets to examine activity to reveal suspicious behavior and quickly trace the origin.

- Knowledge management that will eliminate work product redundancy by reusing, and not reinventing, legal research.

- Cloud computing to reduce costs and operational overhead, and provide greater flexibility through an on-demand, scalable model that fits the agency's needs.

The SEC expects deployment of these new technologies to yield significant annual cost savings.

Conclusion

As the next fiscal year unfolds, the SEC will continue its focus on excellence across the agency, using innovative strategies, seamless coordination among the divisions and offices, the latest technology, and its most important resource – the expertise, dedication, and commitment of its 4,000 hard-working men and women – to meet the challenges ahead.

Financial Highlights

This section provides an analysis of the financial position, results of operations, and the underlying causes for significant changes in balances presented in the SEC's FY 2013 financial statements.

As described further below, the SEC's finances have several main components:

- An annual appropriation from Congress;

- Securities transaction fees, charged in accordance with Section 31 of the Securities Exchange Act, which offset the agency's annual appropriation;

- Securities registration, tender offer and merger fees (also called filing fees), of which $50 million is deposited into the Reserve Fund each year. The Reserve Fund may provide resources up to $100 million to pay for SEC expenses, and are not subject to annual appropriation or apportionment;

- Disgorgement and penalties ordered and collected from violators of the securities laws, some of which are then returned to harmed investors and the balances are transferred to the Treasury; and

- The SEC Investor Protection Fund, which is funded through disgorgement and penalties not distributed to harmed investors, and used to make payments to whistleblowers who give tips to aid the SEC's enforcement efforts in certain circumstances, as well as to cover the expenses of the SEC Office of Inspector General's (OIG) Employee Suggestion Program.

Sequestration Order for FY 2013

On March 1, 2013, the President issued the Sequestration Order for FY 2013 which reduced the new budget authority. Budgetary resources in non-exempt budget accounts were reduced by an amount calculated by the Office of Management and Budget (OMB) in its March 1, 2013 report to the Congress. OMB reported the reductions for the SEC as described below:

Salaries and Expenses Fund, Direct

The budget authority of $1,321 million was reduced by 5 percent or $66 million.

Reserve Fund

The budget authority of $50 million was reduced by 5.1 percent or $2.5 million.

Investor Protection Fund

The budget authority of $90 million was reduced by 5.1 percent or $4.6 million.

Overview of Financial Position

Assets. At September 30, 2013, the SEC's total assets were $9,953 million, an increase of $1,192 million or 14 percent over FY 2012.

Fund Balance with Treasury increased by roughly $711 million mainly because of higher Disgorgement and Penalty collections for the year.

Investments, Net increased $308 million due to large Disgorgement and Penalty collections for cases that were subsequently invested and remained invested at the end of FY 2013. These investments include collections from the following cases:

- J.P. Morgan Securities LLC

- British Petroleum PLC

- Credit Suisse Securities (USA) LLC

- UBS Financial Services Inc. of Puerto Rico

Accounts Receivable, Net increased $150 million due to the remaining Disgorgement and Penalty receivables including British Petroleum PLC in FY 2013, which totaled $175 million as of FY 2013. This increase was offset by a decrease in accounts receivables for Section 31 fees. The decrease of $17 million in Section 31 accounts receivables can be attributed to an overall decrease in transaction volume when comparing September 2013 to September 2012.

Property and Equipment, Net increased $30 million for capitalized information systems and telecommunication equipment during FY 2013, as part of the enterprise server, storage, and backup upgrade project and the modernization of SEC.gov.

CHART 1.3
FY 2013 ASSETS BY TYPE

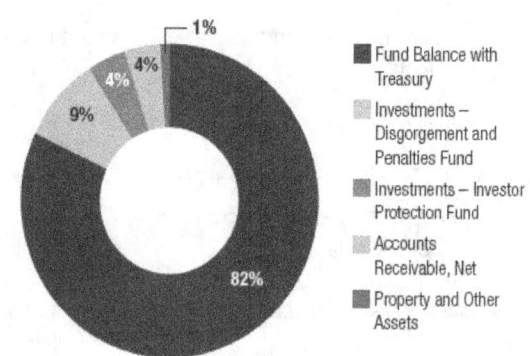

- Fund Balance with Treasury
- Investments – Disgorgement and Penalties Fund
- Investments – Investor Protection Fund
- Accounts Receivable, Net
- Property and Other Assets

TABLE 1.2
ASSETS AS OF SEPTEMBER 30, 2013 AND 2012

(DOLLARS IN MILLIONS)	FY 2013	FY 2012
Fund Balance with Treasury	$ 8,155	$ 7,444
Investments – Disgorgement and Penalties Fund	848	522
Investments – Investor Protection Fund	434	452
Accounts Receivable, Net	387	237
Property and Equipment, Net	127	97
Other Assets	2	9
Total Assets	$ 9,953	$ 8,761

Liabilities. The SEC's total liabilities were $2,298 million at September 30, 2013, an increase of $1,136 million or 98 percent from FY 2012. The change is mainly related to the increase in the liabilities for Disgorgement and Penalty cases recorded in the fourth quarter of FY 2012 and during FY 2013, stemming from amounts assessed against the following cases:

- British Petroleum PLC ($525 million)

- J.P. Morgan Securities LLC ($297 million)

- J.P. Morgan Chase and Company ($200 million)

- Credit Suisse Securities (USA) LLC ($120 million)

- Yusaf Jawed, Grifphon Asset Management LLC, and Grifphon Holdings LLC ($68 million)

For the assets received resulting from judgments, the SEC recognizes a corresponding liability as they are non-entity assets held pending distribution to harmed investors.

Ending Net Position. The SEC's net position, comprised of both unexpended appropriations and the cumulative results of operations, increased by $56 million or 1 percent between September 30, 2012 and September 30, 2013.

The increase is primarily due to the SEC earning fee revenues in excess of program costs in its Salaries and Expenses and Reserve Funds, as discussed in the Results of Operations section on the next page.

CHART 1.4
FY 2013 LIABILITIES BY TYPE

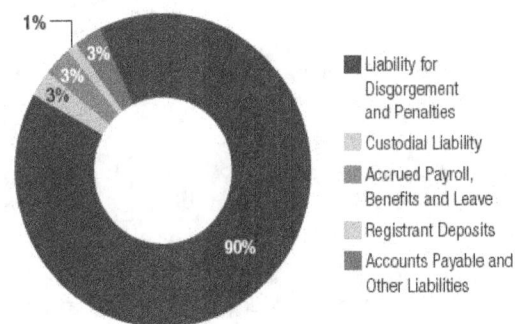

TABLE 1.3
LIABILITIES AS OF SEPTEMBER 30, 2013 AND 2012

(DOLLARS IN MILLIONS)	FY 2013	FY 2012
Liability for Disgorgement and Penalties	$ 2,065	$ 933
Custodial Liability	69	62
Accrued Payroll, Benefits and Leave	70	68
Accounts Payable	44	48
Registrant Deposits	33	34
Other Liabilities	17	17
Total Liabilities	**$ 2,298**	**$ 1,162**

Results of Operations

Earned Revenues. Total earned revenues for the year ended September 30, 2013 increased $116 million over the total for FY 2012. Beginning in FY 2012, and as discussed below, the majority of the SEC's filing fees are no longer used to partially fund the SEC's operations and are now deposited to the U.S. Treasury General Fund upon collection.

Reserve Fund. Section 991(e) of the Dodd-Frank Wall Street Reform and Consumer Protection Act (Dodd-Frank Act) authorized the creation of a Securities and Exchange Commission Reserve Fund (Reserve Fund). Funded from filing fee collections, the SEC can deposit up to $50 million per fiscal year, and the fund cannot hold more than $100 million in total. Excess filing fees are deposited to the U.S. Treasury General Fund.

For the fiscal year ended September 30, 2013, filing fee revenues were $507 million. $50 million was deposited into the Reserve Fund, of which $2.5 million was sequestered. The excess of $457 million was earned on behalf of the U.S. Treasury General Fund.

Filing fees deposited to the Reserve Fund can be used to fund the SEC's operations, create budgetary authority, and are reported as a component of Appropriations (Discretionary and Mandatory) on the SEC's Statement of Budgetary Resources. Filing fees deposited to the U.S. Treasury General Fund cannot be used to fund the SEC's operations. These amounts do not create budgetary authority, and are reported as a component of *Other Financing Sources: Other* on the SEC's Statement of Changes in Net Position.

The Reserve Fund obligated $41 million as of September 30, 2013 for information technology-related projects, leaving a remaining amount of $44.5 million of available resources.

Program Costs. Total Program Costs were $1,331 million for the year ended September 30, 2013, an increase of $133 million or 11 percent when compared to the prior year. Salary and Benefit Expenses increased $56 million, and Other Expenses increased $77 million when comparing FY 2013 to FY 2012.

TABLE 1.4
EARNED REVENUES FOR THE YEARS ENDED SEPTEMBER 30, 2013 AND 2012

(DOLLARS IN MILLIONS)	FY 2013	FY 2012
Section 31 Securities Transaction Fees	$ 1,257	$ 1,270
Securities Registration, Tender Offer, and Merger Fees (Filing Fees)	507	378
Total Earned Revenue	**$ 1,764**	**$ 1,648**

CHART 1.5
FY 2013 FILING FEES REVENUE
(DOLLARS IN MILLIONS)

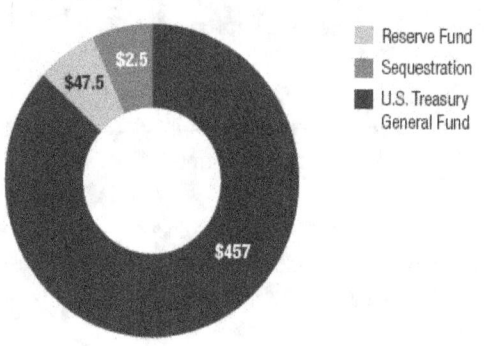

Reserve Fund
Sequestration
U.S. Treasury General Fund

$2.5
$47.5
$457

CHART 1.6
PROGRAM COSTS

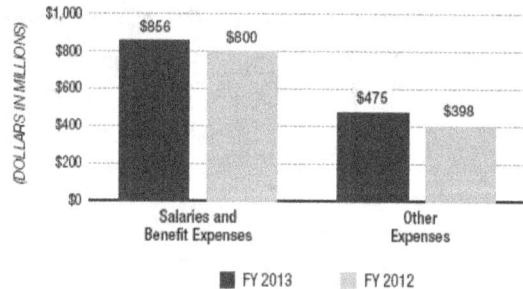

FY 2013   FY 2012

The SEC had increased expenses in the areas of personnel compensation and benefits which correlates to an increase of 238 full-time equivalent employees; information technology service contracts and licensing; capitalized and non-capitalized information systems software and hardware including the modernization of SEC.gov; and whistleblower award payments.

Budgetary Resources

In FY 2013, the SEC's total budgetary resources equaled $1,402 million, a 13 percent increase from the FY 2012 amount of $1,236 million. Significant components of the SEC's Total Budgetary Resources are described below.

Unobligated Balance Brought Forward – Unfunded Lease Obligations. The SEC's unobligated balance, brought forward was $43 million for FY 2013. The balance reflects the funding actions and recoveries related to the unfunded lease obligations plus the carry-over authority in the Salaries and Expenses Fund and the Reserve Fund.

Unfunded lease obligations totaled $441 million as of September 30, 2013. This represents a reduction relative to the FY 2012 amount, because of funding actions of $80 million and $2 million in downward adjustments.

Spending Authority from Offsetting Collections. The Spending Authority from Offsetting Collections balance of $1,208 million in FY 2013 mainly reflects the Section 31 exchange fees collected in the year, reduced by $66 million as a result of the Sequestration Order for FY 2013.

CHART 1.7
FY 2013 SOURCES OF FUNDS

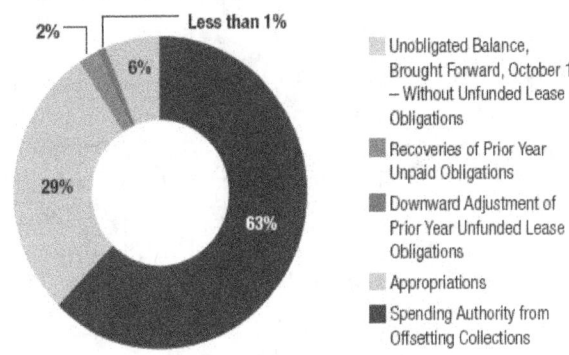

Unobligated Balance, Brought Forward, October 1 – Without Unfunded Lease Obligations

Recoveries of Prior Year Unpaid Obligations

Downward Adjustment of Prior Year Unfunded Lease Obligations

Appropriations

Spending Authority from Offsetting Collections

Percentages do not include the Unobligated Balance Brought Forward, October 1 – Interpretation for Lease Obligations

TABLE 1.5
TOTAL BUDGETARY RESOURCES FOR THE YEARS ENDED SEPTEMBER 30, 2013 AND 2012

(DOLLARS IN MILLIONS)	FY 2013	FY 2012
Unobligated Balance, Brought Forward, October 1:		
Salaries and Expenses Fund – Without Unfunded Lease Obligations	$ 102	$ 47
Salaries and Expenses Fund – Effect of Change in Legal Interpretation for Lease Obligations	(523)	(778)
Reserve Fund	13	–
Investor Protection Fund	451	451
Total Unobligated Balance, Brought Forward, October 1	43	(280)
Recoveries of Prior Year Unpaid Obligations	31	26
Downward Adjustments of Prior Year Unfunded Lease Obligations	2	142
Appropriation (Discretionary and Mandatory)		
Salaries and Expenses Fund	48	33
Reserve Fund	72	25
Investor Protection Fund	(2)	1
Spending Authority from Offsetting Collections	1,208	1,289
Total Budgetary Resources	**$ 1,402**	**$ 1,236**

Spending Authority from Offsetting Collections and Appropriations

During the fiscal year, the SEC receives an appropriation to fund its operations. This appropriation establishes the SEC's new budget authority in its Salaries and Expenses Fund for the fiscal year. The SEC's new budget authority of $1,321 million was reduced by $66 million as a result of the sequestration for FY 2013.

At the end of the fiscal year, SEC's Section 31 fee collections are used to offset the appropriation. On May 25, 2013, the reduction in the Section 31 fee rate from $22.40 to $17.40 per million dollars of securities transacted on exchanges and over-the-counter markets became effective. The SEC's Section 31 fee collections totaled $1,273 million for FY 2013. Therefore, the SEC retained appropriated authority equal to $48 million.

Investor Protection Fund

The SEC prepares stand alone financial statements for the Investor Protection Fund as required by the Dodd-Frank Act. The Investor Protection Fund was established in the fourth quarter of FY 2010 to provide funding for a whistleblower award program and to finance the operations of the SEC Office of Inspector General's Employee Suggestion Program.

The balance of the Investor Protection Fund decreased by $14.2 million between the years ended September 30, 2013 and 2012. The Investor Protection Fund recognized total earnings of $651 thousand during FY 2013. Total earnings include nonexchange revenue of $655 thousand from the interest earned on investments in U.S. Treasury Securities; and gains of $6 thousand less the losses of $10 thousand from the disposition of investments. In addition, the Investor Protection Fund incurred expenses of $14.8 million for whistleblower awards and $51 thousand for salary and benefit costs in the OIG's Employee Suggestion Program.

Additional information regarding the Investor Protection Fund and the Office of the Whistleblower is available in the 2013 Annual Report on the Dodd-Frank Whistleblower Program. This report may be found at *www.sec.gov/whistleblower.*

CHART 1.8
OFFSETTING COLLECTIONS VS. NEW BUDGETARY AUTHORITY
SECTION 31 EXCHANGE AND FILING FEES

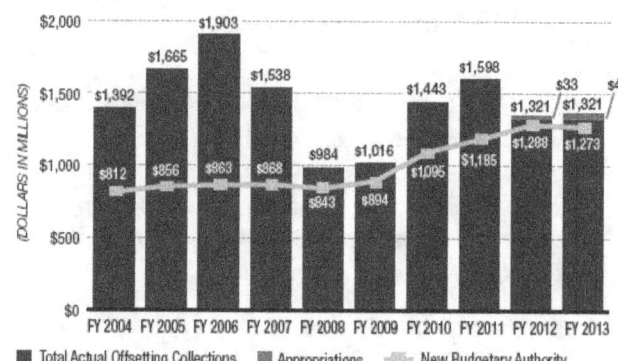

■ Total Actual Offsetting Collections   ■ Appropriations   ⋯ New Budgetary Authority

FY 2004 – FY 2011 Offsetting Collections includes transaction fees and filing fees. FY 2012 and beyond, Offsetting Collections includes transaction fees and $50 million of filing fees.

TABLE 1.6
INVESTOR PROTECTION FUND ACTIVITY
FOR THE YEARS ENDED SEPTEMBER 30, 2013 AND 2012

(DOLLARS IN THOUSANDS)	FY 2013	FY 2012
Balance of Fund at beginning of fiscal year	$453,429	$452,788
Amount deposited into or credited to the Fund during the fiscal year	–	–
Amount of earnings on investments during the fiscal year	651	757
Amount paid from the Fund during the fiscal year to whistleblowers	(14,832)	(46)
Amount paid from the Fund during the fiscal year for expenses incurred by Employee Suggestion Program	(51)	(70)
Balance of the Fund at the end of the preceding fiscal year	**$ 439,197**	**$ 453,429**

Limitations of the Financial Statements

The principal financial statements included in this report have been prepared by SEC management to report the financial position and results of operations of the SEC, pursuant to the requirements of 31 U.S. Code Section 3515(b). While the statements have been prepared from the books and records of the SEC in accordance with generally accepted accounting principles (GAAP) for Federal entities and the formats prescribed by OMB, the statements are in addition to the financial reports used to monitor and control budgetary resources, which are prepared from the same books and records. The statements should be read with the understanding that they are for a component of the U.S. Government, a sovereign entity.

Performance Highlights

The SEC's performance data provides a foundation for both programmatic and organizational decision-making and is critical for gauging the agency's success in meeting its objectives. The SEC is committed to using performance management best practices to promote greater accountability. This section provides information on its key performance measures for FY 2013 – it describes the SEC's data verification and validation process, outlines the SEC's strategic and performance planning framework, provides information on the costs incurred by the agency's four strategic goals and 10 national programs, and highlights the agency's progress toward reaching key performance targets.

The SEC's FY 2013 Annual Performance Report (APR) will be issued with the agency's FY 2015 Congressional Budget Justification, and will provide a complete discussion of all of the agency's strategic goals, including a description of performance goals and objectives, data sources, performance results and trends, and information about internal reviews and evaluations. The SEC's APR is expected to be available in February 2014 at *www.sec.gov/about/secreports.shtml*.

Verification and Validation of Performance Data

The SEC's programs require accurate data to properly assess program performance and to make good management decisions. Data verification and validation is used to evaluate whether data has been generated according to specifications, satisfy acceptance criteria, and are appropriate and consistent with their intended use. Data verification is a systematic process for evaluating performance and compliance of a set of data when compared to a set of standards to ascertain its completeness, correctness, and consistency using the methods and criteria defined in the project documentation. Data validation follows the data verification process and uses information from the project documentation to ascertain the usability of the data in light of its measurement quality objectives and to ensure that results obtained are scientifically defensible.

The SEC ensures that the performance data presented in this report is complete, reliable and accurate based upon the following assessment steps:

(1) The agency develops performance measures through its strategic planning process.

(2) The SEC's divisions and offices perform the following steps to ensure that data used in the calculation of performance measures is accurate and reliable including adequately documenting:

- the sources of the underlying data elements, and the procedures used to gather the data;

- the procedures used to obtain assurance as to the accuracy and reliability of the data;

- the data definitions for reference; and

- documenting and explaining the measure calculations.

(3) The divisions and offices calculate and report the performance measures to the Office of Financial Management, and the measures are approved by division directors and office heads. This process ensures that the data used in the calculation of performance measures is accurate and reliable and that internal control is maintained through the approval process.

Strategic and Performance Planning Framework

The SEC's FY 2013 strategic and performance planning framework is based on the FY 2010 – FY 2015 Strategic Plan, available at *www.sec.gov/about/secstratplan1015f. pdf.* The Strategic Plan outlines the agency's mission, vision, values, and strategic goals and objectives. The SEC's work is structured around four strategic goals, and 12 strategic objectives the agency plans to achieve in support of those four goals. The SEC's goals and priorities in the Strategic Plan are influenced by several external environmental factors, including global, complex and constantly evolving securities markets.

Table 1.7 displays the agency's FY 2013 costs for its four strategic goals and 12 strategic objectives, as well as how these costs are divided among the SEC's programs described in Table 1.1.

TABLE 1.7

Strategic Goal	Strategic Objective	Contributing Programs *($ in millions)*
Foster and enforce compliance with the Federal securities laws **Cost: $711.1 million**	The SEC fosters compliance with the Federal securities laws. Cost: $207.9 million	
	The SEC promptly detects violations of the Federal securities laws. Cost: $134.3 million	
	The SEC prosecutes violations of Federal securities laws and holds violators accountable. Cost: $368.9 million	
Establish an effective regulatory environment **Cost: $139.2 million**	The SEC establishes and maintains a regulatory environment that promotes high-quality disclosure, financial reporting, and governance, and that prevents abusive practices by registrants, financial intermediaries, and other market participants. Cost: $55.1 million	
	The U.S. capital markets operate in a fair, efficient, transparent, and competitive manner, fostering capital formation and useful innovation. Cost: $52.6 million	
	The SEC adopts and administers rules and regulations that enable market participants to understand clearly their obligations under the securities laws. Cost: $31.5 million	
Facilitate access to the information investors need to make informed investment decisions **Cost: $195.7 million**	Investors have access to high-quality disclosure materials that are useful to investment decision making. Cost: $154.7 million	
	Agency rulemaking and investor education programs are informed by an understanding of the wide range of investor needs. Cost: $41 million	
Enhance the Commission's performance through effective alignment and management of human, information, and financial capital **Cost: $284.5 million**	The SEC maintains a work environment that attracts, engages, and retains a technically proficient and diverse workforce that can excel and meet the dynamic challenges of market oversight. Cost: $63.4 million	
	The SEC retains a diverse team of world-class leaders who provide motivation and strategic direction to the SEC workforce. Cost: $65.7 million	
	Information within and available to the SEC becomes a Commission-wide shared resource, appropriately protected, that enables a collaborative and knowledge-based working environment. Cost: $35.3 million	
	Resource decisions and operations reflect sound financial and risk management principles. Cost: $120.1 million	

■ Enforcement   ▨ Compliance Inspections and Examinations   ■ Corporation Finance   ▨ Trading and Markets   ▨ Investment Management
▨ Economic and Risk Analysis   ■ General Counsel   ▨ Other Program Offices   ■ Agency Direction and Administrative Support
▨ Inspector General

Performance Achievements

The SEC expended more than $1,330 million in FY 2013 to achieve its four strategic goals and 12 strategic objectives. Overall, the agency exceeded or met approximately 54 percent of its 72 planned performance targets. The percentage of performance targets that were met or exceeded for each strategic goal are outlined below in Table 1.8. (In calculating these figures, performance metrics for which no data was available were also included in the computation.)

TABLE 1.8

Strategic Goal	Foster and enforce compliance with the Federal securities laws	Establish an effective regulatory environment	Facilitate access to the information investors need to make informed investment decisions	Enhance the Commission's performance through effective alignment and management of human, information, and financial capital
% Performance Goal Targets Met or Exceeded	35%	69%	67%	48%

A detailed explanation of how the agency met or exceeded its planned performance targets, such as through increased efficiencies and improved processes, will be provided in the APR which will be published in February 2014. When a planned performance target was not met, the report will provide a description of actions that will be taken to achieve the target in the future.

The Enforcement program increased the percentage of enforcement actions resolved (Table 1.10). The agency did not meet its target for average months between opening a matter under inquiry or an investigation and commencing an enforcement action (Table 1.9).

TABLE 1.9

PERFORMANCE GOAL
Average months between opening a matter under inquiry or an investigation and commencing an enforcement action

Description: This measure concerns the pace of investigations that lead to the filing of enforcement actions. Specifically, this measure captures average number months between the opening of an investigation and the filing of the first enforcement action arising out of that investigation. If the investigation was preceded by a matter under inquiry, the measure draws on the date of opening of the matter inquiry. In conducting investigations, the enforcement program continually strives to balance the need for complete, effective, and fair investigation with the need to file enforcement actions in as timely a manner as possible.

Fiscal Year	FY 2008	FY 2009	FY 2010	FY 2011	FY 2012	FY 2013 Plan	FY 2013 Actual	FY 2013 Results
Months	Prior-year data not available			22	21	20	21	Not Met

Responsible Division/Office: Division of Enforcement

Data Source: HUB case management and tracking system for the Division of Enforcement

Plan for Improving Performance: The Division is focused on ways to ensure that its enforcement actions are brought quickly, in recognition of the fact that timeliness brings with it an increased deterrent effect. The Division will continue to assess the pace of investigations with an eye towards overall filing speeds, and the Division will continue to seek to identify areas of enforcement in which it may be possible to conduct streamlined, expedited investigations of multiple parties. Additionally, Division management will encourage investigative staff to focus their efforts on core violative conduct, and to seek to expedite meetings with, or testimony of, key witnesses where appropriate.

TABLE 1.10

PERFORMANCE GOAL
Percentage of Enforcement Actions Resolved

Description: This measure assesses the rate at which the SEC's filed enforcement actions are resolved. Specifically, the measure identifies, as to all parties to enforcement actions that were resolved in the fiscal year, the percentage against whom the Commission obtained a judgment or order entered on consent, a default judgment, a judgment of liability on one or more charges, and/or the imposition of monetary or other relief. The Division is currently assessing the value of this metric, and evaluating how to incorporate qualitative considerations of the results of the Division's enforcement actions.

Fiscal Year	FY 2008	FY 2009	FY 2010	FY 2011	FY 2012	FY 2013 Plan	FY 2013 Actual	FY 2013 Results
Percentage	92%	92%	92%	93%	89%	92%	93%	Exceeded

Responsible Division/Office: Division of Enforcement

Data Source: HUB case management and tracking system for the Division of Enforcement

The agency did not meet its targets for the percentage of investment advisors, investment companies, and broker dealers examined during the year (Table 1.11). The staff continued to spend considerable time and effort during the year on improving its risk assessment and surveillance capabilities to ensure that the national examination program is spending its limited time and resources on those firms presenting the highest risk. As part of these efforts, the staff spent significant resources on collecting and analyzing data about all registrants. The results of these efforts help to ensure that the program is focusing on the highest risk entities and selecting appropriate candidates for onsite examination. Examinations of high-risk firms often take significant time to complete and are frequently of large and complex entities. For example, the investment advisers examined in FY 2013 represent more than 25 percent of the overall assets under management of currently registered advisers. In addition, examination resources have been allocated during the past year to other efforts intended to improve the long-term performance of the program, including industry outreach initiatives, rule-making efforts and other program improvement efforts that were identified as part of the program's broad, overarching self-assessment.

TABLE 1.11

PERFORMANCE GOAL
Percentage of investment advisers, investment companies, and broker-dealers examined during the year

Description: This measure indicates the number of registrants examined by the SEC or an SRO as a percentage of the total number of registrants. This measure includes all types of examinations: risk priority examinations, cause inspections to follow up on tips and complaints, limited-scope special inspections to probe emerging risk areas, oversight examinations of broker-dealers to test compliance and the quality of examinations by the Financial Industry Regulatory Authority (FINRA).

Fiscal Year	FY 2008	FY 2009	FY 2010	FY 2011	FY 2012	FY 2013 Plan	FY 2013 Actual	FY 2013 Results
Investment advisers	14%	10%	9%	8%	8%	10%	9%	Not Met
Investment companies	23%	29%	10%	13%	12%	14%	11%	Not Met
Broker-Dealers (exams by SEC and SROs)	57%	54%	44%	58%	49%	50%	46%	Not Met

Responsible Division/Office: Office of Compliance Inspections and Examinations

Data Source: SRO Databases (BD SRO Data); Tracking and Reporting Examinations – National Documentation Systems (TRENDS); and Commission filings

Plan for Improving Program Performance: During FY 2014, the staff will continue to implement improved processes and procedures that have been identified as part of its ongoing self-improvement process. Significant improvement initiatives in the areas of strategy, structure, people, processes, and technology have been completed in the last several years or are currently underway. The agency expects that these improvements, which include further refinements to the exam program's risk assessment processes, will lead to more effective coverage of registered entities. Furthermore, certain targeted initiatives aimed at high risk firms and activities have already been implemented and it is anticipated that these efforts will result in improved coverage levels in FY 2014.

Under the Federal securities laws, issuers are required to disclose material financial and other information to the public. In FY 2013, the SEC continued to meet the requirements of the Sarbanes-Oxley Act (Table 1.12) by reviewing the disclosures of more than 33 percent of all reporting companies and investment company portfolios each year. This volume of disclosure review helped deter fraud and assured that investors had access to relevant information about emerging issues. In addition to reviewing filings of reporting companies, the SEC continued to issue initial comments on Securities Act filings in less than 30 days (Table 1.13).

TABLE 1.12

PERFORMANCE GOAL
Percentage of public companies and investment companies with disclosures reviewed each year

Description: The Sarbanes-Oxley Act requires that the SEC review the disclosures of all companies and investment company portfolios reporting under the Exchange Act at least once every three years. These reviews help improve the information available to investors and may uncover possible violations of the securities laws.

Fiscal Year	FY 2008	FY 2009	FY 2010	FY 2011	FY 2012	FY 2013 Plan	FY 2013 Actual	FY 2013 Results
Corporations	39%	40%	44%	48%	48%	33%	52%	Exceeded
Responsible Division/Office: Division of Corporation Finance								
Data Source: Electronic Data Gathering, Analysis, and Retrieval (EDGAR)/Filing Activity Tracking System								
Investment Company Portfolios	36%	35%	35%	33%	36%	33%	34%	Exceeded
Responsible Division/Office: Division of Investment Management								
Data Source: Microsoft Office Suite Tools								

TABLE 1.13

PERFORMANCE GOAL
Time to issue initial comments on Securities Act filings

Description: The target of 30 days or less has become a de facto industry standard for the maximum time to receive initial comments.

Fiscal Year	FY 2008	FY 2009	FY 2010	FY 2011	FY 2012	FY 2013 Plan	FY 2013 Actual	FY 2013 Results
Days	25.2 days	25.3 days	24.1 days	24.4 days	24.9 days	<30 days	25.6 days	Met
Responsible Division/Office: Division of Corporation Finance								
Data Source: Electronic Data Gathering, Analysis, and Retrieval (EDGAR)								

Management Assurances

In FY 2013, the SEC demonstrated its continued commitment to maintaining strong internal controls. Internal control is an integral component of effective agency management, providing reasonable assurance that the following objectives are being achieved: effectiveness and efficiency of operations, reliability of financial reporting, and compliance with laws and regulations. The Federal Managers' Financial Integrity Act of 1982 (FMFIA) establishes management's responsibility to assess and report on internal accounting and administrative controls. Such controls include program, operational, and administrative areas, as well as accounting and financial management. The FMFIA requires Federal agencies to establish controls that reasonably ensure obligations and costs are in compliance with applicable laws; funds, property, and other assets are safeguarded against waste, loss, unauthorized use, or misappropriation; and revenues and expenditures are properly recorded and accounted for to maintain accountability over the assets. The FMFIA also requires agencies to annually assess and report on the internal controls that protect the integrity of Federal programs (FMFIA § 2) and whether financial management systems conform to related requirements (FMFIA § 4). Guidance for implementing the FMFIA is provided through Office of Management and Budget (OMB) Circular A-123, *Management's Responsibility for Internal Control*. In addition, it requires agencies to provide an assurance statement on the effectiveness of programmatic internal controls and financial system conformance, and internal control over financial reporting.

Section 963 of the Dodd-Frank Wall Street Reform and Consumer Protection Act (Dodd-Frank Act) describes the responsibility of SEC management to establish and maintain adequate internal controls and procedures for financial reporting. The Dodd-Frank Act requires an annual financial controls audit, assessment of the effectiveness of internal control, and attestation by the Chair and the Chief Financial Officer. Section 922 of the Dodd-Frank Act requires the SEC to submit audited financial statements of the Investor Protection Fund to the Committee on Banking, Housing and Urban Affairs of the Senate and the Committee on Financial Services of the House of Representatives.

The Assurance Statement below is issued in accordance with the FMFIA, OMB Circular A-123, and Sections 922 and 963 of the Dodd-Frank Act.

Annual Assurance Statement

Assurance Statement on Internal Control over Operations: The SEC management is responsible for establishing and maintaining effective internal control and financial management systems that meet the objectives of the Federal Managers' Financial Integrity Act of 1982 (FMFIA). In accordance with OMB Circular A-123, the SEC conducted its annual assessment of the effectiveness of internal controls. Based on the results of the assessment for the period ending September 30, 2013, the SEC is able to provide an unqualified statement of assurance that the internal controls and financial systems, both for the agency as a whole and for the Investor Protection Fund, meet the objectives of the FMFIA. No material weaknesses were found in the design or operation of the internal controls for the fiscal year ended September 30, 2013.

Assurance Statement on Internal Control over Financial Reporting: In accordance with Appendix A of OMB Circular A-123, the SEC conducted its assessment of the effectiveness of internal control over financial reporting, which includes safeguarding of assets and compliance with applicable laws and regulations. Based on the results of the assessment, the SEC is able to provide reasonable assurance that internal control over financial reporting, both for the agency as a whole and for the Investor Protection Fund, met the objectives of FMFIA and were operating effectively as of September 30, 2013. No material weaknesses were found in the design or operation of controls.

SEC also conducted reviews of its financial management systems in accordance with OMB Circular A-127, *Financial Management Systems*. Based on the results of these reviews, SEC can provide reasonable assurance that its financial management systems substantially comply with the requirements of the Federal Financial Management Improvement Act (FFMIA) as of September 30, 2013.

Mary Jo White
Chair
December 12, 2013

Kenneth A. Johnson
Chief Financial Officer
December 12, 2013

Management's Responsibility for Internal Control

FMFIA requires the head of the agency, based on the agency's internal evaluation, to provide an annual Statement of Assurance on the effectiveness of their management, administrative, and financial reporting controls. OMB Circular A-123 implements FMFIA and defines management's responsibility for internal control in federal agencies. The FY 2013 annual assurance statements for FMFIA and ICFR are provided on the preceding page.

FMFIA § 2 requires agencies to establish internal controls and financial systems which provide reasonable assurance that the following objectives are achieved:

- Effective and efficient operations,

- Compliance with applicable laws and regulations, and

- Reliability of financial reporting.

The Chair's FMFIA assurance statement is primarily based on individual assurance statements from each division director and office head. The individual statements assessed internal controls related to the effectiveness of the controls over programs and operations, financial reporting, and compliance with laws and regulations. These statements were based on self-assessments and internal reviews supported by enhanced control testing, as well as Office of Inspector General (OIG) and Government Accountability Office (GAO) reviews, audits, inspections and investigations.

The results of these statements were considered with other sources of information when determining whether any management control deficiencies or non-conformances needed to be reported in the annual assurance statement. Other information sources included, but were not limited to, the following:

- An entity-level control assessment;

- Internal management reviews, self-assessments and tests of internal controls;

- Management's personal knowledge gained from daily operations;

- Reports from the GAO and OIG;

- Reviews of financial management systems under OMB Circular A-127, *Financial Management Systems*;

- Reports pursuant to the Federal Information Security Management Act (FISMA) and OMB Circular A-130, *Management of Federal Information Resources*;

- Annual reviews and reports pursuant to the Improper Payments Elimination and Recovery Act (IPERA);

- Reports and other information from Congress or agencies such as OMB, the Office of Personnel Management (OPM), or the General Services Administration (GSA) reflecting the adequacy of internal controls; and

- Additional reviews relating to a division or office's operations, including those discussed in the Other Reviews section below.

FMFIA § 4 requires that agencies annually evaluate and report on whether financial management systems conform to government-wide requirements. The SEC evaluated its financial management systems for the fiscal year ending September 30, 2013, in accordance with the FFMIA and OMB Circular A-127, *Financial Management Systems*, as applicable.

Appendix A of OMB Circular A-123 requires the agency head to provide a separate statement of assurance on the effectiveness of ICFR, in addition to the overall FMFIA assurance statement. SEC management assessed internal control at the entity-level, process, transaction, and application level. This report also provides a Summary of Financial Statement Audits and Management Assurances under the section entitled Other Accompanying Information, as required by OMB Circular A-136, *Financial Reporting Requirements*.

The effectiveness of process level controls was assessed through detailed test procedures related to the agency's financial reporting objectives. As part of this effort, the agency performed a comprehensive risk assessment in which SEC management identified:

- Significant financial reports;

- Significant line items and accounts;

- Major classes of transactions;

- Relevant assertions, risks of material misstatement and control objectives;

- Reporting and regulatory requirements; and

- Existing deficiencies and corrective action plans.

From the results of the risk assessment, SEC management selected processes fundamental to the agency's financial management. SEC management updated documentation of the business processes and control activities designed to mitigate significant financial reporting and compliance risks.

These control activities were tested for design and operating effectiveness. The agency also tested the operating effectiveness of control activities that were found to be deficient in prior years. These test results served as a basis for management's assessment of the effectiveness of ICFR.

The results of testing completed prior to and as of September 30th formed the basis of the annual management assurance statement. SEC management also analyzed the magnitude of the internal control deficiencies and the level of assurance provided under the FMFIA requirements. SEC management analyzed the internal control deficiencies, both individually and in the aggregate, to determine if a material weakness[1] existed in the financial reporting processes. ICFR testing conducted during FY 2013 did not identify any deficiencies that rose to the level of a material weakness.

Significant factors considered for assessing each deficiency included the following:

- Nature of the control deficiency (e.g., design, operation);

- Internal control objectives and activities impacted;

- Potential impact on financial statement line items, accounts and disclosures;

- The interaction of control deficiencies with other deficiencies; and

- The materiality of account balances impacted by the deficiency.

Each year, the agency's Financial Management Oversight Committee (FMOC) advises the Chair as to whether the SEC had any deficiencies in internal control or financial system design significant enough to be reported as a material weakness or non-conformance. This advice is based on the assurance statements from division directors and office heads and other supplemental sources of information.

Other Reviews

The SEC's financial statements were audited by the GAO. The objective of GAO's audit was to express an opinion on the financial statements and on internal control over financial reporting, and to report on tests of compliance with selected laws and regulations.

The OIG conducted nine audits and reviews during FY 2013. The reviews covered 12 of the 38 assessable units (32 percent), to include the Office of the Chair. Some components were subject to multiple reviews.

Financial Management System Conformance

The FFMIA requires that each agency implement and maintain financial management systems that comply substantially with Federal financial management systems requirements, applicable Federal accounting standards, and the U.S. Standard General Ledger at the transaction level. The purpose of the FFMIA is to advance Federal financial management by verifying that financial management systems provide accurate, reliable, and timely financial management information in order to manage daily operations, produce reliable financial statements, maintain effective internal control, and comply with legal and regulatory requirements. Although the SEC is exempt from the requirement to determine substantial compliance with FFMIA, the agency assesses its financial management systems annually for conformance with the requirements of OMB Circular A-127 and other Federal financial system requirements.

The SEC's process to assess its financial management systems was in compliance with the January 9, 2009 revision of OMB Circular A-127 and included the use of an FFMIA risk model which ranked risks from nominal to significant. Based on the results of the FY 2013 review, the SEC concluded that its risk rating was nominal. Upon the review of the criteria in OMB Circular A-127 for agencies with nominal risk, the SEC determined its financial core and mixed systems are in substantial compliance with Section 803(a) of the FFMIA requirements. This was based in part on notable progress made by SEC management and staff in

---

[1] A material weakness is a significant deficiency, or combination of significant deficiencies, that create a reasonable possibility that program objectives are not met, or results in the risk of control failure not being mitigated.

implementing remediation activities in response to significant deficiencies in ICFR noted in FY 2011 and FY 2012. The SEC assessed each of its core and mixed financial systems to determine the risk category. The systems were reviewed individually for compliance, and then collectively a risk rating was determined for the agency's system compliance. The SEC performed an assessment of the FFMIA risk indicators and classified its financial systems as being in the nominal risk category.

Summary of Current Financial System and Future Strategies

The FY 2013 ICFR assessment demonstrated that a nominal rating would be appropriate for the seven risk indicators, and therefore it can be concluded that the agency substantially complied with the requirements of Section 803(a) of the FFMIA. The SEC's core financial system, Delphi, is a Financial Systems Integration Office (FSIO) certified system and met all of the requirements of FFMIA.

FY 2013 was the first full year SEC operated under a Federal Shared Service Provider (FSSP). Through a strong partnership with our FSSP, the SEC will continue to automate, where possible, to eliminate some of its manual processes and consolidate them within the capabilities of the new system. SEC continues to build upon its prior year efforts to subject key non-integrated spreadsheets and databases to risk assessment and tightened controls. With the reduced reliance on manual processes and improved financial reporting, the SEC has reduced its portfolio of user-developed applications.

The SEC legacy financial system, Momentum, is no longer accessible via the general support system (GSS) and is now deemed a historical research tool. This action effectively remediated prior year security controls recommendations affecting the financial systems servers.

While the FY 2013 ICFR assessment noted deficiencies in some areas, there was substantial progress made from the prior year and the assessment identified no significant deficiency in the area of information security.

Federal Information Security Management Act

The Federal Information Security Management Act (FISMA) requires Federal agencies to "develop, document, and implement an agency-wide information security program to provide information security for the information and information systems that support the operations and assets of the agency, including those provided or managed by another agency, contractor, or other source." In addition, FISMA requires Federal agencies to conduct annual assessments of their information security and privacy programs, to develop and implement remediation efforts for identified weaknesses and vulnerabilities, and to report compliance to OMB. The SEC's OIG, Chief Information Security Officer, and Privacy Officer annually perform a joint review of the Commission's compliance with FISMA requirements. The Commission will submit its 2013 report to OMB on November 15, 2013, as required or adjusted, based on the FY 2014 lapse of appropriations.

Oversight and Compliance

The SEC's Office of Information Technology (OIT), collaborating with business owners, completed assessment and authorization activities for 18 reportable systems. As a result, the SEC has now assessed and authorized a total of 63 reportable systems in accordance with OMB policy and guidance from the National Institute of Standards and Technology (NIST). OIT completed contingency testing on the majority of the SEC's authorized systems as part of disaster recovery exercises, unscheduled events, and weather occurrences.

OIT Security's assessment team visited four of the 11 SEC regional offices[2] as part of a three-year review cycle and performed a technical assessment of both the local network infrastructure and physical security. The assessment team also conducted a disaster recovery simulation exercise at the four regional offices. Three of the four regional office exercises included a successful failover to alternate servers.

---

[2] *New York, Miami, Chicago, and Boston*

OIT facilitated the remediation of 258 self-identified deficiencies associated with the SEC's network infrastructure and major applications, closed 47 OIG recommendations and submitted artifacts to support resolution of 15 matters for consideration to GAO.

OIT conducted 65 privacy reviews, which included the approval and publishing of 26 privacy impact assessments (PIAs). OIT also published five systems of records notices in the Federal Register.

Training and Communications

OIT delivered on-line cyber security and privacy awareness training to the SEC user community and achieved 96 percent completion. During the regional office assessments, in-person privacy training focused on the safe handling of personally identifiable information (PII) and was delivered to approximately 75 percent of users in those regional offices. OIT delivered two virtual training conferences to regional office IT Specialists in all 11 offices, which focused on Executive Branch Information Protection and Privacy Requirements and Cyber Security Threats. OIT published monthly newsletters providing guidance and tips about data protection and cyber security tips.

Policy and Technology

OIT began updating governance documentation to address changes in NIST guidance that will become effective in FY 2014.

The SEC continues to safely explore cloud computing technologies and solutions based on Federal information protection requirements. SEC leveraged one cloud provider that has been through the Federal Risk and Authorization Management Program (FedRAMP) and is exploring three additional cloud service providers that are registered in FedRAMP but have not yet received provisional authorization from the Joint Authorization Board (JAB).

FINANCIAL SECTION

This section of the Agency Financial Report contains the U.S. Securities and Exchange Commission's (SEC) financial statements, required supplementary information, financial statements for the Investor Protection Fund, and the related Independent Auditor's Report. Information presented here satisfies the financial reporting requirements of the Accountability of Tax Dollars Act of 2002 and Dodd-Frank Wall Street Reform and Consumer Protection Act (Dodd-Frank Act).

The SEC prepares these statements in conformity with U.S. generally accepted accounting principles (GAAP) for the Federal Government and OMB Circular A-136, *Financial Reporting Requirements*.

The section contains the Government Accountability Office's (GAO) audit opinion, followed by the SEC's response. Then, the section shows the required financial statements for the SEC. The statements provide a comparison of fiscal year (FY) 2013 and FY 2012 information. The SEC prepares the following required financial statements.

- Balance Sheet – presents, as of a specific time, resources owned or managed by the SEC that provide probable economic benefits (assets), amounts owed by the entity (liabilities), and amounts which comprise the difference (net position).

- Statement of Net Cost – presents the gross cost incurred by the SEC less exchange revenue earned from its activities, including registration and filing fees. The SEC presents net cost of operations by program to provide cost information at the program level. The SEC recognizes collections as exchange revenue on the Statement of Net Cost, even when the collections are transferred to other entities.

- Statement of Changes in Net Position – reports the change in net position during the reporting period. This statement presents changes to Cumulative Results of Operations.

- Statement of Budgetary Resources – provides information about how budgetary resources were made available as well as their status at the end of the year.

- Statement of Custodial Activity – reports the collection of revenue for the Treasury General Fund. The SEC accounts for sources and disposition of the collections as custodial activities on this statement. Custodial collections of non-exchange revenue, such as amounts collected from violators of securities laws as a result of enforcement proceedings, are reported only on the Statement of Custodial Activity.

The SEC does not have stewardship over resources or responsibilities for which supplementary stewardship reporting would be required.

Budgetary information aggregated for purposes of the Statement of Budgetary Resources is disaggregated for each of the SEC's major budget accounts and is presented as Required Supplementary Information.

The accompanying Notes to the Financial Statements provide a description of significant accounting policies as well as detailed information on select statement lines.

This section contains stand alone, comparative financial statements and accompanying notes for the Investor Protection Fund as required by the Dodd-Frank Act. These statements include the Balance Sheet, Statement of Net Cost, Statement of Changes in Net Position, and Statement of Budgetary Resources.

Message from the Chief Financial Officer

I am delighted to join Chair White in presenting the SEC's Agency Financial Report (AFR) for fiscal year (FY) 2013. We hope you find the AFR a useful summary of the SEC's use of resources, operating performance, financial stewardship, and internal control.

Our independent auditor, the Government Accountability Office, has issued an unmodified opinion on our financial statements and internal controls. In addition, the SEC successfully downgraded the severity of our two remaining significant deficiencies from FY 2012 related to internal controls over accounting for budgetary resources, and property and equipment. We achieved these results through steps that included:

- Refining the process for recording upward and downward adjustments;

- Improving regular reconciliations between financial sub-systems, subsidiary ledgers, and the general ledger;

- Enhancing the regular agency reviews of undelivered orders (UDOs);

- Instituting daily tie point analyses;

- Implementing a procedure for tracking fixed assets, to ensure that new assets were added timely and accurately;

- Ensuring that all potentially capitalizable assets are reviewed by an accountant prior to recording the asset in the general ledger; and

- Enhancing the SEC's process for performing a full physical inventory.

GAO did identify a new significant deficiency in the area of information security. Specifically, it was noted that we did not consistently implement and evidence effective internal controls related to risk management and project oversight in our information systems operations. We are in the process of implementing corrective actions to ensure consistent application and documentation of our security protocols.

I am also pleased to report that the SEC has successfully completed its first full year of operations under a Federal Shared Service Provider (FSSP) model, engaging with the Department of Transportation's Enterprise Service Center (ESC) to host our financial system and record many of our financial transactions. To adapt to this new model, the SEC's Office of Financial Management (OFM) has reorganized and shifted its emphasis from data entry to focus more on data analysis. For example, OFM instituted procedures to bolster monitoring over transactions affecting financial reporting. The Office also strengthened its program for monitoring internal controls, to enhance accountability and to identify any problems quickly, before they grow in size and scope.

Over the last few years, we have made significant strides forward in the SEC's multi-year path towards a strong, sustainable internal control posture. This progress would not have been possible without the dedication and hard work of many staff across the SEC who manage the SEC's finances and controls. In the coming year, the agency will work to address the ongoing challenge of further improving the systems that support financial processes and controls, together with the Enterprise Service Center. These efforts include ESC's upgrade of the financial system Delphi, ESC's deployment of a new travel system, and the development of a data repository that can bring financial information together for improved analysis and reporting.

This section of the AFR displays the SEC's financial statements and notes, both for the entity as a whole and for the Investor Protection Fund, as required under Section 922 of the Dodd-Frank Act. It also contains the results of the FY 2013 audit conducted by the U.S. Government Accountability Office, as well as the agency's response.

These documents are important because they give the public a window into the state of the SEC's finances and its internal controls over financial reporting. Thank you for taking the time to read these materials, and we hope you will find them both useful and informative.

Sincerely,

Kenneth A. Johnson
Chief Financial Officer
December 12, 2013

Report of Independent Auditors

U.S. GOVERNMENT ACCOUNTABILITY OFFICE

441 G St. N.W.
Washington, DC 20548

Independent Auditor's Report

To the Chair of the United States Securities and Exchange Commission

In our audits of the 2013 and 2012 financial statements of the United States Securities and Exchange Commission (SEC) and the Investor Protection Fund (IPF), we found

- the financial statements as of and for the fiscal years ended September 30, 2013, and 2012, are presented fairly, in all material respects, in accordance with U.S. generally accepted accounting principles;
- although internal controls could be improved, SEC maintained, in all material respects, effective internal control over financial reporting as of September 30, 2013; and
- no reportable noncompliance in fiscal year 2013 with provisions of applicable laws, regulations, contracts, and grant agreements we tested.

The following sections discuss in more detail (1) our report on SEC's and IPF's financial statements and on internal control over financial reporting, and required supplementary information (RSI) and other information included with the financial statements; (2) our report on compliance with laws, regulations, contracts, and grant agreements; and (3) SEC's comments on a draft of this report.

Report on SEC's and IPF's Financial Statements and on Internal Control over Financial Reporting

We agreed, under our audit authority, to audit the financial statements of SEC and IPF. The Securities Exchange Act of 1934, as amended in 2010 by the Dodd-Frank Wall Street Reform and Consumer Protection Act (Dodd-Frank Act), requires that SEC provide separate annual audited financial statements for IPF to Congress.[1] IPF's financial transactions are also included in SEC's overall financial statements. Further, in accordance with the Dodd-Frank Act, we are assessing the effectiveness of SEC's internal control over financial reporting, evaluating SEC's assessment of such effectiveness, and attesting to SEC's assessment of its internal control over financial reporting.[2] SEC's financial statements comprise the balance sheets as of September 30, 2013, and 2012; the related statements of net cost of operations, changes in net position, budgetary resources, and custodial activity for the fiscal years then ended; and the related notes to the financial statements. IPF's financial statements comprise the balance sheets as of September 30, 2013, and 2012; the related statements of net cost of operations, changes in net position, and budgetary resources for the fiscal years then ended; and the related notes to the financial statements. We audited SEC's internal control over financial reporting as of September 30, 2013, based on criteria established under 31 U.S.C. § 3512(c), (d), commonly known as the Federal Managers' Financial Integrity Act (FMFIA).

---

[1]Section 21F(g)(5) of the Securities Exchange Act of 1934, 15 U.S.C. § 78u-6(g)(5).

[2]Pub. L. No. 111-203, § 963(a), (b)(2), 124 Stat. 1376, 1910 (2010), *codified at* 15 U.S.C. § 78d-8(a), (b)(2).

We conducted our audits in accordance with U.S. generally accepted government auditing standards. We believe that the audit evidence we obtained is sufficient and appropriate to provide a basis for our audit opinions.

Management's Responsibility

SEC management is responsible for (1) the preparation and fair presentation of its financial statements and those of IPF in accordance with U.S. generally accepted accounting principles; (2) preparing, measuring, and presenting the RSI in accordance with U.S. generally accepted accounting principles; (3) preparing and presenting other information included in documents containing the audited financial statements and auditor's report, and ensuring the consistency of that information with the audited financial statements and the RSI; (4) maintaining effective internal control over financial reporting, including the design, implementation, and maintenance of internal control relevant to the preparation and fair presentation of financial statements that are free from material misstatement, whether due to fraud or error; (5) evaluating the effectiveness of internal control over financial reporting based on the criteria established under FMFIA; and (6) providing its assertion about the effectiveness of internal control over financial reporting as of September 30, 2013, based on its evaluation, included in the Management Assurance section of the annual financial report (AFR).

Auditor's Responsbility

Our responsibility is to express opinions on SEC's and IPF's financial statements and opinions on SEC's and IPF's internal control over financial reporting based on our audits. U.S. generally accepted government auditing standards require that we plan and perform the audits to obtain reasonable assurance about whether the financial statements are free from material misstatement, and whether effective internal control over financial reporting was maintained in all material respects. We are also responsible for applying certain limited procedures to the RSI and other information included with the financial statements.

An audit of financial statements involves performing procedures to obtain audit evidence about the amounts and disclosures in the financial statements. The procedures selected depend on the auditor's judgment, including the auditor's assessment of the risks of material misstatement of the financial statements, whether due to fraud or error. In making those risk assessments, the auditor considers internal control relevant to the entity's preparation and fair presentation of the financial statements in order to design audit procedures that are appropriate in the circumstances. An audit of financial statements also involves evaluating the appropriateness of the accounting policies used and the reasonableness of significant accounting estimates made by management, as well as evaluating the overall presentation of the financial statements. An audit of internal control over financial reporting includes obtaining an understanding of internal control over financial reporting, assessing the risk that a material weakness exists, evaluating the design and operating effectiveness of internal control over financial reporting based on the assessed risk, and testing relevant internal control over financial reporting. Our audit of internal control also considered the entity's process for evaluating and reporting on internal control over financial reporting based on criteria established under FMFIA. Our audits also included performing such other procedures as we considered necessary in the circumstances.

We did not evaluate all internal controls relevant to operating objectives as broadly established under FMFIA, such as those controls relevant to preparing performance information and ensuring efficient operations. We limited our internal control testing to testing controls over financial reporting. Our internal control testing was for the purpose of expressing an opinion on whether effective internal control over financial reporting was maintained, in all material respects. Consequently, our audit may not identify all deficiencies in internal control over financial reporting that are less severe than a material weakness.[3]

Definitions and Inherent Limitations of Internal Control over Financial Reporting

An entity's internal control over financial reporting is a process effected by those charged with governance, management, and other personnel, the objectives of which are to provide reasonable assurance that (1) transactions are properly recorded, processed, and summarized to permit the preparation of financial statements in accordance with U.S. generally accepted accounting principles, and assets are safeguarded against loss from unauthorized acquisition, use, or disposition, and (2) transactions are executed in accordance with laws governing the use of budget authority and with other applicable laws, regulations, contracts, and grant agreements that could have a direct and material effect on the financial statements.

Because of its inherent limitations, internal control over financial reporting may not prevent, or detect and correct, misstatements due to fraud or error. We also caution that projecting any evaluation of effectiveness to future periods is subject to the risk that controls may become inadequate because of changes in conditions, or that the degree of compliance with the policies or procedures may deteriorate.

Opinion on SEC's Financial Statements

In our opinion, SEC's financial statements present fairly, in all material respects, SEC's financial position as of September 30, 2013, and 2012, and its net cost of operations, changes in net position, budgetary resources, and custodial activity for the fiscal years then ended in accordance with U.S. generally accepted accounting principles.

Opinion on IPF's Financial Statements

In our opinion, IPF's financial statements present fairly, in all material respects, IPF's financial position as of September 30, 2013, and 2012, and its net cost of operations, changes in net position, and budgetary resources for the fiscal years then ended in accordance with U.S. generally accepted accounting principles.

Opinions on Internal Control over Financial Reporting

Although certain internal controls could be improved, SEC maintained, in all material respects, effective internal control over financial reporting as of September 30, 2013, for SEC and IPF based on criteria established under FMFIA.[4] Our opinions on SEC's internal control are consistent with SEC's assertion that its internal controls over financial reporting, both for the

---

[3]A material weakness is a deficiency, or combination of deficiencies, in internal control over financial reporting, such that there is a reasonable possibility that a material misstatement of the entity's financial statements will not be prevented, or detected and corrected, on a timely basis. A deficiency in internal control exists when the design or opera ion of a control does not allow management or employees, in the normal course of performing heir assigned functions, to prevent, or detect and correct, misstatements on a imely basis.

[4]31 U.S.C. § 3512(c), (d).

agency as a whole and for IPF, were operating effectively as of September 30, 2013, and that no material weaknesses were found in the design or operation of the controls.[5]

As discussed in greater detail later in this report, our fiscal year 2013 audit identified continuing and new deficiencies in SEC's internal control over information security that collectively constituted a significant deficiency in SEC's internal control over financial reporting.[6] This significant deficiency pertained to SEC's overall financial reporting, but not that of IPF because of the nature of IPF's financial transactions during fiscal year 2013.

Specifically, SEC was not able to adequately address control deficiencies in information security that we reported in fiscal year 2012.[7] In addition, our work in fiscal year 2013 identified several new control deficiencies in information security. We considered the aggregate of these deficiencies in information security to represent a significant deficiency in SEC's internal control over financial reporting.

However, during fiscal year 2013, SEC made notable progress in addressing other internal control deficiencies we reported in fiscal year 2012. Specifically, SEC sufficiently addressed the deficiencies in its financial reporting for budgetary resources and property and equipment such that we no longer consider the remaining control deficiencies in these areas, individually or collectively, to represent significant deficiencies as of September 30, 2013.

During our 2013 audit, we also identified deficiencies in SEC's internal control over financial reporting that we do not consider to be material weaknesses or significant deficiencies. Nonetheless, these deficiencies warrant SEC management's attention. We have communicated these matters to SEC management and, where appropriate, will report on them separately to SEC, along with recommendations for corrective actions.

Significant Deficiency over Information Security

During our 2013 audit, we found that SEC did not consistently implement effective internal control over its information systems operations, including implementation of some key elements of its information security program across certain financial systems and applications that support financial reporting. Specifically, our fiscal year 2013 testing identified significant configuration issues in a key SEC financial system during transition to SEC's new data center in June 2013. For example, SEC did not always securely configure firewalls; implement mandatory security configuration settings, such as recording failed log-on attempts or logging events to a centralized server; or disable unnecessary services and ports on servers, in accordance with

---

[5]The Dodd-Frank Act requires that (1) SEC submit annual reports to Congress describing management's responsibility for internal control over financial repor ing and assessing the effectiveness of such internal control during the fiscal year, (2) the SEC Chairman and Chief Financial Officer attest to SEC's reports, and (3) GAO attest to and report on the assessment made by SEC. Pub. L. No. 111-203, § 963, 124 Stat. 1376, 1910 (2010), *codified at* 15 U.S.C. § 78d-8. SEC conducted an evaluation of its internal control over financial reporting in accordance wi h the Office of Management and Budget's Circular No. A-123, *Management's Responsibility for Internal Control,* based on criteria established under FMFIA.

[6]A significant deficiency is a deficiency, or a combination of deficiencies, in internal control hat is less severe than a material weakness, yet important enough to merit attention by those charged wi h governance.

[7]GAO, *Management Report: Improvements Needed in SEC's Internal Controls and Accounting Procedures,* GAO-13-274R (Washington, D.C.: Apr. 4, 2013).

SEC policy. Although SEC took prompt action to reduce the risk associated with the improper configurations we identified, the internal control deficiencies indicate that SEC's monitoring process was not always effective in identifying and correcting internal control issues in a timely manner. For example, SEC did not effectively implement a continuous monitoring process over a key SEC financial system, such as enabling and configuring systems logging service and auditing functionalities in accordance with SEC security baseline requirements, or scanning database instances on a timely basis in order to readily detect and correct instances in which SEC policy was not being effectively implemented.

The deficiencies we found also indicate that SEC did not consistently implement effective risk assessment and project oversight related to a key SEC financial system. Specifically, SEC (1) did not consistently implement an effective risk management process, (2) did not always provide adequate contractor oversight for its information technology (IT) project contractors, and (3) did not always apply adequate project management discipline over its IT projects. For example, SEC did not appropriately evaluate and document security risks related to the transition to its new data center. SEC also did not appropriately identify roles, resources, and responsibilities for IT contractor oversight, including assessing contractor performance in completing project deliverables related to the data center transition. Further, SEC did not complete several critical path project tasks identified in its project plan prior to implementation dates for the data center transition, or take remedial actions to address the missed critical path project tasks.

During our 2013 audit, we also identified continuing deficiencies in SEC's information security related to (1) inadequate access control over financial systems operated by SEC related to user identification and authentication, authorization, and audit and monitoring and (2) inconsistent deployment of patches, which could jeopardize the data integrity and confidentiality of SEC's financial information. These deficiencies decreased assurance regarding the reliability of the data processed by key financial systems and increased the risk that unauthorized individuals could gain access to critical hardware or software and intentionally or inadvertently access, alter, or delete sensitive data or computer programs. Consequently, the combination of the continuing and new information security deficiencies existing as of September 30, 2013, considered collectively, represent a significant deficiency in SEC's internal control over information security.

Until SEC consistently implements effective internal control over its information systems operations—including implementation of all key elements of its information security program systematically across all of its financial systems and its general support system, which support financial reporting—increased risk exists that the information that is processed, stored, and transmitted on its systems remains vulnerable to unauthorized use, and management will not have sufficient assurance that financial information is adequately safeguarded from inadvertent or deliberate misuse, fraudulent use, improper disclosure, or destruction.

Other Matters

Required Supplementary Information

U.S. generally accepted accounting principles issued by the Federal Accounting Standards Advisory Board (FASAB) require that RSI be presented to supplement the financial statements.[8]

---

[8]RSI is comprised of "Management's Discussion and Analysis" and he "Combined Statement of Budgetary Resources" that are included wi h the financial statements.

Although not a part of the financial statements, FASAB considers this information to be an essential part of financial reporting for placing the financial statements in appropriate operational, economic, or historical context. We have applied certain limited procedures to the RSI in accordance with U.S. generally accepted government auditing standards, which consisted of inquiries of management about the methods of preparing the RSI and comparing the information for consistency with management's responses to the auditor's inquiries, the financial statements, and other knowledge we obtained during the audit of the financial statements, in order to report omissions or material departures from FASAB guidelines, if any, identified by these limited procedures. We did not audit and we do not express an opinion or provide any assurance on the RSI because the limited procedures we applied do not provide sufficient evidence to express an opinion or provide any assurance.

Other Information

SEC's other information contains a wide range of information, some of which is not directly related to the financial statements.[9] This information is presented for purposes of additional analysis and is not a required part of the financial statements or RSI. We read the other information included with the financial statements in order to identify material inconsistencies, if any, with the audited financial statements. Our audit was conducted for the purpose of forming an opinion on SEC's and IPF's financial statements. We did not audit and do not express an opinion or provide any assurance on the other information.

Report on Compliance with Laws, Regulations, Contracts, and Grant Agreements

In connection with our audits of SEC's and IPF's financial statements, we tested compliance with selected provisions of applicable laws, regulations, contracts, and grant agreements consistent with our auditor's responsbility discussed below. We caution that noncompliance may occur and not be detected by these tests. We performed our tests of compliance in accordance with U.S. generally accepted government auditing standards.

Management's Responsibility

SEC management is responsible for complying with laws, regulations, contracts, and grant agreements applicable to SEC and IPF.

Auditor's Responsbility

Our responsibility is to test compliance with selected provisions of laws, regulations, contracts, and grant agreements applicable to SEC and IPF that have a direct effect on the determination of material amounts and disclosures in the SEC and IPF financial statements, and perform certain other limited procedures. Accordingly, we did not test compliance with all laws, regulations, contracts, and grant agreements applicable to SEC and IPF.

Results of Our Tests for Compliance with Laws, Regulations, Contracts, and Grant Agreements

Our tests for compliance with selected provisions of applicable laws, regulations, contracts, and grant agreements disclosed no instances of noncompliance for fiscal year 2013 that would be reportable under U.S. generally accepted government auditing standards. However, the

---

[9]Other informaion is comprised of other accompanying information, which presents the "Schedule of Spending" and other information included with the financial statements, other than RSI and the auditor's report.

objective of our tests was not to provide an opinion on compliance with laws, regulations, contracts, and grant agreements applicable to SEC and IPF. Accordingly, we do not express such an opinion.

Intended Purpose of Report on Compliance with Laws, Regulations, Contracts, and Grant Agreements

The purpose of this report is solely to describe the scope of our testing of compliance with selected provisions of applicable laws, regulations, contracts, and grant agreements, and the results of that testing, and not to provide an opinion on compliance. This report is an integral part of an audit performed in accordance with U.S. generally accepted government auditing standards in considering compliance. Accordingly, this report on compliance with laws, regulations, contracts, and grant agreements is not suitable for any other purpose.

Agency Comments

In commenting on a draft of this report, SEC's Chair expressed her pleasure that GAO found that SEC had successfully remediated the two significant deficiencies identified in 2012, and attributed this accomplishment to the hard work and dedication of staff in SEC's Office of Financial Management, Office of Acquisitions, and Office of Information Technology. The Chair stated that SEC will continue to optimize its internal controls and further improve the systems that support financial processes and controls, jointly with its shared service provider. The Chair added that SEC will focus on the significant deficiency we reported in the area of information security, specifically by taking corrective actions to consistently implement and evidence effective internal controls related to risk management and project oversight in its information systems operations. The complete text of SEC's comments is reprinted in enclosure I.

James R. Dalkin
Director
Financial Management and Assurance

December 13, 2013

Enclosure I: Management's Response to Audit Opinion

UNITED STATES
SECURITIES AND EXCHANGE COMMISSION
WASHINGTON, D.C. 20549

THE CHAIR

December 11, 2013

Mr. James R. Dalkin
Director
Financial Management and Assurance
United States Government Accountability Office
441 G Street, N.W.
Washington, DC 20548

Dear Mr. Dalkin:

Thank you for the opportunity to review and comment on the audit report of the Government Accountability Office (GAO). I am pleased that the GAO's FY 2013 audit found that the SEC's financial statements and notes were presented fairly in all material respects and in accordance with U.S. generally accepted accounting principles.

I am also pleased the GAO found that the SEC maintained, in all material respects, effective internal controls over financial reporting and, in addition, that we have successfully remediated the two significant deficiencies identified in 2012. This accomplishment was the result of the hard work and dedication of staff in the SEC's Office of Financial Management, Office of Acquisitions, and Office of Information Technology. In 2013, the SEC also successfully completed its first full year of operations under a Federal Shared Service Provider (FSSP) model together with the Department of Transportation's Enterprise Service Center (ESC), which hosts our financial system and records many of our financial transactions.

In 2014, the SEC will continue to optimize our internal controls and further improve the systems that support financial processes and controls, jointly with the Enterprise Service Center. We also will focus on the newly identified significant deficiency in the area of information security. Specifically, we have initiated corrective actions to consistently implement and evidence effective internal controls related to risk management and project oversight in our information systems operations.

I very much appreciate the professional manner in which you and your team conducted the audit for FY 2013. I look forward to continuing our productive dialogue in the coming months on the SEC's efforts to address the areas noted in your report. If you have any questions, please feel free to contact me.

Sincerely,

Mary Jo White
Chair

SEC Financial Statements

Financial Statements

U.S. SECURITIES AND EXCHANGE COMMISSION

Balance Sheets

As of September 30, 2013 and 2012

(DOLLARS IN THOUSANDS)	FY 2013	FY 2012
ASSETS (Note 2):		
Intragovernmental:		
Fund Balance with Treasury (Note 3)	$ 8,154,737	$ 7,443,432
Investments, Net (Note 5)	1,282,642	973,916
Advances and Prepayments	1,623	7,824
Total Intragovernmental	9,439,002	8,425,172
Cash and Other Monetary Assets (Note 4)	389	1,066
Accounts Receivable, Net (Note 6)	387,027	236,691
Property and Equipment, Net (Note 7)	126,871	97,570
Advances and Prepayments	—	235
Total Assets	$ 9,953,289	$ 8,760,734
LIABILITIES (Note 8):		
Intragovernmental:		
Accounts Payable	$ 5,675	$ 8,829
Employee Benefits	3,086	5,184
Unfunded FECA and Unemployment Liability	1,308	1,441
Custodial Liability	68,831	62,497
Liability for Non-Entity Assets	3,069	2,457
Total Intragovernmental	81,969	80,408
Accounts Payable	38,313	39,474
Actuarial FECA Liability	7,155	8,050
Accrued Payroll and Benefits	15,405	13,765
Accrued Leave	51,706	48,531
Registrant Deposits	32,857	33,689
Liability for Disgorgement and Penalties (Note 16)	2,065,202	932,763
Other Accrued Liabilities (Note 8)	5,509	5,765
Total Liabilities	2,298,116	1,162,445
Commitments and Contingencies (Note 10)		
NET POSITION:		
Unexpended Appropriations – All Other Funds	764	764
Cumulative Results of Operations – Funds from Dedicated Collections (Note 11)	7,653,217	7,596,330
Cumulative Results of Operations – All Other Funds	1,192	1,195
Total Net Position – Funds from Dedicated Collections	7,653,217	7,596,330
Total Net Position – All Other Funds	1,956	1,959
Total Net Position	$ 7,655,173	$ 7,598,289
Total Liabilities and Net Position	$ 9,953,289	$ 8,760,734

The accompanying notes are an integral part of these financial statements.

U.S. SECURITIES AND EXCHANGE COMMISSION

Statements of Net Cost

For the years ended September 30, 2013 and 2012

(DOLLARS IN THOUSANDS)	FY 2013	FY 2012
PROGRAM COSTS (Note 12):		
Enforcement	$ 451,072	$ 400,574
Compliance Inspections and Examinations	265,348	235,737
Corporation Finance	141,777	137,441
Trading and Markets	76,213	67,936
Investment Management	50,366	48,238
Economic and Risk Analysis	29,504	20,296
General Counsel	41,417	40,951
Other Program Offices	51,768	48,791
Agency Direction and Administrative Support	216,077	190,314
Inspector General	7,032	7,238
Total Program Costs	1,330,574	1,197,516
Less: Earned Revenue Not Attributed to Programs (Note 12)	1,764,267	1,647,859
Net (Income) Cost from Operations (Note 15)	$ (433,693)	$ (450,343)

The accompanying notes are an integral part of these financial statements.

U.S. SECURITIES AND EXCHANGE COMMISSION

Statements of Changes in Net Position

For the years ended September 30, 2013 and 2012

(DOLLARS IN THOUSANDS)	FY 2013		
	Funds from Dedicated Collections	**All Other Funds**	**Consolidated Total**
CUMULATIVE RESULTS OF OPERATIONS:			
Beginning Balances	$ 7,596,330	$ 1,195	$ 7,597,525
Budgetary Financing Sources:			
Appropriations Used	47,546	—	47,546
Non-Exchange Revenue	655	—	655
Other	6	—	6
Other Financing Sources:			
Transfers In/Out Without Reimbursement	—	—	—
Imputed Financing (Note 13)	32,958	—	32,958
Other (Note 17)	(10)	(457,964)	(457,974)
Total Financing Sources	81,155	(457,964)	(376,809)
Net Income (Cost) from Operations	(24,268)	457,961	433,693
Net Change	56,887	(3)	56,884
Cumulative Results of Operations (Note 11)	7,653,217	1,192	7,654,409
UNEXPENDED APPROPRIATIONS:			
Beginning Balances	—	764	764
Budgetary Financing Sources:			
Appropriations Received	47,641	—	47,641
Other Adjustments	(95)	—	(95)
Appropriations Used	(47,546)	—	(47,546)
Total Budgetary Financing Sources	—	—	—
Total Unexpended Appropriations	—	764	764
Net Position, End of Period	$ 7,653,217	$ 1,956	$ 7,655,173

(DOLLARS IN THOUSANDS)	FY 2012		
	Funds from Dedicated Collections	All Other Funds	Consolidated Total
CUMULATIVE RESULTS OF OPERATIONS:			
Beginning Balances	$ 7,409,186	$ 1,202	$ 7,410,388
Budgetary Financing Sources:			
Appropriations Used	32,601	(29)	32,572
Non-Exchange Revenue	757	—	757
Other	—	—	—
Other Financing Sources:			
Transfers In/Out Without Reimbursement	(784)	784	—
Imputed Financing (Note 13)	30,588	—	30,588
Other (Note 17)	—	(327,123)	(327,123)
Total Financing Sources	63,162	(326,368)	(263,206)
Net Income (Cost) from Operations	123,982	326,361	450,343
Net Change	187,144	(7)	187,137
Cumulative Results of Operations (Note 11)	7,596,330	1,195	7,597,525
UNEXPENDED APPROPRIATIONS:			
Beginning Balances	—	735	735
Budgetary Financing Sources:			
Appropriations Received	32,601	—	32,601
Other Adjustments	—	—	—
Appropriations Used	(32,601)	29	(32,572)
Total Budgetary Financing Sources	—	29	29
Total Unexpended Appropriations	—	764	764
Net Position, End of Period	$ 7,596,330	$ 1,959	$ 7,598,289

The accompanying notes are an integral part of these financial statements.

U.S. SECURITIES AND EXCHANGE COMMISSION

Statements of Budgetary Resources

For the years ended September 30, 2013 and 2012

(DOLLARS IN THOUSANDS)	FY 2013	FY 2012
BUDGETARY RESOURCES:		
Unobligated Balance, Brought Forward, October 1	$ 43,672	$ (279,929)
Recoveries of Prior Year Unpaid Obligations	30,777	26,688
Downward Adjustments of Prior Year Unfunded Lease Obligations (Note 14.C)	2,009	141,933
Unobligated Balance from Prior Year Budget Authority, Net	76,458	(111,308)
Appropriations (Discretionary and Mandatory)	117,811	58,226
Spending Authority from Offsetting Collections (Discretionary and Mandatory)	1,208,208	1,289,139
Total Budgetary Resources	$ 1,402,477	$ 1,236,057
STATUS OF BUDGETARY RESOURCES:		
Obligations Incurred (Note 14):	$ 1,257,711	$ 1,192,385
Unobligated Balance, End of Year:		
Apportioned	518,816	522,993
Exempt from Apportionment	43,749	12,642
Unapportioned	(417,799)	(491,963)
Total Unobligated Balance, End of Year	144,766	43,672
Total Budgetary Resources	$ 1,402,477	$ 1,236,057
CHANGE IN OBLIGATED BALANCE:		
Unpaid Obligations:		
Unpaid Obligations, Brought Forward, October 1 (Gross)	$ 954,598	$ 1,110,634
Obligations Incurred	1,257,711	1,192,385
Outlays (Gross)	(1,324,876)	(1,179,800)
Recoveries of Prior Year Unpaid Obligations	(30,777)	(26,688)
Downward Adjustments of Prior Year Unfunded Lease Obligations (Note 14.C)	(2,009)	(141,933)
Unpaid Obligations, End of Year	854,647	954,598
Uncollected Payments:		
Uncollected Payments, Federal Sources, Brought Forward, October 1	(189)	(47)
Change in Uncollected Payments, Federal Sources	(63)	(142)
Uncollected Payments, Federal Sources, End of Year	(252)	(189)
Obligated Balance, End of Year	854,395	954,409
Memorandum (non-add) entries:		
Obligated Balance, Start of Year	$ 954,409	$ 1,110,587
Obligated Balance, End of Year	$ 854,395	$ 954,409
BUDGET AUTHORITY AND OUTLAYS, NET:		
Budget Authority, Gross (Discretionary and Mandatory)	$ 1,326,019	$ 1,347,365
Actual Offsetting Collections (Discretionary and Mandatory)	(1,274,195)	(1,288,998)
Change in Uncollected Customer Payments from Federal Sources (Discretionary and Mandatory)	(63)	(142)
Budget Authority, Net (Discretionary and Mandatory)	$ 51,761	$ 58,225
Outlays, Gross (Discretionary and Mandatory)	$ 1,324,876	$ 1,179,800
Actual Offsetting Collections (Discretionary and Mandatory)	(1,274,195)	(1,288,998)
Outlays, Net (Discretionary and Mandatory)	50,681	(109,198)
Distributed Offsetting Receipts	(3,150)	(1,123)
Agency Outlays, Net (Discretionary and Mandatory)	$ 47,531	$ (110,321)

The accompanying notes are an integral part of these financial statements.

U.S. SECURITIES AND EXCHANGE COMMISSION

Statements of Custodial Activity

For the years ended September 30, 2013 and 2012

(DOLLARS IN THOUSANDS)	FY 2013	FY 2012
REVENUE ACTIVITY:		
Sources of Cash Collections:		
Disgorgement and Penalties	$ 518,592	$ 377,645
Other	1,355	1,059
Total Cash Collections	519,947	378,704
Accrual Adjustments	6,334	10,633
Total Custodial Revenue	526,281	389,337
DISPOSITION OF COLLECTIONS:		
Amounts Transferred to:		
Department of the Treasury	519,947	378,704
Amounts Yet to be Transferred	6,334	10,633
Total Disposition of Collections	526,281	389,337
NET CUSTODIAL ACTIVITY	$ —	$ —

The accompanying notes are an integral part of these financial statements.

Notes to the Financial Statements

U.S. SECURITIES AND EXCHANGE COMMISSION
As of September 30, 2013 and 2012

NOTE 1. Significant Accounting Policies

A. Reporting Entity

The U.S. Securities and Exchange Commission (SEC) is an independent agency of the U.S. Government established pursuant to the Securities Exchange Act of 1934 (Exchange Act), charged with regulating this country's capital markets. The SEC's mission is to protect investors; maintain fair, orderly, and efficient markets; and facilitate capital formation. The SEC works with Congress, other executive branch agencies, Self Regulatory Organizations (SROs) (e.g., stock exchanges and the Financial Industry Regulatory Authority (FINRA)), accounting and auditing standards setters, state securities regulators, law enforcement officials, and many other organizations in support of the agency's mission.

The agency's programs protect investors and promote the public interest by fostering and enforcing compliance with the Federal securities laws; establishing an effective regulatory environment; facilitating access to the information investors need to make informed investment decisions; and enhancing the SEC's performance through effective alignment and management of human, information, and financial capital.

The SEC consists of five presidentially-appointed Commissioners, with staggered five-year terms. The SEC is organized into five divisions and multiple offices. The five divisions are the Division of Enforcement, the Division of Corporation Finance, the Division of Trading and Markets, the Division of Investment Management, and the Division of Economic and Risk Analysis. The offices include the Office of Compliance Inspections and Examinations, Office of General Counsel, Office of Investor Education and Advocacy, Office of the Chief Accountant, Office of International Affairs, Office of Administrative Law Judges, Office of Credit Ratings, Office of the Investor Advocate, Office of Municipal Securities, Office of Inspector General, eleven regional offices, and various supporting services.

The SEC reporting entity includes the Investor Protection Fund (See *Note 1.T, Investor Protection Fund*). In addition to being included in the SEC's financial statements, the Investor Protection Fund's financial activities and balances are also presented separately as stand-alone financial statements, as required by Exchange Act Section 21F(g)5.

As discussed in *Note 10.A, Commitments: Securities Investor Protection Act*, the SEC reporting entity does not include the Securities Investor Protection Corporation (SIPC).

As discussed in *Note 1.S, Disgorgement and Penalties,* disgorgement funds collected and held by the SEC on behalf of harmed investors are part of the SEC reporting entity. However, disgorgement funds held by the U.S. Courts and by non-Federal receivers on behalf of harmed investors are not part of the SEC reporting entity.

B. Basis of Presentation and Accounting

(1) Basis of Presentation and Accounting

The accompanying financial statements present the financial position, net cost of operations, changes in net position, budgetary resources, and custodial activities of the SEC as required by the Accountability of Tax Dollars Act of 2002. The statements may differ from other financial reports submitted pursuant to Office of Management and Budget (OMB) directives for the purpose of monitoring and controlling the use of the SEC budgetary resources, due to differences in accounting and reporting principles discussed in the following paragraphs. The SEC's books and records serve as the source of the information presented in the accompanying financial statements.

The agency classifies assets, liabilities, revenues, and costs in these financial statements according to the type of entity associated with the transactions. Intragovernmental assets and liabilities are those due from or to other Federal entities. Intragovernmental revenues are earned from other Federal entities. Intragovernmental costs are payments or accruals due to other Federal entities.

The SEC's financial statements are prepared in conformity with generally accepted accounting principles (GAAP) for Federal reporting entities and presented in conformity with OMB Circular A-136, *Financial Reporting Requirements*. The Balance Sheet, Statement of Net Cost, and Statement of Changes in Net Position are prepared using the accrual basis of accounting. Accordingly, revenues are recognized when earned and expenses are recognized when incurred without regard to the receipt or payment of cash. These principles differ from budgetary accounting and reporting principles on which the Statement of Budgetary Resources is prepared. The differences relate primarily to the capitalization and depreciation of property and equipment, as well as the recognition of other assets and liabilities. The Statement of Custodial Activity is presented on the modified cash basis of accounting. Cash collections and amounts transferred to Treasury or the Investor Protection Fund are reported on a cash basis. The change in receivables and related payables are reported on an accrual basis.

The SEC presents net cost of operations by program. OMB Circular A-136 defines the term "major program" as describing an agency's mission, strategic goals, functions, activities, services, projects, processes, or any other meaningful grouping. The presentation by program is consistent with the presentation used by the agency in submitting its budget requests.

Certain prior year amounts presented on the Statement of Budgetary Resources and Required Supplementary Information have been reclassified to conform to the current year presentation required by OMB Circular A-136.

(2) Changes in Presentation

- Statement of Federal Financial Accounting Standards (SFFAS) 43, *Funds from Dedicated Collections: Amending Statement of Federal Financial Accounting Standards 27, Identifying and Reporting Earmarked Funds*, was issued in June 2012 and became effective in FY 2013. As discussed below, the SEC collects transaction fees from SROs and securities registration, tender offer, merger, and other fees from registrants. Except for securities registration, tender offer, merger, and other fees from registrants in excess of $50 million, that the SEC deposits into the Treasury General Fund and transfers to Treasury at the end of the fiscal year, all

of the SEC's collections meet the definition of dedicated collections discussed in SFFAS No. 43. The impact of this statement for the most part is a change in terminology from "earmarked funds" to "funds from dedicated collections," which is reflected in the FY 2013 financial statements and applicable notes.

- OMB Circular A-136 requires the disclosure of future lease payments for non-cancelable operating leases with terms of more than one year. The SEC's Note 9 discloses future lease payments for all non-cancelable leases with terms of more than one year, as well as the non-cancelable portion of cancelable commercial operating leases. Note 9 does not report comparative amounts from the prior fiscal year. In FY 2012, this note reported amounts for cancelable as well as non-cancelable lease periods. The SEC believes that the FY 2013 Note 9 conforms more precisely with the OMB reporting requirements in Circular A-136.

C. Use of Estimates

The preparation of financial statements in conformity with GAAP requires management to make estimates and assumptions that affect the reported amounts of assets and liabilities. These estimates and assumptions include, but are not limited to, the disclosure of contingent liabilities at the date of the financial statements and the reported amounts of revenue and expenses during the reporting period. Actual results may differ from these estimates. Estimates are also used when computing the allowance for uncollectible accounts and in the allocation of costs to the SEC programs presented in the Statement of Net Cost.

D. Intra- and Inter-Agency Relationships

The SEC is comprised of a single Federal agency with limited intra-entity transactions. The Investor Protection Fund can finance the operations of the SEC Office of Inspector General's Employee Suggestion Program and the Office of the Whistleblower on a reimbursable basis. This has given rise to a small amount of intra-entity eliminations of the related revenue and expense transactions between the Investor Protection Fund and the SEC's General Salaries and Expenses Fund.

E. Fund Accounting Structure

The SEC, in common with other Federal agencies, utilizes various Treasury Appropriation Fund Symbols (Funds), to recognize and track appropriation authority provided by Congress, collections from the public and other financial activity. These funds are described below:

(1) Funds from Dedicated Collections:

- **Salaries and Expenses:** Earned revenues from securities transaction fees from SROs are deposited into Fund X0100, *Salaries and Expenses, Securities and Exchange Commission*. These collections are dedicated to carrying out the SEC's mission, functions, and day to day operations and may be used in accordance with spending limits established by Congress. Collections in excess of Congressional spending limits are unavailable by law and reported as Non-Budgetary Fund Balance with Treasury (See *Note 3, Fund Balance with Treasury*).

- **Investor Protection Fund:** The Investor Protection Fund is a fund for dedicated collections that provides funding for the payment of whistleblower awards as required by the Dodd-Frank Act. The Investor Protection Fund is financed by a portion of monetary sanctions collected by the SEC in judicial or administrative actions brought by the SEC. Persons may receive award payments from the Fund if they provide original information to the SEC that results in a successful enforcement action and other conditions are met. In addition, the Fund can be used to finance the operations of the Office of the Whistleblower and the SEC Office of Inspector General's Employee Suggestion Program for the receipt of suggestions for improvements in work efficiency and effectiveness, and allegations of misconduct or mismanagement within the SEC. This activity is recognized in Fund X5567, *Monetary Sanctions and Interest, Investor Protection Fund, Securities and Exchange Commission (Investor Protection Fund)*. See *Note 1.T, Investor Protection Fund*.

- **Reserve Fund:** A portion of SEC registration fee collections up to $50 million in any one fiscal year may be deposited in the Reserve Fund, the balance of which cannot exceed $100 million. The Reserve Fund is a fund for dedicated collections that may be used by the SEC to obligate up to $100 million in one fiscal year as the SEC determines necessary to carry out its functions. Although amounts deposited in the

Reserve Fund are not subject to apportionment, the SEC must notify Congress when funds are obligated. The $100 million cap may be limited by the balance in the fund and Congressional action. Pursuant to the SEC's FY 2012 Appropriations Act, $25 million was temporarily rescinded, leaving $25 million available during FY 2012. The FY 2012 temporary rescission ended on September 30, 2012, leaving that $25 million available starting in FY 2013. The allowable $50 million for FY 2013 was collected in the first quarter of FY 2013. This activity is recognized in Fund X5566, *Securities and Exchange Commission Reserve Fund*.

(2) Miscellaneous Receipt Accounts:

- The Miscellaneous Receipt Accounts hold non-entity receipts and accounts receivable from custodial activities that the SEC cannot deposit into funds under its control. These accounts include registration fee collections in excess of amounts deposited into the Reserve Fund, receipts pursuant to certain SEC enforcement actions and other small collections that will be sent to the U.S. Treasury General Fund upon collection. This activity is recognized in Fund 0850.150, *Registration, Filing, and Transaction Fees, Securities and Exchange Commission*; Fund 1060, *Forfeitures of Unclaimed Money and Property*; Fund 1099, *Fines, Penalties, and Forfeitures, Not Otherwise Classified*; Fund 1435, *General Fund Proprietary Interest, Not Otherwise Classified*; and Fund 3220, *General Fund Proprietary Receipts, Not Otherwise Classified*. Miscellaneous Receipt Accounts are reported as "All Other Funds" on the Statement of Changes in Net Position.

(3) Deposit Funds:

- The Deposit Funds hold disgorgement, penalties, and interest collected and held on behalf of harmed investors, registrant monies held temporarily until earned by the SEC, and collections awaiting disposition or reclassification. This activity is recognized in Fund X6561, *Unearned Fees, Securities and Exchange Commission* and Fund X6563, *Disgorgement and Penalty Amounts Held for Investors, Securities and Exchange Commission*. Deposit Funds do not impact the SEC's Net Position and are not reported on the Statement of Changes in Net Position.

The SEC's lending and borrowing authority is limited to authority to borrow funds from Treasury and loan funds to the Securities and Investor Protection Corporation, as discussed in *Note 10, Commitments and Contingencies*. The SEC has custodial responsibilities, as disclosed in *Note 1.M, Liabilities*.

F. Funds from Dedicated Collections

A fund from dedicated collections is financed by specifically identified revenues, often supplemented by other financing sources, which remain available over time. The SEC collects specifically identified revenues and is required to use those revenues for designated activities, benefits or purposes and to account for them separately from the Government's general revenues. As described in *Note 1.E, Fund Accounting Structure*, the SEC's funds from dedicated collections are deposited into Fund X0100, *Salaries and Expenses*; Fund X5567, *Investor Protection Fund*; and Fund X5566, *Reserve Fund*.

G. Entity and Non-Entity Assets

Entity assets are assets that the SEC may use in its operations.

Non-entity assets are assets that the SEC holds on behalf of another Federal agency or a third party and are not available for the SEC's use. The SEC's non-entity assets include the following: (a) disgorgement, penalties, and interest collected and held or invested by the SEC; (b) disgorgement, penalties, and interest receivable that will be collected by the SEC; (c) securities registration, tender offer, merger, and other fees collected and receivable from registrants, in excess of amounts deposited in the SEC's Reserve Fund, and (d) other miscellaneous receivables and collections.

H. Fund Balance with Treasury

Fund Balance with Treasury (FBWT) reflects amounts the SEC holds in the U.S. Treasury that have not been invested in Federal securities. The components of the SEC's FBWT are in the various funds described in *Note 1.E, Fund Accounting Structure*.

The SEC conducts all of its banking activity in accordance with directives issued by the U.S. Department of the Treasury's Bureau of the Fiscal Service.

I. Investments

The SEC has the authority to invest disgorgement funds in Treasury securities including civil penalties collected under the "Fair Fund" provision of the Sarbanes-Oxley Act of 2002. As the funds are collected, the SEC holds them in a deposit fund account and may invest them in overnight and short-term market-based Treasury securities through the Bureau of the Fiscal Service. The interest earned is subject to taxation under Treasury Regulation Section 1.468B-2, *Taxation of Qualified Settlement Funds and Related Administrative Requirements*.

The SEC also has authority to invest amounts in the Investor Protection Fund in overnight and short-term market-based Treasury securities through the Bureau of the Fiscal Service. The interest earned on the investments is a component of the balance of the Fund and available to be used for expenses of the Investor Protection Fund.

Additional information regarding the SEC's investments is provided in *Note 5, Investments*.

J. Accounts Receivable and Allowance for Uncollectible Accounts

SEC's entity and non-entity accounts receivable consist primarily of amounts due from the public. Entity accounts receivable are amounts that the SEC may retain upon collection. Non-entity accounts receivable are amounts that the SEC will forward to another Federal agency or to the public after the funds are collected.

Entity Accounts Receivable

The bulk of the SEC's entity accounts receivable arise from securities transaction fees. In addition, the SEC has small amounts of activity arising from the sale of services provided by the SEC to other Federal agencies; reimbursement of employee travel by outside organizations; and employee-related debt. Entity accounts receivable balances are normally small at year-end due to the timing and payment requirements relative to the largest categories of accounts receivable activity. Specifically, securities transaction fees are payable to the SEC twice a year: in March for the period September through December, and in September for the period January through August. Accordingly, the year-end accounts receivable accrual generally represents fees payable to the SEC for one month of securities transaction fee activity (September).

Non-Entity Accounts Receivable

Non-entity accounts receivable arise mainly from amounts assessed against violators of securities laws, including disgorgement of illegal gains, civil penalties, and related assessed interest. The SEC is responsible for collection, and recognizes a receivable, when an order of the Commission or a Federal court directs payment to the SEC or the U.S. Treasury.

Interest recognized by the SEC on non-entity accounts receivable includes prejudgment interest specified by the court or administrative order as well as post-judgment interest on collectible accounts. The SEC does not recognize interest revenue on accounts considered to be uncollectible.

The SEC's enforcement investigation and litigation activities often result in court orders directing violators of Federal securities laws to pay amounts assessed to a Federal court or to a non-Federal receiver acting on behalf of harmed investors. These orders are not recognized as accounts receivable by the SEC because the debts are payable to, and collected by, another party.

Securities registration, tender offer, merger, and other fees from registrants (filing fee) collections in excess of those deposited into the SEC's Reserve Fund are not available for the SEC's operations and are transferred to the U.S. Treasury General Fund. Accounts receivable amounts arising from filing fees in excess of those deposited into the Reserve Fund are non-entity and are held on behalf of the U.S. Treasury.

Allowance for Uncollectible Amounts

The SEC calculates the allowance for uncollectible amounts and the related provision for estimated losses for filing fees and other accounts receivable using an analysis of historical collection data. No allowance for uncollectible amounts or related provision for estimated losses has been established for securities transaction fees payable by SROs, as these amounts are fully collectible based on historical experience.

The SEC uses a three-tiered methodology for calculating the allowance for loss on its disgorgement and penalty accounts receivable. The first tier involves making an individual collection assessment of cases that represent at least 65 percent of the portfolio. The second and third tiers are composed of the remaining cases that are equal to or less than 30 days old and over 30 days old, respectively. For the second and third tiers, the SEC applies an allowance rate based on historical collection data analysis.

The SEC writes off receivables aged two or more years by removing the debt amounts from the gross accounts receivable and any related allowance for uncollectible accounts.

K. Other Assets

Payments made in advance of the receipt of goods and services are recorded as advances or prepayments and recognized as expenses when the related goods and services are received.

L. Property and Equipment, Net

The SEC's property and equipment consists of software, general-purpose equipment used by the agency, capital improvements made to buildings leased by the SEC for office space, and, when applicable, internal-use software development costs for projects in development. The SEC reports property and equipment purchases and additions at historical cost. The agency expenses property and equipment acquisitions that do not meet the capitalization criteria as well as normal repairs and maintenance.

The SEC depreciates property and equipment over the estimated useful lives using the straight-line method of depreciation. The agency removes property and equipment from its asset accounts in the period of disposal, retirement, or removal from service. The SEC recognizes the difference between the book value and any proceeds as a gain or loss in the period that the asset is removed.

M. Liabilities

The SEC recognizes liabilities for probable future outflows or other sacrifices of resources as a result of events that have occurred as of the Balance Sheet date. The SEC's liabilities consist of routine operating accounts payable, accrued payroll and benefits, registrant deposit accounts that have not been returned to registrants, liabilities for disgorgement and penalties, legal liabilities, and liabilities for amounts collected or receivable on behalf of the U.S. Treasury.

Enforcement Related Liabilities

A liability for disgorgement and penalties arises when an order is issued for the SEC to collect disgorgement, penalties, and interest from securities law violators. When the Commission or court issues such an order, the SEC establishes an accounts receivable due to the SEC offset by a liability. The presentation of this liability on the Balance Sheet is dependent upon several factors. If the court or Commission order indicates that collections are to be retained by the Federal Government, either by transfer to the U.S. Treasury General Fund or to the Investor Protection Fund, the liabilities are classified as custodial (that is, collected on behalf of the Government) and intragovernmental. If the order indicates that the funds are eligible for distribution to harmed investors, the SEC will recognize a Governmental liability (that is, a liability of the Government to make a payment to the public). This liability is not presented as a custodial liability. The SEC does not record liabilities on its financial statements for disgorgement and penalty amounts that another Government entity such as a court, or a non-governmental entity, such as a receiver, has collected or will collect.

In accordance with the provisions of the Dodd-Frank Act, collections not distributed to harmed investors may be transferred to either the Investor Protection Fund or the U.S. Treasury General Fund. Collections not distributed to harmed investors are transferred to the Investor Protection Fund if the Fund's balance does not exceed $300 million at the time of collection. Refer to *Note 16, Disgorgement and Penalties* for additional information.

Liability Classification

The SEC recognizes liabilities that are covered by budgetary resources, liabilities that are not covered by budgetary resources, and liabilities that do not require the use of budgetary resources.

Liabilities that are covered by budgetary resources are liabilities incurred for which budgetary resources are available to the SEC during the reporting period without further Congressional action.

The SEC also recognizes liabilities not covered by budgetary resources. Budgetary and financial statement reporting requirements sometimes differ on the timing for the required recognition of an expense. For example, in the financial statements, annual leave expense must be accrued in the reporting period when the annual leave is earned. However, in the budget, annual leave is required to be recognized and funded in the fiscal year when the annual leave is either used or paid out to a separating employee, not when recognized in the financial statements. As a result of this timing difference, accrued annual leave liability is classified as a liability "not covered by budgetary resources" as of the financial statement date.

Amounts that do not require the use of budgetary resources include registrant deposit accounts that have not been returned to registrants and the offsetting liability that corresponds to assets the SEC holds relating to collections from disgorgements and penalties and receivables. Liabilities that do not require the use of budgetary resources are covered by assets that do not represent budgetary resources to the SEC. Refer to *Note 8, Liabilities Covered and Not Covered by Budgetary Resources* for more information.

N. Employee Retirement Systems and Benefits

The SEC's employees may participate in either the Civil Service Retirement System (CSRS) or the Federal Employees Retirement System (FERS), depending on when they started working for the Federal Government. FERS and Social Security automatically cover most employees hired after December 31, 1983. Employees who are rehired after a break in service of more than one year and who had five years of Federal civilian service prior to 1987 are eligible to participate in the CSRS offset retirement system or may elect to join FERS.

All employees are eligible to contribute to a Thrift Savings Plan (TSP). For those employees participating in FERS, the TSP is automatically established, and the SEC makes a mandatory 1 percent contribution to this plan. In addition, the SEC matches contributions ranging from 1 to 4 percent for FERS-eligible employees who contribute to their TSP. Employees participating in CSRS do not receive matching contributions to their TSP. The SEC contributes the employer's matching amount to the Social Security Administration under the Federal Insurance Contributions Act, which fully covers FERS participating employees.

The SEC does not report CSRS, FERS, Federal Employees Health Benefits Program, Federal Employees Group Life Insurance Program assets, or accumulated plan benefits; the U.S. Office of Personnel Management (OPM) reports this information.

O. Injury and Post-employment Compensation

The Federal Employees' Compensation Act (FECA), administered by the U.S. Department of Labor (DOL), provides income and medical cost protection to covered Federal civilian employees harmed on the job or who have contracted an occupational disease, and dependents of employees whose death is attributable to a job-related injury or occupational disease. The DOL bills the SEC annually as claims are paid, and the

SEC in turn accrues a liability to recognize the future payments. Payment on these bills is deferred for two years to allow for funding through the budget process. Similarly, employees that the SEC terminates without cause may receive unemployment compensation benefits under the unemployment insurance program also administered by the DOL, which bills each agency quarterly for paid claims.

In addition, the SEC records an estimate for the FECA actuarial liability using the DOL's FECA model. The model considers the average amount of benefit payments incurred by the SEC for the past three fiscal years, multiplied by the medical and compensation liability to benefits paid ratio for the whole FECA program.

P. Annual, Sick, and Other Leave

The SEC accrues annual leave and compensatory time as earned and reduces the accrual when leave is taken. The balances in the accrued leave accounts reflect current leave balances and pay rates. No portion of this liability has been obligated because budget execution rules do not permit current or prior year funding to be used to pay for leave earned but not yet either taken or paid as a lump sum upon termination during the reporting period. Accordingly, such accrued leave is reported as "not covered by budgetary resources." Refer to *Note 8, Liabilities Covered and Not Covered by Budgetary Resources*. The SEC expenses sick leave and other types of non-vested leave as used.

Q. Revenue and Other Financing Sources

The SEC's revenue and financing sources include exchange revenues, which are generated from transactions in which both parties give and receive value, and non-exchange revenues, which arise from the Federal Government's ability to demand payment.

Exchange Revenue

The SEC's exchange revenue consists primarily of collections of securities transaction fees from SROs and of securities registration, tender offer, merger, and other fees from registrants (filing fees). The fee rates are calculated by the SEC's Division of Economic and Risk Analysis and established by the SEC in accordance with Federal law and are applied to volumes of activity reported by SROs or to filings submitted by registrants. Fees are recognized as exchange revenue on the effective date of transaction or filing. These fee collections are the primary source of the SEC's funding and may be used up to limits established by Congress. See *Note 1.E, Fund Accounting Structure.*

The SEC recognizes amounts remitted by registrants in advance of the transaction or filing date as a liability until earned by the SEC or returned to the registrant. Federal regulation requires the return of registrant advance deposits when an account is dormant for three years, except in certain cases where refunds are not permitted. The Securities Act of 1933 and the Exchange Act do not permit refunds to registrants for securities that remain unsold after the completion, termination, or withdrawal of an offering. However, Code of Federal Regulations (CFR) Title 17 Chapter II, Part 230, Section 457(p) permits filers to offset a fee paid (filing fee offset) for a subsequent registration statement (offering) filed within five years of the initial filing date of the earlier registration statement. The total aggregate dollar amount of the filing fee associated with the unsold securities may be offset against the total filing fee due on the subsequent offering. Unused filing fee offsets are not a liability to the SEC because registrants cannot obtain refunds of fees or additional services in relation to securities that remain unsold. However, filing fee offsets may reduce revenue earned in future accounting periods.

Non-exchange Revenue

The SEC's non-exchange revenue mainly consists of amounts collected from violators of securities laws as a result of enforcement proceedings. These amounts may take the form of disgorgement of illegal gains, civil penalties, and related interest. Amounts collected may be paid to injured investors, transferred to the Investor Protection Fund, or transferred to the U.S. Treasury General Fund, based on established policy and regulation.

All non-exchange revenue expected to be forwarded to either the U.S. Treasury General Fund or Investor Protection Fund is recognized on the Statement of Custodial Activity. The Investor Protection Fund recognizes non-exchange revenue on the Statement of Changes in Net Position when funds are transferred into the Investor Protection Fund. The result is that, in accordance with Federal accounting standards, the entire amount of custodial activity is presented on the Statement of Custodial Activity to document the movement of funds, and the portion retained by the SEC is recognized as SEC activity.

The SEC does not recognize amounts collected and held by another government entity, such as a court registry, or a non-government entity, such as a receiver.

R. Budgets and Budgetary Accounting

The SEC is subject to certain restrictions on the use of securities transaction fees. The SEC deposits securities transaction fee revenue in a designated account at Treasury. However, the SEC may use funds from this account only as authorized by Congress and made available by OMB apportionment, upon issuance of a Treasury warrant. Revenue collected in excess of appropriated amounts is restricted from use by the SEC. Funds appropriated that the SEC does not use in a given fiscal year are maintained in a designated account for use in future periods in accordance with the requirements of the SEC's appropriation. Collection of fees arising from securities registration, tender offer, merger, and other fees from registrants, other than those that are deposited in the Reserve Fund, are not available to be used in the operations of the SEC. Refer to *Note 1. E, Fund Accounting Structure*.

Salaries and Expenses

Each fiscal year, the SEC receives Category A apportionments, which are quarterly distributions of budgetary resources made by OMB. The SEC also receives a small amount of Category B funds related to reimbursable activity, which are exempt from quarterly apportionment.

Investor Protection Fund

The Investor Protection Fund is a special fund that has the authority to retain revenues and other financing sources not used in the current period for future use. The Dodd-Frank Act provides that the Fund is available to the SEC without further appropriation or fiscal year limitation for the purpose of funding the activities of the Office of the Whistleblower and the Office of Inspector General's Employee Suggestion Program. However, the SEC is required to request and obtain an annual apportionment from OMB to use these funds. All of the funds are Category B, exempt from quarterly apportionment.

Reserve Fund

The Reserve Fund is a special fund that has the authority to retain certain revenues not used in the current period for future use. The Dodd-Frank Act provides that the Fund is available to the SEC without further appropriation or fiscal year limitation "to carry out the functions of the Commission." Amounts in the Reserve Fund are exempt from apportionment.

S. Disgorgement and Penalties

The SEC maintains non-entity assets related to disgorgements and penalties ordered pursuant to civil injunctive and administrative proceedings. The SEC also recognizes an equal and offsetting liability for these assets as discussed in *Note 1.M, Liabilities*. These non-entity assets consist of disgorgement, penalties, and interest assessed against securities law violators where the Commission or a Federal court has determined that the SEC should return such funds to harmed investors or may be transferred to the Investor Protection Fund or the U.S. Treasury General Fund. The SEC does not record on its financial statements any asset amounts that another government entity such as a court, or a non-governmental entity, such as a receiver, has collected or will collect. Additional details regarding disgorgement and penalties are presented in *Note 11, Funds from Dedicated Collections* and *Note 16, Disgorgement and Penalties*.

T. Investor Protection Fund

The Investor Protection Fund was established through a permanent indefinite appropriation to provide financing for payments to whistleblowers and can be used for the expenses of the Office of the Whistleblower and the SEC Office of Inspector General's Employee Suggestion Program. The Investor Protection Fund is financed by transferring a portion of monetary sanctions collected by the SEC in judicial or administrative actions brought by the SEC under the securities laws that are not added to a disgorgement fund or other funds intended for harmed investors under Section 308 of the Sarbanes Oxley Act of 2002 (15 U.S.C. 7246). Sanctions collected by the Commission payable either to the SEC or the U.S. Treasury General Fund will be transferred to the Investor Protection Fund if the balance in that fund is less than $300 million on the day of collection.

The SEC may request the Secretary of the Treasury to invest Investor Protection Fund amounts in Treasury securities. Refer to *Note 1.I, Investments*, for additional details.

NOTE 2. Entity and Non-Entity Assets

Entity assets are assets that the SEC may use in its operations.

Non-entity assets are assets that the SEC holds on behalf of another Federal agency or a third party and are not available for the SEC's use. The SEC's non-entity assets include the following: (a) disgorgement, penalties, and interest collected and held or invested by the SEC; (b) disgorgement, penalties, and interest receivable that will be collected by the SEC; (c) securities registration, tender offer, merger, and other fees collected and receivable from registrants, in excess of amounts deposited in the SEC's Reserve Fund; and (d) other miscellaneous receivables. Additional details are provided in *Note 16, Disgorgement and Penalties*.

At September 30, 2013, SEC entity and non-entity assets consisted of the following:

(DOLLARS IN THOUSANDS)	Entity	Non-Entity	Total
Intragovernmental:			
Fund Balance with Treasury:			
SEC Funds	$ 7,133,643	$ —	$ 7,133,643
Registrant Deposits	—	32,857	32,857
Disgorgement and Penalties (Note 16)	—	988,237	988,237
Investments, Net:			
Disgorgement and Penalties (Note 16)	—	848,441	848,441
Investor Protection Fund	434,201	—	434,201
Advances and Prepayments	1,623	—	1,623
Total Intragovernmental Assets	7,569,467	1,869,535	9,439,002
Cash and Other Monetary Assets:			
SEC Funds	2	—	2
Disgorgement and Penalties (Note 16)	—	387	387
Accounts Receivable, Net:			
SEC Funds	86,628	—	86,628
Disgorgement and Penalties (Note 16)	—	297,098	297,098
Custodial and Other Non-Entity Assets	—	3,301	3,301
Property and Equipment, Net (Note 7)	126,871	—	126,871
Advances and Prepayments	—	—	—
Total Assets	$ 7,782,968	$ 2,170,321	$ 9,953,289

At September 30, 2012, SEC entity and non-entity assets consisted of the following:

(DOLLARS IN THOUSANDS)	Entity	Non-Entity	Total
Intragovernmental:			
Fund Balance with Treasury:			
SEC Funds	$ 7,067,857	$ —	$ 7,067,857
Registrant Deposits	—	33,689	33,689
Disgorgement and Penalties (Note 16)	—	341,886	341,886
Investments, Net:			
Disgorgement and Penalties (Note 16)	—	521,444	521,444
Investor Protection Fund	452,472	—	452,472
Advances and Prepayments	7,824	—	7,824
Total Intragovernmental Assets	7,528,153	897,019	8,425,172
Cash and Other Monetary Assets:			
SEC Funds	8	—	8
Disgorgement and Penalties (Note 16)	—	1,058	1,058
Accounts Receivable, Net:			
SEC Funds	103,312	—	103,312
Disgorgement and Penalties (Note 16)	—	130,616	130,616
Custodial and Other Non-Entity Assets	—	2,763	2,763
Property and Equipment, Net (Note 7)	97,570	—	97,570
Advances and Prepayments	235	—	235
Total Assets	$ 7,729,278	$ 1,031,456	$ 8,760,734

NOTE 3. Fund Balance with Treasury

The Fund Balance with Treasury by type of fund and Status of Fund Balance with Treasury as of September 30, 2013 and 2012 consists of the following:

(DOLLARS IN THOUSANDS)	FY 2013	FY 2012
Fund Balances:		
General Funds	$ 7,053,301	$ 7,016,900
Special Funds	80,342	50,957
Other Funds	1,021,094	375,575
Total Fund Balance with Treasury	$ 8,154,737	$ 7,443,432
Status of Fund Balance with Treasury:		
Unobligated Balance:		
Available	$ 128,327	$ 84,943
Unavailable	96,422	56,249
Obligated Balance not Yet Disbursed	413,616	431,386
Non-Budgetary Fund Balance with Treasury	7,516,372	6,870,854
Total Fund Balance with Treasury	$ 8,154,737	$ 7,443,432

Special Funds consist of the Investor Protection Fund and the Reserve Fund. Refer to *Note 1.E, Fund Accounting Structure*, for additional information.

Other Funds consist of Fund Balance with Treasury held in deposit funds.

Obligated and unobligated balances reported for the status of Fund Balance with Treasury differ from the amounts reported in the Statement of Budgetary Resources due to the fact that budgetary balances are supported by amounts other than Fund Balance with Treasury. These amounts include Investor Protection Fund investments, uncollected payments from Federal sources, and the impact of the change in legal interpretation for leases (see *Note 14.C, Other Budgetary Disclosures, Change in Legal Interpretation for Lease Obligations*). Pursuant to the SEC's FY 2012 Appropriations Act, $25 million in Reserve Fund collections were temporarily rescinded and are included in the unavailable balance reported for FY 2012. The FY 2012 temporary recission ended on September 30, 2012, leaving that $25 million available starting in FY 2013. Refer to *Note 1.E, Fund Accounting Structure, Funds from Dedicated Collections: Reserve Fund*.

Non-Budgetary Fund Balance with Treasury is comprised of amounts in deposit funds and offsetting collections temporarily precluded from obligation in the SEC's General Salaries and Expenses Fund (X0100). Amounts temporarily precluded from obligation represent offsetting collections in excess of appropriated amounts related to securities transactions fees, as well as securities registration, tender offer, merger, and other fees from registrants (filing fees) collected in fiscal years 2011 and prior.

There were no significant differences between the Fund Balance reflected in the SEC's financial statements and the balance in the Treasury accounts.

NOTE 4. Cash and Other Monetary Assets

The SEC had a cash balance of $389 thousand as of September 30, 2013. The SEC receives disgorgement and penalties collections throughout the year. Any collections received after the U.S. Treasury Department cut-off for deposit of checks are treated as deposits in transit and recognized as Cash on the Balance Sheet. The SEC had a cash balance of $1.1 million as of September 30, 2012.

NOTE 5. Investments

The SEC invests funds in overnight and short-term non-marketable market-based Treasury securities. The SEC records the value of its investments in Treasury securities at cost and amortizes any premium or discount on a straight-line basis (S/L) through the maturity date of these securities. Non-marketable market-based Treasury securities are issued by the Bureau of the Fiscal Service to Federal agencies. They are not traded on any securities exchange but mirror the prices of similar Treasury securities trading in the Government securities market.

At September 30, 2013, investments consisted of the following:

(DOLLARS IN THOUSANDS)	Cost	Amortization Method	Amortized (Premium) Discount	Interest Receivable	Investment, Net	Market Value Disclosure
Non-Marketable Market-Based Securities						
Disgorgement and Penalties	$ 849,368	S/L	$ (3,932)	$ 3,005	$ 848,441	$ 845,551
Investor Protection Fund – Entity	434,009	S/L	56	136	434,201	434,211
Total	$ 1,283,377		$ (3,876)	$ 3,141	$ 1,282,642	$ 1,279,762

At September 30, 2012, investments consisted of the following:

(DOLLARS IN THOUSANDS)	Cost	Amortization Method	Amortized (Premium) Discount	Interest Receivable	Investment, Net	Market Value Disclosure
Non-Marketable Market-Based Securities						
Disgorgement and Penalties	$ 520,297	S/L	$ (891)	$ 2,038	$ 521,444	$ 519,526
Investor Protection Fund – Entity	454,119	S/L	(2,875)	1,228	452,472	451,319
Total	$ 974,416		$ (3,766)	$ 3,266	$ 973,916	$ 970,845

Intragovernmental Investments in Treasury Securities

The Federal Government does not set aside assets to pay future benefits or other expenditures associated with the investment by Federal agencies in non-marketable Federal securities. The balances underlying these investments are deposited in the U.S. Treasury, which uses the cash for general Government purposes. Treasury securities are issued to the SEC as evidence of these balances. Treasury securities are an asset of the SEC and a liability of the U.S. Treasury. Because the SEC and the U.S. Treasury are both components of the Government, these assets and liabilities offset each other from the standpoint of the Government as a whole. For this reason, the investments presented by the SEC do not represent an asset or a liability in the U.S. Government-wide financial statements.

Treasury securities provide the SEC with authority to draw upon the U.S. Treasury to make future payments from these accounts. When the SEC requires redemption of these securities to make expenditures, the Government finances those expenditures out of accumulated cash balances, by raising taxes or other receipts, by borrowing from the public or repaying less debt, or by curtailing other expenditures. This is the same manner in which the Government finances all expenditures.

NOTE 6. Accounts Receivable, Net

At September 30, 2013, accounts receivable consisted of the following:

(DOLLARS IN THOUSANDS)	Gross Receivables	Allowance	Net Receivables
Entity Accounts Receivable:			
Securities Transaction Fees	$ 86,295	$ —	$ 86,295
Other	333	—	333
Non-Entity Accounts Receivable:			
Disgorgement and Penalties (Note 16)	1,660,940	1,363,842	297,098
Filing Fees	4,477	1,411	3,066
Other	1,222	987	235
Total Accounts Receivable	$ 1,753,267	$ 1,366,240	$ 387,027

At September 30, 2012, accounts receivable consisted of the following:

(DOLLARS IN THOUSANDS)	Gross Receivables	Allowance	Net Receivables
Entity Accounts Receivable:			
Securities Transaction Fees	$ 103,009	$ —	$ 103,009
Other	372	69	303
Non-Entity Accounts Receivable:			
Disgorgement and Penalties (Note 16)	1,715,267	1,584,651	130,616
Filing Fees	4,304	1,853	2,451
Other	2,158	1,846	312
Total Accounts Receivable	$ 1,825,110	$ 1,588,419	$ 236,691

Refer to *Note 1.J, Accounts Receivable and Allowance for Uncollectible Accounts* for methods used to estimate allowances. The SEC estimates that accumulated interest on accounts receivable considered to be uncollectible is $985 thousand and $1.8 million, respectively, as of September 30, 2013 and 2012. This estimate does not include interest accumulated on debts written off or officially waived.

As of September 30, 2013 and 2012, the balances include disgorgement and penalty accounts receivable, net of allowance, of $68.6 million and $62.2 million, respectively designated as payable to the U.S. Treasury General Fund per court order. As discussed in *Note 1.M, Liabilities*, these receivables, their offsetting liabilities, and the associated revenues, are classified as custodial.

As discussed in *Note 1.J, Accounts Receivable and Allowance for Uncollectible Accounts*, pursuant to Section 991(e) of the Dodd-Frank Act, accounts receivable for securities registration, tender offer, merger, and other fees from registrants in excess of the amounts deposited into the Reserve Fund are held on behalf of the U.S. Treasury and are transferred to the U.S. Treasury General Fund upon collection.

NOTE 7. Property and Equipment, Net

At September 30, 2013, property and equipment consisted of the following:

Class of Property (DOLLARS IN THOUSANDS)	Depreciation/ Amortization Method	Capitalization Threshold for Individual Purchases	Capitalization Threshold for Bulk Purchases	Service Life (Years)	Acquisition Cost	Accumulated Depreciation/ Amortization	Book Value
Furniture and Equipment	S/L	$ 50	$ 50	3-5	$ 134,392	$ 71,120	$ 63,272
Software	S/L	300	300	3-5	132,845	98,202	34,643
Leasehold Improvements	S/L	300	N/A	10	95,634	66,678	28,956
Total					$ 362,871	$ 236,000	$ 126,871

At September 30, 2012, property and equipment consisted of the following:

Class of Property (DOLLARS IN THOUSANDS)	Depreciation/ Amortization Method	Capitalization Threshold for Individual Purchases	Capitalization Threshold for Bulk Purchases	Service Life (Years)	Acquisition Cost	Accumulated Depreciation/ Amortization	Book Value
Furniture and Equipment	S/L	$ 15	$ 50	3-5	$ 96,240	$ 56,715	$ 39,525
Software	S/L	300	300	3-5	109,480	87,109	22,371
Leasehold Improvements	S/L	300	N/A	10	92,556	56,882	35,674
Total					$ 298,276	$ 200,706	$ 97,570

In FY 2013, the capitalization threshold for individual purchases of Furniture and Equipment was changed from $15,000 to $50,000.

NOTE 8. Liabilities Covered and Not Covered by Budgetary Resources

The SEC recognizes liabilities that are covered by budgetary resources, liabilities that are not covered by budgetary resources, and liabilities that do not require the use of budgetary resources.

Liabilities that are covered by budgetary resources are liabilities incurred for which budgetary resources are available to the SEC during the reporting period without further Congressional action.

The SEC also recognizes liabilities not covered by budgetary resources. Budgetary and financial statement reporting requirements sometimes differ on the timing for the required recognition of an expense. For example, in the financial statements, annual leave expense must be accrued in the reporting period when the annual leave is earned. However, in the budget, annual leave is required to be recognized and funded in the fiscal year when the annual leave is either used or paid out to a separating employee, not when recognized in the financial statements. As a result of this timing difference, accrued annual leave liability is classified as a liability "not covered by budgetary resources" as of the financial statement date.

Liabilities that do not require the use of budgetary resources include registrant deposit accounts that have not been returned to registrants and the offsetting liability that corresponds to assets the SEC holds relating to collections from disgorgements and penalties and receivables as discussed in *Note 1.M, Liabilities*. Liabilities that do not require the use of budgetary resources are covered by assets that do not represent budgetary resources to the SEC.

At September 30, 2013, liabilities consisted of the following:

(DOLLARS IN THOUSANDS)	Liabilities Covered by Budgetary Resources	Liabilities Not Covered by Budgetary Resources	Liabilities Not Requiring Budgetary Resources	Total
Intragovernmental:				
Accounts Payable	$ 5,675	$ —	$ —	$ 5,675
Other Intragovernmental Liabilities				
Accrued Employee Benefits	3,086	—	—	3,086
Unfunded FECA and Unemployment Liability	—	1,308	—	1,308
Custodial Liability	—	—	68,831	68,831
Liability for Non-Entity Assets	—	—	3,069	3,069
Subtotal – Other Intragovernmental Liabilities	3,086	1,308	71,900	76,294
Total Intragovernmental	8,761	1,308	71,900	81,969
Accounts Payable	38,313	—	—	38,313
Actuarial FECA Liability	—	7,155	—	7,155
Other Liabilities				
Accrued Payroll and Benefits	15,405	—	—	15,405
Accrued Leave	—	51,706	—	51,706
Registrant Deposits	—	—	32,857	32,857
Liability for Disgorgement and Penalties (Note 16)	—	—	2,065,202	2,065,202
Other Accrued Liabilities				
Recognition of Lease Liability (Note 9)	—	5,145	—	5,145
Other	2	—	362	364
Subtotal – Other Liabilities	15,407	56,851	2,098,421	2,170,679
Total Liabilities	$ 62,481	$ 65,314	$ 2,170,321	$ 2,298,116

Other Liabilities (Intragovernmental and Governmental) totaled $2,247 million as of September 30, 2013, of which all but $57 million is current. The non-current portion of Other Liabilities includes the appropriate portions of Accrued Employee Benefits, Unfunded FECA and Unemployment Liability, Accrued Leave, Contingent Liabilities, and Lease Liability. Current liabilities not covered by budgetary resources totaled $1.3 million as of September 30, 2013.

At September 30, 2012, liabilities consisted of the following:

(DOLLARS IN THOUSANDS)	Liabilities Covered by Budgetary Resources	Liabilities Not Covered by Budgetary Resources	Liabilities Not Requiring Budgetary Resources	Total
Intragovernmental:				
Accounts Payable	$ 8,829	$ —	$ —	$ 8,829
Other Intragovernmental Liabilities				
Accrued Employee Benefits	2,426	2,758	—	5,184
Unfunded FECA and Unemployment Liability	—	1,441	—	1,441
Custodial Liability	—	—	62,497	62,497
Liability for Non-Entity Assets	—	—	2,457	2,457
Subtotal – Other Intragovernmental Liabilities	2,426	4,199	64,954	71,579
Total Intragovernmental	11,255	4,199	64,954	80,408
Accounts Payable	39,474	—	—	39,474
Actuarial FECA Liability	—	8,050	—	8,050
Other Liabilities				
Accrued Payroll and Benefits	13,765	—	—	13,765
Accrued Leave	—	48,531	—	48,531
Registrant Deposits	—	—	33,689	33,689
Liability for Disgorgement and Penalties (Note 16)	—	—	932,763	932,763
Other Accrued Liabilities				
Recognition of Lease Liability (Note 9)	—	5,708	—	5,708
Other	7	—	50	57
Subtotal – Other Liabilities	13,772	54,239	966,502	1,034,513
Total Liabilities	$ 64,501	$ 66,488	$ 1,031,456	$ 1,162,445

Other Liabilities (Intragovernmental and Governmental) totaled $1,106 million as of September 30, 2012, of which all but $57 million was current. The non-current portion of Other Liabilities includes the appropriate portions of the Unfunded FECA and Unemployment Liability, Accrued Leave, and Lease Liability. Current liabilities not covered by budgetary resources totaled $1.4 million as of September 30, 2012.

NOTE 9. Leases

Operating Leases

At September 30, 2013, the SEC leased office space at 16 locations under operating lease agreements that expire between FY 2013 and FY 2029. The SEC paid $103 million annually for rent for the years ended September 30, 2013 and 2012, respectively.

The following table details expected future lease payments for (a) the full term of all non-cancelable leases with terms of more than one year and (b) the non-cancelable portion of all cancelable commercial leases with terms of more than one year. This listing excludes leases with the General Services Administration (GSA). "Non-cancelable" leases are leases for which the lease agreements do not provide an option for the lessee to cancel the lease prior to the end of the lease term. The total expected future lease payments reflect an estimate of base rent and contractually required costs.

Under existing commitments, expected future lease payments through FY 2019 and thereafter are as follows:

Fiscal Year (DOLLARS IN THOUSANDS)	Non-Cancelable Expected Future Lease Payments
2014	$ 87,658
2015	81,466
2016	77,239
2017	78,332
2018	78,613
2019 and thereafter	117,895
Total	$ 521,203

As discussed in Note 14.C, Other Budgetary Disclosures, $441 million of the above $521 million are unfunded obligations.

Expense Recognition of "Rent Holiday"

In FY 2005, the SEC moved into temporary office space in New York due to renovations in the new leased office space. This temporary space was provided to the SEC for only the lessor's operating costs. As a result, the SEC recognized $8 million of rent expense discount, which is being amortized on a straight-line basis over the 15 year life of the new lease. Amortization of the discount recognized in FY 2013 and FY 2012 totaled $533 thousand in each year, respectively.

The unamortized balance of this location's discount totaled $4.0 million and $4.5 million, at September 30, 2013 and 2012 respectively.

In November 2011, the SEC occupied leased office space in Atlanta, Georgia. The lease term is 15 years and includes a one year rent payment holiday. The SEC expects to amortize $1.4 million of rent expense discount over the non-cancelable term of the lease which is 10 years. Amortization of the discount as an adjustment of rent payments began in November 2012. The unamortized balance of this location's discount totaled $1.1 million at September 30, 2013.

NOTE 10. Commitments and Contingencies

A. Commitments: Securities Investor Protection Act

The Securities Investor Protection Act of 1970 (SIPA), as amended, created the Securities Investor Protection Corporation (SIPC) to restore funds and securities to investors and to protect the securities markets from disruption following the failure of broker-dealers. Generally, if a brokerage firm is not able to meet its obligations to customers, then customers' cash and securities held by the brokerage firm are returned to customers on a pro rata basis. If sufficient funds are not available at the firm to satisfy customer claims, the reserve funds of SIPC are used to supplement the distribution, up to a ceiling of $500,000 per customer, including a maximum of $250,000 for cash claims.

SIPA authorizes SIPC to create a fund to maintain all monies received and disbursed by SIPC. SIPA gives SIPC the authority to borrow up to $2.5 billion from the SEC in the event that the SIPC Fund is or may appear insufficient for purposes of SIPA. To borrow the funds, SIPC must file with the SEC a statement of the uses of such a loan and a repayment plan, and then the SEC must certify to the Secretary of the Treasury that the loan is necessary to protect broker-dealer customers and maintain confidence in the securities markets and that the repayment plan provides as reasonable assurance of prompt repayment as may be feasible under the circumstances. The Treasury would make these funds available to the SEC through the purchase of notes or other obligating instruments issued by the SEC. Such notes or other obligating instruments would bear interest at a rate determined by the Secretary of the Treasury. As of

September 30, 2013, the SEC had not loaned any funds to the SIPC, and there are no outstanding notes or other obligating instruments issued by the SEC.

Based on the estimated costs to complete ongoing customer protection proceedings, the current size of the SIPC Fund supplemented by SIPC's ongoing assessments on brokers is expected to provide sufficient funds to cover acknowledged customer claims. There are several broker-dealers that are being liquidated under SIPA or that have been referred to SIPC for liquidation that may result in additional customer claims. In the event that the SIPC Fund is or may reasonably appear to be insufficient for the purposes of SIPA, SIPC may seek a loan from the SEC.

B. Commitments and Contingencies: Investor Protection Fund

As mentioned in *Note 1.E, Fund Accounting Structure*, the Investor Protection Fund is used to pay awards to whistle-blowers if they voluntarily provide original information to the SEC and meet other conditions. The legislation allows whistleblowers to receive between 10 and 30 percent of the monetary sanctions collected in the covered action or in a related action, with the actual percentage being determined at the discretion of the SEC using criteria provided in the legislation and the related rules to implement the legislation adopted by the SEC.

A Preliminary Determination is a first assessment, made by the Claims Review Staff, as to whether the claim should be allowed or denied and, if allowed, what the proposed award percentage amount should be. A contingent liability is recognized in instances where a positive Preliminary Determination (payment of award is probable) has been made by the Claims Review Staff in the Office of the Whistleblower and the amount can be reasonably estimated. Liabilities are recognized in instances where a collection has been received and a positive Proposed Final Determination has been reached by the Claims Review Staff. However, the actual payment of the whistleblower award would not occur until after the final order was issued by the Commission. The SEC did not recognize a contingent liability (not covered by budgetary resources) for potential whistleblower awards as of September 30, 2012 or September 30, 2013.

C. Other Commitments

In addition to future lease commitments discussed in *Note 9, Leases*, the SEC is obligated for the purchase of goods and services that have been ordered, but not received. As of September 30, 2013 net obligations for all of the SEC's activities were $854.4 million, of which $62.5 million was delivered and unpaid. As of September 30, 2012, net obligations for all of SEC's activities were $954.4 million, of which $64.5 million was delivered and unpaid.

D. Other Contingencies

The SEC recognizes contingent liabilities when a past event or exchange transaction has occurred, a future outflow or other sacrifice of resources is probable, and the future outflow or sacrifice of resources is measurable. The SEC is party to various routine administrative proceedings, legal actions, and claims brought against it, including threatened or pending litigation involving labor relations claims, some of which may ultimately result in settlements or decisions against the Federal Government.

NOTE 11. Funds from Dedicated Collections

The SEC's funds from dedicated collections consist of transactions and balances recorded in its Salaries and Expenses Fund, Investor Protection Fund, and Reserve Fund. See *Note 1.F, Funds from Dedicated Collections*. Also see *Note 5, Investments*, for additional information about intragovernmental investments in Treasury securities.

For FY 2013, the assets, liabilities, net position, and net income from operations relating to funds from dedicated collections consisted of the following:

(DOLLARS IN THOUSANDS)	Salaries & Expenses	Investor Protection Fund	Reserve Fund	Eliminations	Total Funds From Dedicated Collections
Balance Sheet as of September 30, 2013					
ASSETS					
Fund Balance with Treasury	$7,052,538	$ 4,996	$ 75,346	$ —	$7,132,880
Cash and Other Monetary Assets	2	—	—	—	2
Investments, Net	—	434,201	—	—	434,201
Accounts Receivable, Net	86,628	—	—	—	86,628
Property and Equipment, Net	109,957	—	15,721	—	125,678
Advances and Prepayments	1,623	—	—	—	1,623
Total Assets	$7,250,748	$ 439,197	$ 91,067	$ —	$7,781,012
LIABILITIES					
Accounts Payable	$ 39,407	$ —	$ 4,581	$ —	$ 43,988
FECA and Unemployment Liability	8,463	—	—	—	8,463
Accrued Payroll and Benefits	18,491	—	—	—	18,491
Accrued Leave	51,706	—	—	—	51,706
Other Accrued Liabilities	5,147	—	—	—	5,147
Total Liabilities	123,214	—	4,581	—	127,795
NET POSITION					
Cumulative Results of Operations	7,127,534	439,197	86,486	—	7,653,217
Total Net Position	7,127,534	439,197	86,486	—	7,653,217
Total Liabilities and Net Position	$7,250,748	$ 439,197	$ 91,067	$ —	$7,781,012
Statement of Net Cost for the year ended September 30, 2013					
Gross Program Costs	$1,302,673	$ 14,883	$ 13,504	$ (51)	$1,331,009
Less Earned Revenues Not Attributable to Program Costs	1,256,792	—	50,000	(51)	1,306,741
Net (Income) Cost from Operations	$ 45,881	$ 14,883	$ (36,496)	$ —	$ 24,268
Statement of Changes in Net Position for the year ended September 30, 2013					
Cumulative Results of Operations:					
Net Position, Beginning of Period	$7,092,911	$ 453,429	$ 49,990	$ —	$7,596,330
Budgetary Financing Sources:					
Appropriations Used	47,546	—	—	—	47,546
Non-Exchange Revenue	—	655	—	—	655
Transfers In/Out Without Reimbursement	—	—	—	—	—
Other	—	6	—	—	6
Other Financing Sources:					
Imputed Financing	32,958	—	—	—	32,958
Other	—	(10)	—	—	(10)
Net Income (Cost) from Operations	(45,881)	(14,883)	36,496	—	(24,268)
Net Change	34,623	(14,232)	36,496	—	56,887
Cumulative Results of Operations	7,127,534	439,197	86,486	—	7,653,217
Unexpended Appropriations:					
Budgetary Financing Sources:					
Appropriations Received	47,641	—	—	—	47,641
Other Adjustments (Recissions, etc.)	(95)	—	—	—	(95)
Appropriations Used	(47,546)	—	—	—	(47,546)
Total Unexpended Appropriations	—	—	—	—	—
Net Position, End of Period	$7,127,534	$ 439,197	$ 86,486	$ —	$7,653,217

For FY 2012, the assets, liabilities, net position, and net income from operations relating to funds from dedicated collections consisted of the following:

(DOLLARS IN THOUSANDS)	Salaries & Expenses	Investor Protection Fund	Reserve Fund	Eliminations	Total Funds From Dedicated Collections
Balance Sheet as of September 30, 2012					
ASSETS					
Fund Balance with Treasury	$7,016,133	$ 957	$ 50,000	$ —	$7,067,090
Cash and Other Monetary Assets	8	—	—	—	8
Investments, Net	—	452,472	—	—	452,472
Accounts Receivable, Net	103,312	—	—	—	103,312
Property and Equipment, Net	96,374	—	—	—	96,374
Advances and Prepayments	8,059	—	—	—	8,059
Total Assets	$7,223,886	$ 453,429	$ 50,000	$ —	$7,727,315
LIABILITIES					
Accounts Payable	$ 48,289	$ —	$ 10	$ —	$ 48,299
FECA and Unemployment Liability	9,491	—	—	—	9,491
Accrued Payroll and Benefits	18,949	—	—	—	18,949
Accrued Leave	48,531	—	—	—	48,531
Other Accrued Liabilities	5,715	—	—	—	5,715
Total Liabilities	130,975	—	10	—	130,985
NET POSITION					
Cumulative Results of Operations	7,092,911	453,429	49,990	—	7,596,330
Total Net Position	7,092,911	453,429	49,990	—	7,596,330
Total Liabilities and Net Position	$7,223,886	$ 453,429	$ 50,000	$ —	$7,727,315
Statement of Net Cost for the year ended September 30, 2012					
Gross Program Costs	$1,195,721	$ 116	$ 10	$ (70)	$1,195,777
Less Earned Revenues Not Attributable to Program Costs	1,269,829	—	50,000	(70)	1,319,759
Net (Income) Cost from Operations	$ (74,108)	$ 116	$ (49,990)	$ —	$ (123,982)
Statement of Changes in Net Position for the year ended September 30, 2012					
Cumulative Results of Operations:					
Net Position, Beginning of Period	$6,956,398	$ 452,788	$ —	$ —	$7,409,186
Budgetary Financing Sources:					
Appropriations Used	32,601	—	—	—	32,601
Non-Exchange Revenue	—	757	—	—	757
Transfers In/Out Without Reimbursement	(784)	—	—	—	(784)
Other	—	—	—	—	—
Other Financing Sources:					
Imputed Financing	30,588	—	—	—	30,588
Other	—	—	—	—	—
Net Income (Cost) from Operations	74,108	(116)	49,990	—	123,982
Net Change	136,513	641	49,990	—	187,144
Cumulative Results of Operations	7,092,911	453,429	49,990	—	7,596,330
Unexpended Appropriations:					
Budgetary Financing Sources:					
Appropriations Received	32,601	—	—	—	32,601
Other Adjustments (Recissions, etc.)	—	—	—	—	—
Appropriations Used	(32,601)	—	—	—	(32,601)
Total Unexpended Appropriations	—	—	—	—	—
Net Position, End of Period	$7,092,911	$ 453,429	$ 49,990	$ —	$7,596,330

NOTE 12. Intragovernmental Costs and Exchange Revenue

The Statement of Net Cost presents the SEC's results of operations for its major programs. The SEC assigns all costs incurred to ten programs, consistent with its budget submissions. The full cost of the SEC's programs is the sum of (1) the costs of resources directly or indirectly consumed by those programs, and (2) the costs of identifiable supporting services provided by other responsibility segments within the agency. Typical examples of indirect costs include costs of general administrative services, technical support, security, rent, and operating and maintenance costs for buildings, equipment, and utilities. The SEC allocates support costs to its programs using activity-based cost accounting.

Intragovernmental costs arise from purchases of goods and services from other components of the Federal Government. In contrast, public costs are those which arise from the purchase of goods and services from non-Federal entities.

Exchange revenue is not directly assignable to a specific program and is presented in total. The Statements of Net Cost, for the years ended September 30, 2013 and 2012, with a breakout of intragovernmental and public costs is presented below.

	FY 2013		
(DOLLARS IN THOUSANDS)	Intragovernmental Gross Cost	Gross Cost with the Public	Total
SEC Programs:			
Enforcement	$ 75,436	$ 375,636	$ 451,072
Compliance Inspections and Examinations	44,376	220,972	265,348
Corporation Finance	23,711	118,066	141,777
Trading and Markets	12,745	63,468	76,213
Investment Management	8,423	41,943	50,366
Economic and Risk Analysis	4,934	24,570	29,504
General Counsel	6,926	34,491	41,417
Other Program Offices	8,658	43,110	51,768
Agency Direction and Administrative Support	36,136	179,941	216,077
Inspector General	1,176	5,856	7,032
Total Program Costs	$ 222,521	$ 1,108,053	1,330,574
Less: Exchange Revenues			
Securities Transaction Fees			1,256,644
Securities Registration, Tender Offer, and Merger Fees			507,473
Other			150
Total Exchange Revenues			1,764,267
Net (Income) Cost from Operations			$ (433,693)

(DOLLARS IN THOUSANDS)	FY 2012		
	Intragovernmental Gross Cost	Gross Cost with the Public	Total
SEC Programs:			
Enforcement	$ 73,629	$ 326,945	$ 400,574
Compliance Inspections and Examinations	43,331	192,406	235,737
Corporation Finance	25,263	112,178	137,441
Trading and Markets	12,487	55,449	67,936
Investment Management	8,866	39,372	48,238
Economic and Risk Analysis	3,730	16,566	20,296
General Counsel	7,528	33,423	40,951
Other Program Offices	8,968	39,823	48,791
Agency Direction and Administrative Support	34,982	155,332	190,314
Inspector General	1,330	5,908	7,238
Total Program Costs	$ 220,114	$ 977,402	1,197,516
Less: Exchange Revenues			
Securities Transaction Fees			1,269,612
Securities Registration, Tender Offer, and Merger Fees			378,028
Other			219
Total Exchange Revenues			1,647,859
Net (Income) Cost from Operations			$ (450,343)

Intragovernmental exchange revenue was $97 thousand for the year ended September 30, 2013. Intragovernmental exchange revenue was $147 thousand for the year ended September 30, 2012.

NOTE 13. Imputed Financing

A portion of the retirement, health, and life insurance benefits provided to SEC employees is funded by OPM. In accordance with Federal accounting standards, the SEC recognizes identified costs paid by OPM on behalf of the SEC as an expense. The funding for this expense is reflected as imputed financing on the Statement of Changes in Net Position. Costs paid by OPM on behalf of the SEC were $33 million and $30.5 million in FY 2013 and FY 2012, respectively.

NOTE 14. Status of Budgetary Resources

A. Apportionment Categories of Obligations Incurred

Category A funds are those amounts that are subject to quarterly apportionment by OMB, meaning that a portion of the annual appropriation is not available to the agency until apportioned each quarter. Category B funds represent budgetary resources distributed by a specified time period, activity, project, object, or a combination of these categories. The SEC's Category B funds represent amounts apportioned at the beginning of the fiscal year for the SEC's reimbursable and Investor Protection Fund activities. The SEC's Reserve Fund is exempt from apportionment. For additional information, see *Note 1.E, Fund Accounting Structure*, and *Note 1.R, Budgets and Budgetary Accounting*. For the years ended September 30, 2013 and 2012, the SEC incurred obligations against Category A, Category B, and Exempt funds as follows:

Obligations Incurred *(DOLLARS IN THOUSANDS)*	FY 2013	FY 2012
Direct Obligations		
Category A	$ 1,201,369	$ 1,179,640
Category B — Investor Protection Fund	14,883	116
Exempt From Apportionment — Reserve Fund	41,343	12,358
Total Direct Obligations	1,257,595	1,192,114
Reimbursable Obligations		
Category B	116	271
Total Obligations Incurred	$ 1,257,711	$ 1,192,385

In addition, the amounts of budgetary resources obligated for undelivered orders include $792.2 million and $890.1 million at September 30, 2013 and 2012, respectively.

B. Explanation of Differences between the Statement of Budgetary Resources and the Budget of the U.S. Government

A comparison between the FY 2013 Statement of Budgetary Resources (SBR) and the actual FY 2013 data in the President's budget cannot be presented, as the FY 2015 President's budget which will contain FY 2013 actual data is not yet available. The comparison will be presented in next year's financial statements. The comparison as of September 30, 2012 is presented below:

(DOLLARS IN MILLIONS)	Budgetary Resources	Obligations Incurred	Distributed Offsetting Receipts	Outlays, Net
Combined Statement of Budgetary Resources	$ 1,236	$ 1,192	$ (1)	$ (109)
FY 2012 Ending Balance: Comptroller General Decision B 322160, *Recording of Obligation for Multiple Year Contract*	523	—	—	—
OMB's application of cumulative unobligated balances used to liquidate deficiency	(102)	—	—	—
Rounding	1	—	—	—
Budget of the U.S. Government for FY 2014	$ 1,658	$ 1,192	$ (1)	$ (109)

The differences between the FY 2012 SBR and the prior year column of the FY 2014 Budget exist because certain data elements are reported on the SBR differently than those same data elements are reported in the Budget.

The data elements reported differently are those used to report the SEC's recording of obligations in FY 2011 to reflect the impact of Comptroller General Decision B 322160, Securities and Exchange Commission--Recording of Obligation for Multiple-Year Contract and the subsequent adjustment and liquidation of those obligations. In consultation with OMB, in FY 2011 the SEC recognized obligations for leases entered into in FY 2010 and prior. The recognition of these lease obligations resulted in an unfunded obligation (deficiency) of $778 million.

In the Budget, the unfunded obligation is not included in the beginning of the year unobligated balance brought forward, but instead is reported in a separate schedule of the President's Budget titled "Unfunded Deficiencies."

A detailed reconciliation of the data elements follows:

- Based on an agreement with OMB, the SEC is funding the deficiency over time as the prior year unfunded lease obligation amounts are recovered, and as new budget authority becomes available for current year lease operations. At the end of FY 2012, the SEC's SBR reported $523 million in remaining unfunded obligations after the SEC funded $113 million and recorded a downward adjustment of $142 million to previously unfunded obligations. The SEC's SBR presents the unfunded obligations as part of the beginning of the year unobligated balance brought forward.

- At the end of FY 2012, the "Unfunded Deficiencies" schedule in the SEC's section of the President's Budget reported $421 million in remaining unfunded obligations. The $102 million difference in remaining unfunded obligations reflects the difference in presentation between the SEC's SBR and the President's Budget: the "Unfunded Deficiencies" schedule in the President's Budget applies the FY 2011 year-end unobligated balance ($47 million) as a reduction in the beginning of year unfunded deficiency and the FY 2012 unobligated balance ($55 million) as part of new budget authority used to liquidated deficiencies.

- A portion of the activity in the "Unfunded Deficiencies" schedule is also reflected in the Budgetary Resources section of the SEC's Salaries and Expense Account in the President's Budget. The $310 million in "New budget authority used to liquidate deficiencies" in the "Unfunded Deficiencies" schedule is broken out in the SEC's Salaries and Expense Account as follows: $142 million in "Adjustment for unfunded deficiencies"(downward adjustments) and $168 million in "Adjustments for new budget authority used to liquidate deficiencies." The $142 million downward adjustments include $137.7 million resulting from an agreement signed in June 2012 transferring responsibility for the Constitution Center from the SEC to GSA. The $168 million resulted from $113 million used to liquidate the lease obligations plus the $55 million unobligated balance at the end of FY 2012 considered to be applied to the unfunded obligations in the "Unfunded Deficiencies" schedule.

C. Other Budgetary Disclosures

General Provisions of Appropriation

The SEC's annual Appropriations Act contains general provisions that limit the amount that can be obligated for international conferences, International Organization of Securities Commission (IOSCO) dues, and representation expenses. The act also requires the SEC to fund its Office of Inspector General with a minimum of $6,795,000 . This amount was reduced by $339,750 (5%) to a new figure of $6,455,250 by the sequestration outlined in the OMB Report to the Congress on the Joint Committee Sequestration for Fiscal Year 2013. However, the amount for the Office of Inspector General is a "not less than" item; therefore, the sequestration order does not require a reduction in the funding provided but instead lowers the minimum amount that must be provided.

The SEC's FY 2012 appropriation bill included a provision that temporarily rescinded $25 million in appropriations recognized in SEC's Reserve Fund until FY 2013. Refer to *Note 1.E, Fund Accounting Structure, "Reserve Fund,"* for more information.

Change in Legal Interpretation for Lease Obligations

The SEC was granted independent leasing authority in 1990. Based on a legal review of its statutory authority at the time, the SEC adopted a policy of obligating only the annual portion of lease payments due each year. On October 3, 2011, the Government Accountability Office (GAO) issued a decision that this longstanding practice of recording lease obligations only on an annual basis violated the recording statute, 31 U.S.C. sect. 1501(a)(1). Specifically, the GAO's decision was that the SEC lacks statutory authority to obligate an amount less than the Government's total obligation. If the SEC lacks sufficient budget authority to cover this obligation, the SEC should report a violation of the Antideficiency Act (ADA).

The SEC recorded obligations in the same manner for all its leasing actions between the time the agency was granted independent leasing authority in 1990 and 2010. Further, the agency did not have sufficient remaining unobligated funds in the years in which the various leases were entered to cover the full obligations associated with those leases. As a result, the agency recorded unfunded obligations totaling $778 million for leases executed between 1990 and 2010 in FY 2011. The SEC appropriately obligated the Government's total financial responsibility for lease actions that were executed in FY 2011 and FY 2012.

Unfunded lease obligations totaled $441 million and $523 million as of September 30, 2013 and 2012, respectively. The change in unfunded obligations is due to the SEC funding previously unfunded obligations totaling $80.2 million and also recording downward adjustments to previous year unfunded lease obligations totaling $2 million. Accrual accounting requires expenses to be recognized in the period in which the expenses are incurred. Because future lease expenses are not an expense of the current fiscal year, they are not reported as expenses or liabilities in the current fiscal year. See *Note 9, Leases*, for additional information.

See *Note 10.A, Commitments: Securities Investor Protection Act*, for information on the SEC's borrowing authority.

NOTE 15. Reconciliation of Net Cost of Operations to Budget

For the years ended September 30, 2013 and 2012:

(DOLLARS IN THOUSANDS)	FY 2013	FY 2012
RESOURCES USED TO FINANCE ACTIVITIES:		
Budgetary Resources Obligated:		
Obligations Incurred (Note 14)	$ 1,257,711	$ 1,192,385
Less: Spending Authority from Offsetting Collections, Recoveries, and Downward Adjustments to Prior Year Unfunded Lease Obligations	(1,307,044)	(1,457,761)
Less: Reserve Fund Appropriations	(50,000)	(50,000)
Net Obligations	(99,333)	(315,376)
Other Resources:		
Imputed Financing from Cost Absorbed by Others (Note 13)	32,958	30,588
Total Resources Used to Finance Activities	(66,375)	(284,788)
RESOURCES USED TO FINANCE ITEMS NOT PART OF THE NET COST OF OPERATIONS:		
Change in Budgetary Resources Obligated for Goods, Services, and Benefits Ordered But Not Yet Provided	104,435	141,372
Resources that Finance the Acquisition of Assets Capitalized on the Balance Sheet	(83,218)	(40,684)
Total Resources Used to Finance Items Not Part of the Net Cost of Operations	21,217	100,688
Total Resources Used to Finance the Net Cost of Operations	(45,158)	(184,100)
COMPONENTS OF NET COST OF OPERATIONS THAT WILL NOT REQUIRE OR GENERATE RESOURCES IN THE CURRENT PERIOD:		
Components Requiring or Generating Resources in Future Periods:		
Change in Accrued Leave Liability	3,175	3,059
Change in Revenue Receivables Not Generating Resources Until Collected	16,684	18,814
Change in Lease Liability	(563)	(548)
Change in Legal Liability	—	(956)
Change in Unfunded Liability	(3,786)	2,674
Total Components of Net Cost of Operations that will Require or Generate Resources in Future Periods	15,510	23,043
Components not Requiring or Generating Resources:		
Depreciation and Amortization	53,801	36,607
Revaluation of Assets or Liabilities	117	446
Non-Entity Filing Fee Revenue, Net	(457,915)	(326,284)
Other Costs that will not Require or Generate Resources	(48)	(55)
Total Components of Net Cost of Operations that will not Require or Generate Resources in Future Periods	(404,045)	(289,286)
Total Components of Net Cost of Operations that will not Require or Generate Resources in the Current Period	(388,535)	(266,243)
Net (Income) Cost from Operations	$ (433,693)	$ (450,343)

Components of net cost of operations that will not require or generate budgetary resources represent required timing differences in the Statement of Net Cost and the Statement of Budgetary Resources.

For example, as noted in *Note 1. M, Liabilities*, annual leave that is earned but not either taken or paid out to separating employees by the end of the fiscal year is required to be reported as an expense in the financial statements in the year when it is earned, but it is required to be funded by budgetary resources in the future fiscal year when it is either used or paid out to separating employees. In the reconciliation above, it is reported as a component of net cost that will not require resources in the current period. Another example is depreciation expense. In budgetary reporting, the entire cost of a depreciable asset is recognized in the period when the asset is purchased. However, in financial statement reporting, accrual accounting requires the cost of such assets to be allocated among the reporting periods that represent the estimated useful life of the asset. In the reconciliation above, depreciation is recognized as a "component not requiring or generating resources."

NOTE 16. Disgorgement and Penalties

The SEC's non-entity assets include disgorgement, penalties, and interest assessed against securities law violators by the Commission or a Federal court. The SEC also recognizes an equal and offsetting liability for these non-entity assets, as discussed in *Note 1.M, Liabilities*.

When the Commission or court issues an order for the SEC to collect disgorgement, penalties, and interest from securities law violators, the SEC establishes an account receivable due to the SEC. Upon collection, the SEC may (a) hold receipts in the Disgorgement and Penalty Deposit Fund as FBWT or Treasury investments pending distribution to harmed investors, (b) deposit receipts in the U.S. Treasury General Fund or, (c) transfer amounts to the Investor Protection Fund. The situations where funds would not be held for distribution to harmed investors arise when the SEC either determines it is not practical to return funds to investors or when court orders expressly state that funds are to be remitted to the U.S. Treasury. The determination as to whether funds not held for distribution to harmed investors will be deposited in the U.S. Treasury or transferred to the Investor Protection Fund is made in accordance with the provisions of the Dodd-Frank Act, and is dependent on the balance in the Investor Protection Fund on the day the amounts are collected. (See *Note 1.T, Investor Protection Fund*).

Disbursements related to disgorgements and penalties include distributions to harmed investors, payments to tax authorities, and fees paid to plan administrators and the Bureau of the Fiscal Service. The SEC does not record accounts receivable on its financial statements for any amounts ordered to another Government entity such as a court, or a non-governmental entity such as a receiver. Additional details regarding disgorgement and penalties are presented in *Note 1.S, Disgorgement and Penalties*, and *Note 2, Entity and Non-Entity Assets*.

At September 30, the net inflows and outflows for FBWT, Investments, and Accounts Receivable related to disgorgement and penalties consisted of the following:

(DOLLARS IN THOUSANDS)	FY 2013	FY 2012
Fund Balance with Treasury:		
Beginning Balance	$ 341,886	$ 73,929
Collections	1,545,037	622,529
Purchases and Redemptions of Treasury Securities	(326,159)	228,513
Disbursements	(53,935)	(205,440)
Transfers and Deposits to the U.S. Treasury General Fund	(518,592)	(377,645)
Total Fund Balance with Treasury (Note 2)	988,237	341,886
Cash and Other Monetary Assets:		
Beginning Balance	1,058	—
Net Activity	(671)	1,058
Total Cash and Other Monetary Assets (Notes 2 and 4)	387	1,058
Investments, Net:		
Beginning Balance	521,444	749,810
Net Activity	326,997	(228,366)
Total Investments, Net (Notes 2 and 5)	848,441	521,444
Accounts Receivable, Net:		
Beginning Balance	130,616	90,982
Net Activity	166,482	39,634
Total Accounts Receivable, Net (Notes 2 and 6)	297,098	130,616
Total Disgorgement and Penalties	$ 2,134,163	$ 995,004

NOTE 17. Statement of Changes in Net Position

In FY 2013, the negative $457,974 thousand in "Other" Financing Sources reported in the Statement of Changes in Net Position consists of $457,915 thousand in securities registration, tender offer, merger, and other fees from registrants ("filing fees") and $49 thousand in Freedom of Information Act (FOIA) fees collected, or to be collected, for deposit into the U.S. Treasury General Fund, and $10 thousand in losses on the sale of investments in U.S. Treasury securities.

In FY 2012, the negative $327,123 thousand consists of $327,068 thousand in filing fees and $55 thousand in FOIA revenues collected, or to be collected, for deposit into the U.S. Treasury General Fund.

Required Supplementary Information (Unaudited)

This section provides the Required Supplementary Information as prescribed by OMB Circular A-136, *Financial Reporting Requirements*.

U.S. SECURITIES AND EXCHANGE COMMISSION

Statements of Budgetary Resources by Fund
For the year ended September 30, 2013:

(DOLLARS IN THOUSANDS)	Salaries and Expenses and Other Funds	Investor Protection Fund	Reserve Fund	Total
	X0100, 09/10 0100, 1435, 3220	5567	5566	
BUDGETARY RESOURCES:				
Unobligated Balance, Brought Forward, October 1	$ (420,430)	$ 451,460	$ 12,642	$ 43,672
Recoveries of Prior Year Unpaid Obligations	30,777	—	—	30,777
Downward Adjustments of Prior Year Unfunded Lease Obligations (Note 14.C)	2,009	—	—	2,009
Unobligated Balance from Prior Year Budget Authority, Net	(387,644)	451,460	12,642	76,458
Appropriations (Discretionary and Mandatory)	47,546	(2,185)	72,450	117,811
Spending Authority from Offsetting Collections (Discretionary and Mandatory)	1,208,208	—	—	1,208,208
Total Budgetary Resources	$ 868,110	$ 449,275	$ 85,092	$ 1,402,477
STATUS OF BUDGETARY RESOURCES:				
Obligations Incurred (Note 14)	$ 1,201,485	$ 14,883	$ 41,343	$ 1,257,711
Unobligated Balance, End of Year:				
Apportioned	84,424	434,392	—	518,816
Exempt from Apportionment	—	—	43,749	43,749
Unapportioned	(417,799)	—	—	(417,799)
Total Unobligated Balance, End of Year	(333,375)	434,392	43,749	144,766
Total Budgetary Resources	$ 868,110	$ 449,275	$ 85,092	$ 1,402,477
CHANGE IN OBLIGATED BALANCE:				
Unpaid Obligations:				
Unpaid Obligations, Brought Forward, October 1 (Gross)	$ 942,240	$ —	$ 12,358	$ 954,598
Obligations Incurred	1,201,485	14,883	41,343	1,257,711
Outlays (Gross)	(1,285,339)	(14,883)	(24,654)	(1,324,876)
Recoveries of Prior Year Unpaid Obligations	(30,777)	—	—	(30,777)
Downward Adjustments of Prior Year Unfunded Lease Obligations (Note 14.C)	(2,009)	—	—	(2,009)
Unpaid Obligations, End of Year	825,600	—	29,047	854,647
Uncollected Payments:				
Uncollected Payments, Federal Sources, Brought Forward, October 1	(189)	—	—	(189)
Change in Uncollected Payments, Federal Sources	(63)	—	—	(63)
Uncollected Payments, Federal Sources, End of Year	(252)	—	—	(252)
Memorandum (non-add) entries:				
Obligated Balance, Start of Year	$ 942,051	$ —	$ 12,358	$ 954,409
Obligated Balance, End of Year	$ 825,348	$ —	$ 29,047	$ 854,395
BUDGET AUTHORITY AND OUTLAYS, NET:				
Budget Authority, Gross (Discretionary and Mandatory)	$ 1,255,754	$ (2,185)	$ 72,450	$ 1,326,019
Actual Offsetting Collections (Discretionary and Mandatory)	(1,274,195)	—	—	(1,274,195)
Change in Uncollected Customer Payments from Federal Sources (Discretionary and Mandatory)	(63)	—	—	(63)
Budget Authority, Net (Discretionary and Mandatory)	$ (18,504)	$ (2,185)	$ 72,450	$ 51,761
Outlays, Gross (Discretionary and Mandatory)	$ 1,285,339	$ 14,883	$ 24,654	$ 1,324,876
Actual Offsetting Collections (Discretionary and Mandatory)	(1,274,195)	—	—	(1,274,195)
Outlays, Net (Discretionary and Mandatory)	11,144	14,883	24,654	50,681
Distributed Offsetting Receipts	(745)	(2,405)	—	(3,150)
Agency Outlays, Net (Discretionary and Mandatory)	$ 10,399	$ 12,478	$ 24,654	$ 47,531

The accompanying notes are an integral part of these financial statements.

For the year ended September 30, 2012:

(DOLLARS IN THOUSANDS)	Salaries and Expenses and Other Funds X0100, 09/10 0100, 1435, 3220	Investor Protection Fund 5567	Reserve Fund 5566	Total
BUDGETARY RESOURCES:				
Unobligated Balance, Brought Forward, October 1	$ (730,880)	$ 450,951	$ —	$ (279,929)
Recoveries of Prior Year Unpaid Obligations	26,688	—	—	26,688
Downward Adjustments of Prior Year Unfunded Lease Obligations (Note 14.C)	141,933	—	—	141,933
Unobligated Balance from Prior Year Budget Authority, Net	(562,259)	450,951	—	(111,308)
Appropriations (Discretionary and Mandatory)	32,601	625	25,000	58,226
Spending Authority from Offsetting Collections (Discretionary and Mandatory)	1,289,139	—	—	1,289,139
Total Budgetary Resources	$ 759,481	$ 451,576	$ 25,000	$ 1,236,057
STATUS OF BUDGETARY RESOURCES:				
Obligations Incurred (Note 14)	$ 1,179,911	$ 116	$ 12,358	$ 1,192,385
Unobligated Balance, End of Year:				
Apportioned	71,533	451,460	—	522,993
Exempt from Apportionment	—	—	12,642	12,642
Unapportioned	(491,963)	—	—	(491,963)
Total Unobligated Balance, End of Year	(420,430)	451,460	12,642	43,672
Total Budgetary Resources	$ 759,481	$ 451,576	$ 25,000	$ 1,236,057
CHANGE IN OBLIGATED BALANCE:				
Unpaid Obligations:				
Unpaid Obligations, Brought Forward, October 1 (Gross)	$ 1,110,634	$ —	$ —	$ 1,110,634
Obligations Incurred	1,179,911	116	12,358	1,192,385
Outlays (Gross)	(1,179,684)	(116)	—	(1,179,800)
Recoveries of Prior Year Unpaid Obligations	(26,688)	—	—	(26,688)
Downward Adjustments of Prior Year Unfunded Lease Obligations (Note 14.C)	(141,933)	—	—	(141,933)
Unpaid Obligations, End of Year	942,240	—	12,358	954,598
Uncollected Payments:				
Uncollected Payments, Federal Sources, Brought Forward, October 1	(47)	—	—	(47)
Change in Uncollected Payments, Federal Sources	(142)	—	—	(142)
Uncollected Payments, Federal Sources, End of Year	(189)	—	—	(189)
Memorandum (non-add) entries:				
Obligated Balance, Start of Year	$ 1,110,587	$ —	$ —	$ 1,110,587
Obligated Balance, End of Year	$ 942,051	$ —	$ 12,358	$ 954,409
BUDGET AUTHORITY AND OUTLAYS, NET:				
Budget Authority, Gross (Discretionary and Mandatory)	$ 1,321,740	$ 625	$ 25,000	$ 1,347,365
Actual Offsetting Collections (Discretionary and Mandatory)	(1,288,998)	—	—	(1,288,998)
Change in Uncollected Customer Payments from Federal Sources (Discretionary and Mandatory)	(142)	—	—	(142)
Budget Authority, Net (Discretionary and Mandatory)	$ 32,600	$ 625	$ 25,000	$ 58,225
Outlays, Gross (Discretionary and Mandatory)	$ 1,179,684	$ 116	$ —	$ 1,179,800
Actual Offsetting Collections (Discretionary and Mandatory)	(1,288,998)	—	—	(1,288,998)
Outlays, Net (Discretionary and Mandatory)	(109,314)	116	—	(109,198)
Distributed Offsetting Receipts	(498)	(625)	—	(1,123)
Agency Outlays, Net (Discretionary and Mandatory)	$ (109,812)	$ (509)	$ —	$ (110,321)

The accompanying notes are an integral part of these financial statements.

INVESTOR PROTECTION FUND
FINANCIAL STATEMENTS

Investor Protection Fund Financial Statements

U.S. SECURITIES AND EXCHANGE COMMISSION
INVESTOR PROTECTION FUND

Balance Sheets

As of September 30, 2013 and 2012

(DOLLARS IN THOUSANDS)	FY 2013	FY 2012
ASSETS:		
Intragovernmental:		
Fund Balance with Treasury (Note 2)	$ 4,996	$ 957
Investments, Net (Note 3)	434,201	452,472
Total Assets	$ 439,197	$ 453,429
LIABILITIES:		
Commitments and Contingencies (Note 4)		
NET POSITION:		
Cumulative Results of Operations - Funds from Dedicated Collections	439,197	453,429
Total Net Position - Funds from Dedicated Collections	439,197	453,429
Total Net Position	439,197	453,429
Total Liabilities and Net Position	$ 439,197	$ 453,429

The accompanying notes are an integral part of these financial statements.

U.S. SECURITIES AND EXCHANGE COMMISSION
INVESTOR PROTECTION FUND

Statements of Net Cost

For the years ended September 30, 2013 and 2012

(DOLLARS IN THOUSANDS)	FY 2013	FY 2012
PROGRAM COSTS (Note 5):		
Payments to Whistleblowers	$ 14,832	$ 46
Employee Suggestion Program	51	70
Total Program Costs	14,883	116
Net (Income) Cost from Operations	$ 14,883	$ 116

The accompanying notes are an integral part of these financial statements.

U.S. SECURITIES AND EXCHANGE COMMISSION
INVESTOR PROTECTION FUND

Statements of Changes in Net Position
For the years ended September 30, 2013 and 2012

(DOLLARS IN THOUSANDS)	FY 2013	FY 2012
CUMULATIVE RESULTS OF OPERATIONS – FUNDS FROM DEDICATED COLLECTIONS:		
Beginning Balances	$ 453,429	$ 452,788
Budgetary Financing Sources:		
Non-Exchange Revenue	655	757
Other	6	—
Other Financing Sources:		
Other	(10)	—
Total Financing Sources	651	757
Net Income (Cost) from Operations	(14,883)	(116)
Net Change	(14,232)	641
Cumulative Results of Operations	439,197	453,429
Net Position, End of Period	$ 439,197	$ 453,429

The accompanying notes are an integral part of these financial statements.

U.S. SECURITIES AND EXCHANGE COMMISSION
INVESTOR PROTECTION FUND

Statements of Budgetary Resources
For the years ended September 30, 2013 and 2012

(DOLLARS IN THOUSANDS)	FY 2013	FY 2012
BUDGETARY RESOURCES:		
Unobligated Balance, Brought Forward, October 1	$ 451,460	$ 450,951
Appropriations (Discretionary and Mandatory)	(2,185)	625
Total Budgetary Resources	$ 449,275	$ 451,576
STATUS OF BUDGETARY RESOURCES:		
Obligations Incurred - Category B (Note 6)	$ 14,883	$ 116
Unobligated Balance, End of Year:		
Apportioned	434,392	451,460
Total Unobligated Balance, End of Year	434,392	451,460
Total Budgetary Resources	$ 449,275	$ 451,576
CHANGE IN OBLIGATED BALANCE:		
Unpaid Obligations:		
Obligations Incurred	$ 14,883	$ 116
Outlays (Gross)	(14,883)	(116)
Unpaid Obligations, End of Year (Note 6)	$ —	$ —
BUDGET AUTHORITY AND OUTLAYS, NET:		
Budget Authority, Gross (Discretionary and Mandatory)	$ (2,185)	$ 625
Budget Authority, Net (Discretionary and Mandatory)	$ (2,185)	$ 625
Outlays, Gross (Discretionary and Mandatory)	$ 14,883	$ 116
Outlays, Net (Discretionary and Mandatory)	14,883	$ 116
Distributed Offsetting Receipts	(2,405)	(625)
Agency Outlays, Net (Discretionary and Mandatory)	$ 12,478	$ (509)

The accompanying notes are an integral part of these financial statements.

Notes to the Investor Protection Fund Financial Statements

U.S. SECURITIES AND EXCHANGE COMMISSION
As of September 30, 2013 and 2012

NOTE 1. Significant Accounting Policies

A. Reporting Structure

The U.S. Securities and Exchange Commission (SEC) is an independent agency of the U.S. Government established pursuant to the Securities Exchange Act of 1934 (Exchange Act), charged with regulating this country's capital markets. The Dodd-Frank Wall Street Reform and Consumer Protection Act of 2010 (Dodd-Frank Act) established the Securities and Exchange Commission Investor Protection Fund. The Investor Protection Fund provides funding for a Whistleblower Award Program and finances the operations of the SEC Office of Inspector General's (OIG) Employee Suggestion Program. The Investor Protection Fund is a fund within the SEC, and these financial statements present a segment of the SEC's financial activity.

B. Basis of Presentation and Accounting

The accompanying financial statements present the financial position, net cost of operations, changes in net position, and budgetary resources of the Investor Protection Fund as required by Exchange Act Section 21F(g)(5). The Act requires a complete set of financial statements that includes a balance sheet, income statement, and cash flow analysis. The Investor Protection Fund is a Federal reporting entity. As such, its financial statements are prepared in conformity with generally accepted accounting principles (GAAP) for the Federal Government, and are presented in conformity with OMB Circular A-136, *Financial Reporting Requirements*. The legislative requirements to prepare an income statement and cash flow analysis are addressed by the Statement of Net Cost and *Note 2, Fund Balance with Treasury*, respectively.

The SEC's books and records serve as the source of the information presented in the accompanying financial statements.

The agency classifies assets, liabilities, revenues, and costs in these financial statements according to the type of entity associated with the transactions. Intragovernmental assets and liabilities are those due from or to other Federal entities, including those activities within the SEC. Intragovernmental revenues and costs result from transactions with other Federal entities.

The Balance Sheet, Statement of Net Cost and Statement of Changes in Net Position are prepared using the accrual basis of accounting. Accordingly, revenues are recognized when earned and expenses are recognized when incurred without regard to the receipt or payment of cash. These principles differ from budgetary accounting and reporting principles on which the Statement of Budgetary Resources is prepared. The statements may differ from other financial reports submitted pursuant to Office of Management and Budget (OMB) directives for the purpose of monitoring and controlling the use of budgetary resources, due to differences in applicable accounting and reporting principles discussed in the following paragraphs. Conceptually, the differences relate primarily to the capitalization and depreciation of property and equipment, as well as the recognition of other assets and liabilities.

C. Use of Estimates

The preparation of financial statements in conformity with GAAP requires management to make estimates and assumptions that affect the reported amounts of assets and liabilities. These estimates and assumptions include the disclosure of contingent assets and liabilities at the date of the financial statements, and the reported amounts of revenues and expenses during the reporting period. Actual results may differ from these estimates.

D. Intra- and Inter-Agency Relationships

Transactions with Other SEC Entities

The Investor Protection Fund is comprised of a single Federal Treasury Fund Symbol. The Investor Protection Fund is the recipient of non-exchange revenues collected by the SEC. Amounts transferred to the Investor Protection Fund are classified as "retained by the SEC" because the Investor Protection

Fund is a fund within the SEC. The Investor Protection Fund can finance the operations of the SEC Office of Inspector General's Employee Suggestion Program and the Office of the Whistleblower on a reimbursable basis.

Accounts receivable that may be used to fund the Investor Protection Fund are recognized as assets of the SEC. These resources are not assets of the Investor Protection Fund until the determination is made to deposit collections in the Investor Protection Fund.

Transactions with Other Federal Agencies

Whistleblower payments may be made from the Investor Protection Fund as a result of monetary sanctions paid to other Federal agencies in related actions, but only if there has been a Commission enforcement action resulting in sanctions of a million dollars or greater and the Commission has determined that the whistleblower is eligible for an award and recommended the percentage. In those instances, the SEC remains liable for paying the whistleblower. However, in instances where a whistleblower has already received an award from the Commodity Futures Trading Commission (CFTC), the whistleblower is not entitled to an award from the SEC.

E. Funds from Dedicated Collections

A fund from dedicated collections is financed by specifically identified revenues, often supplemented by other financing sources, which remain available over time. Investor Protection Fund resources are funds from dedicated collections and may only be used for the purposes specified by the Dodd-Frank Act.

F. Entity Assets

Assets that an agency is authorized to use in its operations are entity assets. The SEC is authorized to use all funds in the Investor Protection Fund for its operations. Accordingly, all assets are recognized as entity assets.

G. Fund Balance with Treasury

Fund Balance with Treasury reflects amounts the Investor Protection Fund holds in the U.S. Treasury that have not been invested in Federal securities. The SEC conducts all of its banking activity in accordance with directives issued by the U.S. Department of the Treasury's Bureau of the Fiscal Service.

H. Investments

The SEC has authority to invest amounts in the Investor Protection Fund in overnight and short-term, market-based Treasury securities. The interest earned on the investments is a component of the Fund and is available to be used for expenses of the Investor Protection Fund. Additional details regarding Investor Protection Fund investments are provided in *Note 3, Investments*.

I. Liabilities

The SEC records liabilities for probable future outflows or other sacrifices of resources as a result of events that have occurred as of the Balance Sheet date. The Investor Protection Fund's liabilities consist of amounts payable to whistleblowers and reimbursable expenses that the Office of Inspector General incurs to operate the Employee Suggestion Program.

The Dodd-Frank Act and the SEC implementing regulations establish the eligibility criteria for whistleblower awards. Refer to *Note 4, Commitments and Contingencies* for additional information regarding the disclosure and recognition of actual and contingent liabilities for whistleblower awards.

J. Program Costs

The Investor Protection Fund reimburses the SEC's General Fund (X0100) for expenses incurred by the Office of Inspector General to administer the Employee Suggestion Program. The Investor Protection Fund also finances payments to whistleblowers under Section 21F of the Exchange Act.

K. Non-Exchange Revenue

Disgorgement and Penalty Transfers

Non-exchange revenue arises from the Government's ability to demand payment. The Investor Protection Fund is financed through the receipt of portions of monetary sanctions collected by the SEC in judicial or administrative actions brought by the SEC under the securities laws that are not either: (1) added to the disgorgement fund or other fund under Section 308 of the Sarbanes-Oxley Act of 2002 (15 U.S.C. 7246) or (2) otherwise distributed to victims of a violation of the securities laws. The Investor Protection Fund recognizes non-exchange revenue for disgorgement and penalty amounts transferred into the fund from the SEC's Disgorgement and

Penalties Fund (X6563). No sanction collected by the SEC can be deposited into the Investor Protection Fund if the balance in the fund exceeds $300 million on the day of collection.

Interest Earnings on Investments with Treasury

Interest earned from investments in U.S. Treasury securities is classified in the same way as the predominant source of revenue to the fund. The Investor Protection Fund is financed through the receipt of non-exchange revenues and thus interest earnings are also recognized as non-exchange revenues.

L. Budgets and Budgetary Accounting

The Investor Protection Fund (Fund X5567) is a special fund established through a permanent indefinite appropriation that has the authority to retain revenues and other financing sources not used in the current period for future use. The Dodd-Frank Act provides that the Fund is available to the SEC without further appropriation or fiscal year limitation for the purpose of paying awards to whistleblowers and funding the activities of the OIG's employee suggestion program. However, the SEC is required to request and obtain an annual apportionment from OMB to use these funds.

The resources of the Investor Protection Fund are apportioned under Category B authority, which means that the funds represent budgetary resources distributed by a specified project and are not subject to quarterly apportionment. Thus, all obligations incurred as presented on the Statement of Budgetary Resources are derived from Category B funds.

NOTE 2. Fund Balance with Treasury

The Fund Balance with Treasury by type of fund and Status of Fund Balance with Treasury as of September 30, 2013 and 2012 consisted of the following:

(DOLLARS IN THOUSANDS)	FY 2013	FY 2012
Fund Balances:		
Special Fund	$ 4,996	$ 957
Total Fund Balance with Treasury	$ 4,996	$ 957
Status of Fund Balance with Treasury:		
Unobligated Balance		
Available	$ 406	$ 957
Unavailable	4,590	—
Subtotal	4,996	957
Total Fund Balance with Treasury	$ 4,996	$ 957

Unobligated balances reported for the status of Fund Balance with Treasury do not agree with the amounts reported in the Statement of Budgetary Resources due to the fact that unobligated balances are not reduced when investments are purchased.

There were no differences between the Fund Balance reflected in the Investor Protection Fund financial statements and the balance in the Treasury accounts.

Cash flow

The Investor Protection Fund cash flows are reflected in investments and in the Statement of Budgetary Resources. Such cash flows during FY 2013 consisted of net investment redemptions of $16.4 million, net interest received of $2.5 million (which includes $3.2 million of interest collections, $765 thousand of premiums paid, and $89 thousand in discounts received), payments to whistleblowers totaling $14.8 million, and the cost of operating the OIG Employee Suggestion Program of $51 thousand.

Cash flows during FY 2012 consisted of net investment redemptions of $375 thousand, net interest received of $625 thousand (which includes $4.2 million of interest collections and $3.6 million of premiums paid), payments to whistleblowers totaling $46 thousand, and the cost of operating the OIG Employee Suggestion Program of $70 thousand.

NOTE 3. Investments

The SEC invests funds in overnight and short-term non-marketable market-based Treasury bills. The SEC records the value of its investments in Treasury bills at cost and amortizes any premium or discount on a straight-line basis (S/L) through the maturity date of these securities. Non-marketable market-based Treasury securities are issued by the Bureau of the Fiscal Service to Federal agencies. They are not traded on any securities exchange but mirror the prices of similar Treasury securities trading in the Government securities market.

Intragovernmental Investments in Treasury Securities

Market-based Treasury securities are debt securities that the U.S. Treasury issues to Federal entities without statutorily determined interest rates. Although the securities are not marketable, the terms (prices and interest rates) mirror the terms of marketable Treasury securities.

The Federal Government does not set aside assets to pay future benefits or other expenditures associated with the investment by Federal agencies in non-marketable Federal securities. The balances underlying these investments are deposited in the U.S. Treasury, which uses the cash for general Government purposes. Treasury securities are issued to the SEC as evidence of these balances. Treasury securities are an asset of the SEC and a liability of the U.S. Treasury. Because the SEC and the U.S. Treasury are both components of the Government, these assets and liabilities offset each other from the standpoint of the Government as a whole. For this reason, the investments presented by the SEC do not represent an asset or a liability in the U.S. Government-wide financial statements.

Treasury securities provide the SEC with authority to draw upon the U.S. Treasury to make future payments from these accounts. When the SEC requires redemption of these securities to make expenditures, the Government finances those expenditures out of accumulated cash balances, by raising taxes or other receipts, by borrowing from the public or repaying less debt, or by curtailing other expenditures. This is the same manner in which the Government finances all expenditures.

At September 30, 2013, investments consisted of the following:

(DOLLARS IN THOUSANDS)	Cost	Amortization Method	Amortized (Premium) Discount	Interest Receivable	Investment, Net	Market Value Disclosure
Non-Marketable Market-Based Securities						
Investor Protection Fund – Entity	$ 434,009	S/L	$ 56	$ 136	$ 434,201	$ 434,211

At September 30, 2012, investments consisted of the following:

(DOLLARS IN THOUSANDS)	Cost	Amortization Method	Amortized (Premium) Discount	Interest Receivable	Investment, Net	Market Value Disclosure
Non-Marketable Market-Based Securities						
Investor Protection Fund – Entity	$ 454,119	S/L	$ (2,875)	$ 1,228	$ 452,472	$ 451,319

NOTE 4. Commitments and Contingencies

Commitments and Contingencies: Whistleblower Program

As mentioned in *Note 1.I, Liabilities*, the Investor Protection Fund is used to pay awards to whistleblowers if they voluntarily provide original information to the SEC and meet other conditions. The legislation allows whistleblowers to receive between 10 and 30 percent of the monetary sanctions collected in the covered action or in a related action, with the actual percentage being determined at the discretion of the SEC using criteria provided in the legislation and the related rules to implement the legislation adopted by the SEC.

A Preliminary Determination is a first assessment, made by the Claims Review Staff, as to whether the claim should be allowed or denied, and if allowed, what the proposed award percentage amount should be. A contingent liability is recognized in instances where a positive Preliminary Determination (payment of award is probable) has been made by the Claims Review Staff in the Office of the Whistleblower and the amount can be reasonably estimated. Liabilities are recognized in instances where a collection has been received and a positive Proposed Final Determination has been reached by the Claims Review Staff. However, the actual payment of the Whistleblower award would not occur until after the final order was issued by the Commission. The SEC did not recognize a contingent liability for potential whistleblower awards as of September 30, 2013 or September 30, 2012.

The SEC believes that approximately $500,000 in additional whistleblower awards may be paid in future periods relating to covered actions for which monetary sanctions were collected and award applications were filed during FY 2013, but a Preliminary Determination had not been rendered during FY 2013 or prior to the issuance of the FY 2013 financial statements. Such claims do not meet the criteria for recognition as contingent liabilities in FY 2013.

NOTE 5. Intragovernmental Costs

The Statement of Net Cost presents the Investor Protection Fund's results of operations for its two activities: the Employee Suggestion Program and Payments to Whistleblowers. Intragovernmental costs arise from purchases of goods and services from other components of the Federal Government (including other SEC funds). In contrast, public costs are those which arise from the purchase of goods and services from non-Federal entities. Payments to whistleblowers are categorized as "costs with the public."

In FY 2013, the Employee Suggestion Program incurred $51 thousand of intragovernmental costs. The Payments to Whistleblowers program incurred $14.8 million of costs with the public (payments to whistleblowers) in FY 2013.

In FY 2012, the Employee Suggestion Program incurred $70 thousand of intragovernmental costs. The Payments to Whistleblowers program incurred $46 thousand of costs with the public (payments to whistleblowers) in FY 2012.

NOTE 6. Status of Budgetary Resources

A. Explanation of Differences between the Statement of Budgetary Resources and the Budget of the U.S. Government

A comparison between the FY 2013 Statement of Budgetary Resources (SBR) and the actual FY 2013 data in the President's budget cannot be presented, as the FY 2015 President's budget which will contain FY 2013 actual data is not yet available; the comparison will be presented in next year's financial statements. There are no differences between the FY 2012 SBR and the FY 2012 data in the President's budget.

B. Other Budgetary Disclosures

There were no budgetary resources obligated for undelivered orders as of September 30, 2013 and 2012.

There are no legal arrangements affecting the use of unobligated balances of budget authority, such as time limits, purpose, and obligation limitations.

NOTE 7. Reconciliation of Net Cost of Operations to Budget

For the years ended September 30, 2013 and 2012, Obligations Incurred equaled the Net Cost of Operations and there were no reconciling items.

OTHER INFORMATION

This section provides additional information regarding the U.S. Securities and Exchange Commission's (SEC) financial and performance management. It includes the Schedule of Spending which provides an overview of how the SEC spent its resources based on amounts available to the SEC; a statement prepared by the agency's Office of Inspector General (OIG) summarizing what the OIG considers to be the most serious management and performance challenges facing the agency. The section also includes a response from the SEC Chair, outlining the agency's progress in addressing the challenges.

The Summary of Financial Statement Audit and Management Assurances clearly lists each material weakness and non-conformance found and/or resolved during the U.S. Government Accountability Office's audit. Additionally, this section provides a detailed explanation of any significant erroneous payments, as required by the Improper Payments Information Act of 2002, as amended.

Schedule of Spending

The Schedule of Spending presents a more detailed summary of the "Obligations Incurred" line presented on the Statement of Budgetary Resources, and how these amounts agreed to be spent compare to the SEC's total resources after factoring amounts available and unavailable to be spent. The SEC's obligations are categorized by major program and object class.

In an additional effort to improve the quality of data reported on USASpending.gov for public transparency, the SEC has also begun reconciliation efforts between obligations reported on the financial statements and spending reported on the website. The majority of obligations included on the financial statements that are not included on USASpending.gov include the following: personnel compensation and benefits, leases, interagency agreements, travel, and training. Differences may also exist due to timing differences between obligations reported in SEC's financial reporting system and data transmitted to USASpending.gov through the central Federal Procurement Data System.

U.S. SECURITIES AND EXCHANGE COMMISSION

Schedule of Spending

For the year ended September 30, 2013

(DOLLARS IN THOUSANDS)	FY 2013
What Money is Available to Spend?	
Total Resources	$ 1,402,477
Less Amount Available but Not Agreed to be Spent	562,565
Less Amount Not Available to be Spent	(417,799)
Total Amounts Agreed to be Spent	$ 1,257,711
How was the Money Spent/Issued?	
Enforcement	
Personnel Compensation and Benefits	$ 271,202
Contractual Services	138,883
Acquisition of Assets	19,376
Other	4,679
	434,140
Compliance Inspections and Examinations	
Personnel Compensation and Benefits	178,607
Contractual Services	52,047
Acquisition of Assets	4,803
Other	3,271
	238,728
Corporation Finance	
Personnel Compensation and Benefits	95,607
Contractual Services	26,398
Acquisition of Assets	6,850
Other	1,712
	130,567
Trading and Markets	
Personnel Compensation and Benefits	51,755
Contractual Services	13,968
Acquisition of Assets	3,536
Other	929
	70,188

(continued on next page)

Schedule of Spending *(continued)*

For the year ended September 30, 2013

(DOLLARS IN THOUSANDS)	FY 2013
Investment Management	
Personnel Compensation and Benefits	35,029
Contractual Services	8,828
Acquisition of Assets	2,101
Other	596
	46,554
Economic and Risk Analysis	
Personnel Compensation and Benefits	17,414
Contractual Services	16,152
Acquisition of Assets	7,104
Other	317
	40,987
General Counsel	
Personnel Compensation and Benefits	28,428
Contractual Services	7,554
Acquisition of Assets	1,730
Other	587
	38,299
Other Program Offices	
Personnel Compensation and Benefits	35,209
Contractual Services	10,222
Acquisition of Assets	2,164
Other	646
	48,241
Agency Direction and Administrative Support	
Personnel Compensation and Benefits	109,668
Contractual Services	81,829
Acquisition of Assets	9,371
Other	2,765
	203,633
Inspector General	
Personnel Compensation and Benefits	3,877
Contractual Services	2,166
Acquisition of Assets	257
Other	74
	6,374
Total Amounts Agreed to be Spent	$ 1,257,711
Who did the Money go to?	
Non-Federal	$ 1,199,233
Federal	58,478
Total Amounts Agreed to be Spent	$ 1,257,711

Inspector General's Statement on Management and Performance Challenges

**OFFICE OF
INSPECTOR GENERAL**

UNITED STATES
SECURITIES AND EXCHANGE COMMISSION
WASHINGTON, D.C. 20549

The Inspector General's Statement on the U.S. Securities and Exchange Commission's Management and Performance Challenges

Carl W. Hoecker
Inspector General
September 30, 2013

The Reports Consolidation Act of 2000 requires the U.S. Securities and Exchange Commission (SEC or Commission) Office of Inspector General (OIG), to identify and report annually on the most serious management challenges that the SEC faces. To identify management challenges, we routinely review past and ongoing audit, investigation, and evaluation work to identify material weaknesses, significant deficiencies, and vulnerabilities. We compiled this statement on the basis of the work that we completed over the past year; our knowledge of the SEC's programs and operations; and feedback from SEC staff and the Government Accountability Office (GAO) auditors who conduct the SEC's annual financial statement audit.

MANAGEMENT AND PERFORMANCE CHALLENGES

Information Security

Although the Office of Information Technology (OIT) has established policies for handling and safeguarding sensitive and nonpublic information, and requires SEC employees, contractors, and interns to complete annual security awareness training, information security[1] continues to be a management challenge at the SEC. Specifically, OIT's compliance with FISMA remains a management challenge this year because OIT has not fully addressed the findings and recommendations that were identified in the OIG's previously issued FISMA reports. For example, in the *2012 FISMA Executive Summary Report*, Report No. 512, issued March 29, 2013, the OIG found that OIT had not fully addressed three findings and six recommendations that were included in the *2011 FISMA Executive Summary Report*, Report No. 501, issued February 2, 2012. The OIG found that OIT had not fully implemented compliance scanning for network devices,

---

[1] The Federal Information Security Management Act (FISMA) provides that "[t]he term 'information security' means protecting information and information systems from unauthorized access, use, disclosure, disruption, modification, or destruction in order to provide- (A) integrity, which means guarding against improper information modification or destruction, and includes ensuring information nonrepudiation and authenticity; (B) confidentiality, which means preserving authorized restrictions on access and disclosure, including means for protecting personal privacy and proprietary information; and (C) availability, which means ensuring timely and reliable access to and use of information." 44 U.S.C. § 3542(b)(1).

multifactor authentication for the SEC's personal identity verification program, and baseline security controls that are tailored for specific information technology (IT) systems.

While the conditions found in the 2012 FISMA report could expose the SEC to threats should layered controls break down, OIT made progress this year in addressing the findings and recommendations that posed a greater risk to the SEC's IT environment. However, OIT has not fully addressed some outstanding significant findings and recommendations.

Information security is a particularly difficult management challenge because the SEC not only shares information internally among its divisions and offices, but also shares information externally with the regulated community and financial regulators. This sharing of external information is necessary to accomplish the SEC's mission of protecting investors and maintaining fair, orderly, and efficient markets that facilitate capital formation. We will continue to review OIT's security controls over the SEC's information systems during the upcoming annual FISMA assessment. We will also continue to review the SEC's handling of sensitive, nonpublic information.

Procurement and Contracting

Since we first identified the SEC's process for procurement and contracting as a management challenge in fiscal year 2008, the Office of Acquisitions (OA) has improved its internal controls in this area. Most recently, in July 2013, OA published a revised administrative regulation and operating procedure on the management and administration of service contracts. The revised regulation provides direction for the avoidance of contracting for inherently governmental functions or personal services, as well as appropriate management procedures for acquiring and managing functions closely associated with inherently governmental functions and critical functions. The operating procedure is designed to assist the SEC in addressing service contracts and personal services, and to avoid the contracting out of inherently governmental functions.

Despite those improvements, the OIG has found that the SEC's monitoring of its contracts is a continuing challenge. Specifically, the OIG has obtained information indicating that there may be insufficient controls over the tracking of funds or the approval of invoices for certain contracts and/or interagency agreements, as well as inconsistencies between the nature of the services provided and the requirements of the applicable task order. We are planning audit work in this area and will continue to monitor it closely.

Financial Management

The GAO's audit of the SEC's fiscal year 2012 financial statements[2] found that the SEC's

---

[2] GAO's fiscal year 2012 financial statement audit included SEC's general purpose and Investor Protection Fund (IPF) financial statements.

financial statements were fairly presented, in all material respects, in conformity with U.S. generally accepted accounting principles. That audit also found that, although internal controls could be improved, the SEC maintained, in all material respects, effective internal controls over financial reporting. However, the GAO identified significant deficiencies in accounting for budgetary resources and property and equipment. The GAO found that these deficiencies are related, in part, to the SEC's transition of its core financial system to the Department of Transportation's Enterprise Service Center Federal Shared Service Provider (FSSP).

In fiscal year 2012, the OIG identified the inherent risks that are associated with transitioning to a new financial system as a management challenge. In its management report to the SEC issued in April 2013, the GAO noted:

> [I]n April 2012, SEC migrated its core financial system operations to a shared service provider. ...[W]e identified new control deficiencies during our fiscal year 2012 audit related to SEC's monitoring controls over the service provider's core financial system operations, including those related to budgetary accounting and reporting activities.[3]

Further, the GAO stated that the "SEC did not develop monitoring procedures over property and equipment transactions recorded by its service provider at the time of its transition to the FSSP's general ledger system."[4] We will continue to monitor the SEC's use of the FSSP.

Human Capital Management

Section 962 of the Dodd-Frank Act required the GAO to report on the SEC's personnel management. In its report issued in July 2013, the GAO concluded:

> Based on analysis of views from Securities and Exchange Commission (SEC) employees and previous studies from GAO, SEC, and third parties, GAO determined that SEC's organizational culture is not constructive and could hinder its ability to effectively fulfill its mission. Organizations with constructive cultures are more effective and employees also exhibit a stronger commitment to mission focus. In describing SEC's culture, many current and former SEC employees cited low morale, distrust of management, and the compartmentalized, hierarchical, and risk-averse nature of

---

[3] GA0-13-274R, *Management Report Improvements Needed in SEC's Internal Controls and Accounting Procedures*, April 4, 2013, p. 3 (footnote omitted).

[4] *Id.*, p. 7.

the organization. According to an Office of Personnel Management (OPM) survey of federal employees, SEC currently ranks 19 of 22 similarly sized federal agencies based on employee satisfaction and commitment. GAO's past work on managing for results indicates that an effective personnel management system will be critical for transforming SEC's organizational culture.[5]

One key area that the GAO report highlighted as needing improvement was workforce planning. The GAO noted that the "SEC has not yet developed a comprehensive workforce plan" and, as a result, "will not be able to make well-informed decisions on how to best meet current and future agency needs."[6] The GAO further found that while the SEC has made efforts to improve communication and collaboration, it "has not yet fully addressed barriers."[7] The SEC has recently launched the SEC Local Labor Management Forum under Executive Order 13522, *Creating Labor-Management Forums to Improve Delivery of Government Services*, to foster a cooperative and productive form of labor-management relations. The OIG will continue to review the progress of this and other efforts to improve the SEC's management of human capital.

---

[5] GA0-13-621, *Securities and Exchange Commission Improving Personnel Management Is Critical for Agency's Effectiveness*, July 2013.

[6] *Id.*

[7] *Id.*

Management's Response to Inspector General's Statement

UNITED STATES
SECURITIES AND EXCHANGE COMMISSION
WASHINGTON, D.C. 20549

THE CHAIR

December 12, 2013

Mr. Carl W. Hoecker
Inspector General
U.S. Securities and Exchange Commission
Washington, D.C. 20549

Dear Mr. Hoecker:

Thank you for your "Statement on the U.S. Securities and Exchange Commission's Management and Performance Challenges," issued on September 30, 2013. We remain committed to enhancing the financial and operational effectiveness of the SEC and appreciate the Office of Inspector General's role in the effort. Below is an overview of the actions—taken and planned to be taken—to address each of the challenges identified in your statement.

Information Security

I appreciate your assessment and appreciation of the inherent challenges in information security management and performance. Information security is an important priority at the SEC. We know that the threat landscape is constantly changing, and we must frequently evaluate our controls and approaches to information security. Thank you for acknowledging the progress we have made this year in addressing issues of great risk to the IT environment. Our Office of Information Technology (OIT) will continue to apply a risk-based approach to prioritize our efforts.

By December 31, 2013, we plan to complete the recommendations related to Report No. 512, issued in March 2013, concerning assessment and continuous monitoring. The OIT security team has put forth a significant amount of effort in 2013 to build an infrastructure supporting an efficient and effective risk management program, including periodic assessments and continuous monitoring. OIT will refine the agency's formal documentation—internal policies and procedures—to account for these new capabilities. Compliance scanning for network devices is now occurring.

OIT has also taken steps to implement multi-factor authentication to our Personal Identity Verification (PIV) program. OIT is taking advantage of a significant and pre-requisite Active Directory clean-up effort that is scheduled for completion in FY 2014, to allow for PIV authentication while minimizing the impact on our end users.

Procurement and Contracting

I am pleased that your office recognized the progress and improvement in the agency's approach to procurement and contracting. The Office of Acquisitions (OA) continues to work diligently to address all OIG concerns.

We are deeply committed to remediating the remaining management challenges identified by the OIG in the SEC's processes for procurement and contracting. During the course of FY 2013, the SEC improved processes surrounding service contracts, stabilized the organizational structure within OA, and provided formal training to agency staff. In FY 2014, OA will continue to utilize its oversight program and conduct internal contract management reviews. We will leverage resources to identify instances where improvements should be made in the areas of funds tracking, invoice approvals or disconnects between contract requirements and services provided.

Financial Management

The SEC just completed its first full year of operations on the Delphi financial system, a Federal Shared Service Provider (FSSP) hosted by the Department of Transportation's (DOT) Enterprise Services Center (ESC). We appreciate your recognizing the challenges associated with migrating a core financial system, particularly to a third party service-provider. Among these challenges is the need to continuously monitor the activities of ESC to ensure completeness and accuracy of SEC data.

To address these challenges, we have adopted a comprehensive approach to continuously assessing the effectiveness of our internal controls over financial reporting, as well as reviewing the daily processing of transactions performed by ESC. The SEC has made significant strides in refining its processes under the FSSP model, both to tighten controls and to make them more efficient.

In 2012, the Government Accountability Office (GAO) identified two significant deficiencies in SEC's internal controls: (1) accounting for budgetary resources; and (2) property and equipment. In its 2013 audit report, the GAO noted that both of these significant deficiencies were remediated. The SEC made significant improvements and strengthened controls in these areas, as specified below.

Budgetary Resources: The SEC addressed a backlog of deobligations and contract closeouts. In addition, the agency refined its process for recording upward and downward adjustments, developed additional monthly reconciliations, implemented a quarterly review of undelivered orders (UDOs), and conducted daily tie point analyses.

Property and Equipment: The SEC implemented a Fixed Asset worksheet tracking log procedure to ensure that new assets were added timely and accurately, implemented a policy to ensure that all potentially capitalizable assets are reviewed by an accountant prior to recording them in the general ledger, reconciled the subsidiary ledger to the general ledger on a monthly basis, and tightened the process for the annual physical inventory. In FY 2014, the SEC will strive to automate many property-related processes, to help tighten controls further in this area.

Human Capital Management

The GAO report of the SEC's personnel management practices and organizational culture contains useful recommendations to help us further strengthen these areas. The SEC concurred with the GAO's recommendations pertaining to the areas identified in your statement, specifically, workforce planning and communication and collaboration.

As the report states, both SEC staff and external stakeholders have started to see some positive effects from the agency's recent efforts to bolster communication and collaboration but continued work is needed to break down existing "silos" within the agency. Steps are well underway to improve intra-agency communication. Initiatives such as the creation of a cross-agency communications group to enhance information and knowledge sharing, the establishment of working groups to address rulemaking and economic analysis requirements, and the development of liaisons in our major divisions and offices to facilitate the sharing of information demonstrate the SEC's commitment to improvements in this area.

To further address this challenge, the Office of the Chief Operating Officer and the Office of Public Affairs are collaborating with the Office of Human Resources (OHR) to devise communication and change management plans to support implementation of human capital-related initiatives. The plans will increase and track multi-channel, internal messaging that specifically recognizes and reinforces awareness of exceptional staff achievements, awards, or other successful outcomes while seeking to promote a sense of agency pride and accomplishment. In FY 2014, the SEC also will implement technology improvements to centralize all human capital information, news and resources. Staff will be able to find tools, forms, guidance and support needed, by accessing one centralized Intranet location. The technology improvements will also allow us to share open meeting fact sheets and other important documents and materials with agency staff more promptly. Plans are underway to initiate a number of other communication strategies that will promote employee engagement and a more open organizational culture.

With respect to workforce planning, GAO found that the SEC had not yet developed a comprehensive workforce plan, including a plan to identify the agency's future leaders. Although we have taken some steps, such as identifying competency gaps and conducting leadership training, these efforts did not reflect all of the elements of effective workforce planning described in the Office of Personnel Management's guidance on this topic.

The SEC's most recent progress in this area includes establishing and staffing a workforce and succession planning function within OHR. This team of three staff members has primary responsibility for providing tools, systems, and reports for analyzing the agency's workforce supply and demand to determine gaps and risks. OHR anticipates fully operationalizing this function in FY 2014. OHR will further address GAO's recommendation by improving databases and systems that support workforce analysis and planning efforts.

During FY 2014, the OHR plans to develop standardized reports for workforce planning and to work with organizational units to customize their workforce planning needs. OHR will also begin developing an effective succession planning program for key positions to address potential attrition. It should be noted that the SEC's attrition rate remains low (approximately 6 percent for FY 2013), and that OHR has enhanced several key human capital programs (*e.g.*, recruitment and retention programs and various training initiatives) directed at maintaining that rate.

* * * *

I hope that the actions outlined in this letter demonstrate our commitment to strengthening internal control and improving the agency's performance. We look forward to working with you to further address these challenges.

Sincerely,

Mary Jo White
Chair

Summary of Financial Statement Audit and Management Assurances

TABLE 3.1
SUMMARY OF FINANCIAL STATEMENT AUDIT

Audit Opinion: Unmodified
Restatement: No

Material Weaknesses	Beginning Balance	New	Resolved	Consolidated	Ending Balance
Total Material Weaknesses	—	—	—	—	—

TABLE 3.2
SUMMARY OF MANAGEMENT ASSURANCES

Effectiveness of Internal Control over Financial Reporting (FMFIA § 2)

Statement of Assurance: Unqualified

Material Weaknesses	Beginning Balance	New	Resolved	Consolidated	Reassessed	Ending Balance
Total Material Weaknesses	—	—	—	—	—	—

Effectiveness of Internal Control over Operations (FMFIA § 2)

Statement of Assurance: Unqualified

Material Weaknesses	Beginning Balance	New	Resolved	Consolidated	Reassessed	Ending Balance
Total Material Weaknesses	—	—	—	—	—	—

Conformance with Financial Management System Requirements (FMFIA § 4)

Statement of Assurance: Conformance

Material Weaknesses	Beginning Balance	New	Resolved	Consolidated	Reassessed	Ending Balance
Total Non-Conformances	—	—	—	—	—	—

Improper Payments Elimination and Recovery Act Reporting Details

The Improper Payments Information Act (IPIA) of 2002, as amended by the Improper Payments Elimination and Recovery Act (IPERA) of 2010 and Improper Payments Elimination and Recovery Improvement Act (IPERIA) of 2012, requires agencies to review all programs and activities they administer and identify those which may be susceptible to significant erroneous payments. For all programs and activities in which the risk of erroneous payments is significant, agencies are to estimate the annual amount of erroneous payments made in those programs. Office of Management and Budget (OMB) Circular A-136 and Appendix C of Circular A-123 requires agencies to report detailed information related to their Improper Payments Elimination Program.

Risk Assessment

In fiscal year (FY) 2013, the U.S. Securities and Exchange Commission (SEC) reviewed its programs and activities to identify those which may be susceptible to significant erroneous payments. The risk assessment included: (1) consideration of certain risk factors that are likely to contribute to a susceptibility to significant improper payments, and (2) transaction testing on a sample basis of payments made during the first six months of FY 2013. A risk assessment was performed for the following programs:

- Vendor payments (includes credit card payments);

- Disgorgement and penalty distributions (made by SEC to fund and tax administrators and directly to harmed investors); and

- Returned deposits of registration filing fees under Section 6b of the Securities Act of 1933 and Sections 13 and 14 of the Securities Exchange Act of 1934.

Travel payments, included in prior years testing, were removed from improper payment testing for FY 2013 due to a decrease in the susceptibility to significant erroneous payments, identified during the prior year risk assessment. The SEC continued to cover travel payments for FY 2013 through its monthly continuous monitoring.

Based on the results of transaction testing applied to a sample of payments, consideration of risk factors, and reliance on the internal controls in place over the payment, refund, and distribution process, the SEC determined that none of its programs and activities are susceptible to significant improper payments at or above the threshold levels set by OMB. Significant erroneous payments are defined as annual erroneous payments in the program exceeding both $10 million and 1.5 percent of total program outlays, or $100 million of improper payments if less than 1.5 percent of total annual program outlays. In accordance with Appendix C of Circular A-123, the SEC is not required to determine a statistically valid estimate of erroneous payments or develop a corrective action plan if the program is not susceptible to significant improper payments.

In FYs 2007 and 2008, SEC's testing of its largest programs resulted in improper payment percentages that were well below one-half percent and less than $30,000 for each program. In FYs 2009 through 2012, the SEC performed a risk assessment for all programs and determined that its programs are not susceptible to significant erroneous payments.

If the level of risk in each program is determined to be low and baseline estimates have been established, the SEC is only required to conduct a formal risk assessment every three years unless the program experiences a significant change in legislation and/or a significant increase in funding level. The SEC will conduct a follow-on review in FY 2014 of its programs and activities to determine whether the programs have experienced any significant changes in legislation or funding levels. If so, the SEC will reassess the programs' risk susceptibility and make a statistically valid estimate of erroneous payments for any programs determined to be susceptible to significant erroneous payments.

Recapture of Improper Payments

In FY 2013, the SEC did not administer any grants, benefits or loan programs. Implementation of recapture auditing, if determined to be cost-effective, would apply to vendor payments, disgorgement and penalty distributions, and refunds of registration filing fee deposits. Per the IPERA legislation a payment is any transfer or commitment for future transfer of Federal funds to any non-Federal person or entity. As such, the SEC is not required to review, and has not reviewed, intragovernmental transactions and payments to employees.

The SEC has determined that implementing a payment recapture audit program for vendor payments, disgorgement and penalty distributions, and refunds of registration filing fee deposits is not cost-effective. That is, the benefits or recaptured amounts associated with implementing and overseeing the program do not exceed the costs, including staff time and resources, or payments to a contractor for implementation, of a payment recapture audit program. In making this determination, the SEC considered its low improper payment rate based on testing conducted over the past six years. The SEC also considered whether sophisticated software and other cost-efficient matching techniques could be used to identify significant overpayments at a low cost per overpayment, or if labor intensive manual reviews of paper documentation would

be required. In addition, the SEC considered the availability of tools to efficiently perform the payment recapture audit and minimize payment recapture audit costs.

The SEC will continue to monitor its improper payments across all programs and activities it administers and assess whether implementing payment recapture audits for each program is cost-effective. If the SEC determines, through future risk assessments, that a program is susceptible to significant improper payments and implementing a payment recapture program is cost-beneficial, the SEC will implement a pilot payment recapture audit to measure the likelihood of cost-effective payment recapture audits on a larger scale.

Even though the SEC has determined that implementing a payment recapture audit program for its programs is not cost-effective, the agency strives to recover any overpayments identified through other sources, such as payments identified through statistical samples conducted under the IPIA. The amounts identified and recovered, by program, are shown in Table 3.3 below.

TABLE 3.3

OVERPAYMENTS RECAPTURED OUTSIDE OF PAYMENT RECAPTURE AUDITS *(IN DOLLARS)*

Source	Amount Identified (CY)	Amount Recovered (CY)	Amount Identified (PYs)	Amount Recovered (PYs)	Cumulative Amount Identified (CY+PYs)	Cumulative Amount Recovered (CY+PYs)
Vendor Payments						
Improper Payments Sampling	$ 46,322	$ —	$ 13,573	$ 13,085	$ 59,895	$ 13,084
Disgorgement and Penalty Distributions						
Improper Payments Sampling	$ —	$ —	$ —	$ —	$ —	$ —
Refunds of Registration Filing Fee Deposits						
Improper Payments Sampling	$ —	$ —	$ 321	$ 321	$ 321	$ 321

APPENDICES

APPENDIX A: Chair and Commissioners
Provides biographies of the SEC Chair and Commissioners.

APPENDIX B: Major Enforcement Cases
Outlines the major enforcement cases of FY 2013.

APPENDIX C: SEC Divisions and Offices
Provides contact information for SEC's headquarters and regional offices.

APPENDIX D: Glossary of Selected Terms
Definitions provided of select technical terms used throughout this report.

APPENDIX E: Acronyms
Defines acronyms cited in the report. Acronyms are listed in alphabetical order.

Appendix A: Chair and Commissioners

Mary Jo White
CHAIR

Mary Jo White was sworn in as the 31st Chair of the SEC on April 10, 2013. She was nominated to be SEC Chair by President Barack Obama on February 7, 2013, and confirmed by the U.S. Senate on April 8, 2013.

Chair White arrived at the SEC with decades of experience as a federal prosecutor and securities lawyer. As the U.S. Attorney for the Southern District of New York from 1993 to 2002, she specialized in prosecuting complex securities and financial institution frauds and international terrorism cases. Under her leadership, the office earned convictions against the terrorists responsible for the 1993 bombing of the World Trade Center and the bombings of American embassies in Africa. She is the only woman to hold the top position in the 200-year-plus history of that office.

Prior to becoming the U.S. Attorney for the Southern District of New York, Chair White served as the First Assistant U.S. Attorney and later Acting U.S. Attorney for the Eastern District of New York from 1990 to 1993. She previously served as an Assistant U.S. Attorney for the Southern District of New York from 1978 to 1981 and became Chief Appellate Attorney of the Criminal Division.

After leaving her U.S. Attorney post, Chair White became chair of the litigation department at Debevoise & Plimpton in New York, where she led a team of more than 200 lawyers. Chair White previously was a litigation partner at the firm from 1983 to 1990 and worked as an associate from 1976 to 1978.

Chair White earned her undergraduate degree, Phi Beta Kappa, from William & Mary in 1970, and her master's degree in psychology from The New School for Social Research in 1971. She earned her law degree in 1974 at Columbia Law School, where she was an officer of the Law Review. She served as a law clerk to the Honorable Marvin E. Frankel of the U.S. District Court for the Southern District of New York.

Chair White has won numerous awards in recognition of her outstanding work both as a prosecutor and a securities lawyer. The 2012 Chambers USA Women in Law Awards named her Regulatory Lawyer of the Year. Among other honors she has received are the Margaret Brent Women Lawyers of Achievement Award, the George W. Bush Award for Excellence in Counterterrorism, the Sandra Day O'Connor Award for Distinction in Public Service, and the "Women of Power and Influence Award" given by the National Organization for Women.

Chair White is a fellow in the American College of Trial Lawyers and the International College of Trial Lawyers. She also has served as a director of The NASDAQ Stock Exchange and on its executive, audit, and policy committees. Chair White is a member of the Council on Foreign Relations.

Luis A. Aguilar
COMMISSIONER

Luis A. Aguilar has been a Commissioner at the U.S. Securities and Exchange Commission since July 31, 2008. He was appointed by President George W. Bush and was reappointed by President Barack Obama.

Prior to his appointment, his practice included matters pertaining to general corporate and business law, international transactions, investment companies and investment advisers, securities law, and corporate finance.

Commissioner Aguilar represents the Commission as its liaison to both the North American Securities Administrators Association and to the Council of Securities Regulators of the Americas.

Commissioner Aguilar has received various honors and awards, including: recipient of Honorary Doctor of Public Service, awarded by Georgia Southern University (2013); recipient of the Atlanta Falcons "2012 NFL Hispanic Heritage Leadership Award" (2012); named by Poder.Hispanic Magazine as one of the "100 Most Influential Hispanics in the Nation" (2011); named by Latino Leaders Magazine as one of the "Top 101 Most Influential Latinos in the United States" (2009, 2010, 2011 and 2012); named to the NACD Directorship 100, the Who's Who of the Boardroom (2009, 2010 and 2011); recipient of The Center for Accounting Ethics, Governance, and the Public Interest "Accounting in the Public Interest Award" (2010); and listed in Best Lawyers in America (2005, 2006, 2007 and 2008).

He is a graduate of the University of Georgia School of Law, and also received a master of laws degree in taxation from Emory University.

Commissioner Aguilar serves as sponsor of the SEC's Hispanic and Latino Opportunity, Leadership, and Advocacy Committee, the African American Council, and the Caribbean American Heritage Committee.

Daniel M. Gallagher
COMMISSIONER

Commissioner Gallagher was confirmed by the Senate on October 21, 2011, and returned to the Securities and Exchange Commission, where he had previously served, on November 7, 2011.

Commissioner Gallagher was on the staff of the SEC beginning in January 2006, when he served as a counsel to SEC Commissioner Paul S. Atkins and later as a counsel to SEC Chairman Christopher Cox. He worked primarily on major matters before the Commission involving the Division of Trading and Markets and the Division of Enforcement.

He joined the Division of Trading and Markets as a Deputy Director in 2008, where he played a key role in the SEC's response to the financial crisis and other significant issues before the Commission, including those involving credit rating agencies and credit default swaps. He served as an Acting Director of the Trading and Markets Division from April 2009 to January 2010, after which he left the agency to become a partner in the Washington, DC office of WilmerHale.

Prior to his initial SEC service, Commissioner Gallagher was the General Counsel and Senior Vice President of Fiserv Securities, Inc., where he was responsible for managing all of the firm's legal and regulatory matters. Commissioner Gallagher began his career in private practice, advising clients on broker-dealer regulatory issues and representing clients in SEC and SRO enforcement proceedings.

Commissioner Gallagher earned his J.D. degree, magna cum laude, from the Catholic University of America, where he was a member of the law review. He graduated from Georgetown University with a B.A. degree in English.

Kara M. Stein
COMMISSIONER

Kara M. Stein was appointed by President Barack Obama to the U.S. Securities and Exchange Commission and was sworn in on August 9, 2013.

Ms. Stein joined the Commission after serving as Legal Counsel and Senior Policy Advisor for securities and banking matters to Senator Jack Reed. From 2009 to 2013, she was Staff Director of the Securities, Insurance, and Investment Subcommittee of the Senate Committee on Banking, Housing, and Urban Affairs. During that time, Ms. Stein played an integral role in drafting and negotiating significant provisions of the Dodd-Frank Wall Street Reform and Consumer Protection Act.

As Staff Director for the Senate Banking Subcommittee of primary jurisdiction over the SEC, Ms. Stein also organized and participated in over twenty hearings on such issues as the:

- evolution of market microstructure,
- regulation of exchange traded products,
- state of the securitization markets,
- risks to investors in capital raising processes, including through public offerings,
- role of the accounting profession in preventing another financial crisis,
- establishment of swap execution facilities, and
- role of the tri-party repurchase markets in the financial marketplace.

Ms. Stein was Legal Counsel and Senior Policy Advisor to Senator Reed from 2007 to 2009 and served as both the Majority and Minority Staff Director on the Banking Committee's Subcommittee on Housing and Transportation from 2001 to 2006. She served as Legal Counsel to Senator Reed from 1999 to 2000, following two years as a Legislative Assistant to Senator Chris Dodd.

Before working on Capitol Hill, Ms. Stein was an associate at the law firm of Wilmer, Cutler & Pickering, a Skadden Public Interest Fellow, an Advocacy Fellow with the Georgetown University Law Center, and an assistant professor with the University of Dayton School of Law.

Ms. Stein received her B.A. from Yale College and J.D. from Yale Law School.

Michael S. Piwowar
COMMISSIONER

Michael S. Piwowar was appointed by President Barack Obama to the U.S. Securities and Exchange Commission and was sworn in on August 15, 2013.

Most recently, Dr. Piwowar was the Republican chief economist for the U.S. Senate Committee on Banking, Housing, and Urban Affairs under Senators Mike Crapo and Richard Shelby. He was the lead Republican economist on the four SEC-related titles of the Dodd-Frank Act and the JOBS Act. Dr. Piwowar also worked on a number of important SEC-related oversight issues under the jurisdiction of the Committee.

During the financial crisis and its immediate aftermath, Dr. Piwowar served in a one-year fixed-term position at the White House as a senior economist at the President's Council of Economic Advisers (CEA) in both the George W. Bush and Barack Obama Administrations. While at the CEA, he also served as a staff economist for the Financial Regulatory Reform Working Group of the President's Economic Recovery Advisory Board (PERAB). Before joining the White House, Dr. Piwowar worked as a Principal at the Securities Litigation and Consulting Group (SLCG).

Dr. Piwowar's first tenure at the SEC was in the Office of Economic Analysis (now called the Division of Economic and Risk Analysis) as a visiting academic scholar on leave from Iowa State University and as a senior financial economist. Dr. Piwowar was an assistant professor of finance at Iowa State University where he focused his research on market microstructure and taught undergraduate and graduate courses in corporate finance and investments. He published a number of articles in leading academic publications and received several teaching and research awards.

Dr. Piwowar received a B.A. in Foreign Service and International Politics from the Pennsylvania State University, an M.B.A. from Georgetown University, and a Ph.D. in Finance from the Pennsylvania State University.

Appendix B: Major Enforcement Cases

Introduction

In order to help protect investors and maintain fair markets, the U.S. Securities and Exchange Commission (SEC) brings enforcement actions against individuals and organizations for alleged securities laws violations. As the SEC's largest division, the Division of Enforcement investigates potential violations of the Federal securities laws and brings civil charges in Federal district court and administrative proceedings. Through the Division of Enforcement, the Commission stops fraud, seeks appropriate penalties and disgorgement from wrongdoers, and returns funds to injured investors. Successful enforcement actions also result in orders barring wrongdoers from working in the securities industry. In fiscal year (FY) 2013, the Division of Enforcement continued to leverage its increasing specialization and expertise, as well as the creativity and doggedness of its staff, resulting in the Division bringing even more complex cases than in previous years. Further, the amount of money ordered in penalties and disgorgement as a result of enforcement actions filed increased in FY 2013 as compared to FY 2012. The actions filed in FY 2013 spanned the full spectrum of securities laws violations. This performance comes just two years after the most significant structural reforms in the Division's history. This section outlines the major enforcement cases of FY 2013. For further information on selected enforcement cases, please see "Litigation Releases" at *www.sec.gov/litigation/litreleases.shtml.*

Actions Related to the Financial Crisis

Building on a strong record in this area, identifying and holding accountable those individuals and institutions whose misconduct led to or arose from the financial crisis continued to be a high priority of the SEC in FY 2013. To date, the SEC has filed 96 enforcement actions involving wrongdoing generally associated with the financial crisis, including: (a) concealing from investors risks, terms, and improper pricing of collateralized debt obligations (CDOs) and other complex structured products; (b) misleading disclosures to investors

about mortgage-related risks; and (c) concealing the extent of risky mortgage-related and other high-risk investments in mutual funds and other financial products.

In total, the SEC's financial crisis related cases have resulted in charges against 161 individuals and entities, including 66 Chief Executive Officers (CEOs), Chief Financial Officers (CFOs), and other senior corporate officers. These cases have resulted in more than $2.73 billion of monetary relief being ordered or agreed to, most of which has been or is in the process of being returned to harmed investors. In addition, 37 individuals have been barred from the securities industry, from serving as officers and directors of public companies, and/or from appearing or practicing before the Commission.

In a set of cases tied to the financial crisis, the SEC, in coordination with the Federal-state Residential Mortgage-Backed Securities (RMBS) Working Group, charged J.P. Morgan Securities LLC and Credit Suisse Securities (USA) with misleading investors in RMBS offerings.[1] The SEC charged J.P. Morgan with misstating information about the delinquency status of mortgage loans that served as collateral for an RMBS offering it underwrote. J.P. Morgan was also charged with securities laws violations rising from misconduct by Bear Stearns – with whom J.P. Morgan merged – wherein Bear Stearns failed to disclose its practice of negotiating discounted cash settlements with loan originators and keeping the proceeds without paying anything to the RMBS trusts who owned the loans. The SEC brought charges against Credit Suisse for similar activity, alleging that Credit Suisse failed to disclose its practice of retaining cash from settlements with loan originators, and for making misleading statements to investors in SEC filings about when it would repurchase mortgage loans from trusts if borrowers missed the first payment due. Both banks settled the SEC's charges, with J.P. Morgan paying $296.9 million and Credit Suisse paying $120 million.

In December, the SEC brought charges against eight former members of the boards of directors overseeing five mutual funds managed by Morgan Keegan for violating their asset

---

[1] *SEC v. J. P. Morgan Securities, et al., SEC v. Credit Suisse Securities (USA) LLC, et al., Press Rel. 2012-233 (November 16, 2012)* www.sec.gov/News/PressRelease/Detail/PressRelease/1365171486012

pricing responsibilities under the Federal securities laws.[2] The funds, which were invested in some securities backed by subprime mortgages, fraudulently overstated the value of their securities as the housing market was on the brink of financial crisis in 2007. The SEC's Order Instituting Administrative and Cease-and-Desist Proceedings (OIP) alleged that the former directors delegated their fair valuation responsibility to a valuation committee without providing meaningful substantive guidance on how fair valuation determinations should be made. The fund directors then made no meaningful effort to learn how fair values were being determined, received only limited information about the factors involved with the funds' fair value determinations, and obtained almost no information explaining why particular fair values were assigned to portfolio securities. In June, the former directors settled by agreeing to cease-and-desist from committing any future violations of the Investment Company Act.

In another case tied to the financial crisis, the SEC brought charges against two investment advisory firms, Claymore Advisors LLC and Fiduciary Asset Management LLC (FAMCO), and two portfolio managers, Mohammed Riad and Kevin Swanson, for their roles in the failure to adequately inform investors about the fund's risky derivative strategies that contributed to the collapse of the Fiduciary/Claymore Dynamic Equity Fund (HCE) during the financial crisis.[3] In its settled order, the SEC found that FAMCO made misleading statements to investors about HCE's performance and its exposure to downside risk, and managed HCE in a manner inconsistent with the fund's registration statement. Claymore failed to reasonably supervise FAMCO as required by the firms' investment advisory agreements, and caused HCE's failure to provide adequate disclosure. Both Claymore and FAMCO agreed to settle the SEC's charges, with Claymore establishing a distribution plan to fully reimburse shareholders for the more than $45 million in losses that were incurred by

HCE. The SEC's action against Riad and Swanson, the two portfolio managers, is ongoing.

In April, the SEC charged Capital One Financial Corporation and two former senior executives for understating millions of dollars in auto loan losses incurred during the months leading into the financial crisis.[4] The SEC found that Capital One failed to incorporate the results of its internal loss forecasting tool in its financial reporting as credit markets began to deteriorate, understating its losses by approximately 18 percent in the second quarter of 2007 and 9 percent in the third quarter. The SEC's order concluded that Capital One's material understatements of its loan loss expense and internal controls failures violated the reporting, books and records, and internal controls provisions of the Federal securities laws, and former Chief Risk Officer Peter Schnall and former Divisional Credit Officer David LaGassa violated securities laws by indirectly causing Capital One's books and records violations by deviating from established policies and procedures and failing to implement proper internal controls. To settle the SEC's charges, Capital One agreed to pay a $3.5 million penalty, Schnall agreed to an $85,000 penalty, and LaGassa agreed to a $50,000 penalty. Capital One and the two executives neither admitted nor denied the findings in consenting to the SEC's order requiring them to cease and desist from committing or causing any violations of these Federal securities laws.

In another RMBS related case, the SEC charged Bank of America and two subsidiaries with defrauding investors in an offering by failing to disclose key risks and misrepresenting facts about the underlying mortgages.[5] The SEC alleged that Bank of America deceived investors about the details of an RMBS offering called BOAMS 2008-A, selling BOAMS 2008-A as a "prime" securitization appropriate for the most conservative RMBS investors, when in fact, Bank of America knew that more than 70 percent of the mortgages backing BOAMS 2008-A originated from "wholesale" mortgage brokers unaffiliated with the bank. Bank of America knew that such wholesale

---

2 *In the Matter of J. Kenneth Alderman, CPA, et al., Press Rel. 2012-259 (December 10, 2012)*
   www.sec.gov/News/PressRelease/Detail/PressRelease/1365171486708

3 *In the Matter of Claymore Advisors, LLC; In the Matter of Fiduciary Asset Management, LLC; In the Matter of Mohammed Riad and Kevin Timothy Swanson, Press Rel. 2012-272 (December 19, 2012) www.sec.gov/News/PressRelease/Detail/PressRelease/1365171487082*

4 *In the Matter of Capital One Financial Corporation, Peter A. Schnall, and David A. LaGassa, Press Rel. 2013-72 (April 24, 2013)*
   www.sec.gov/News/PressRelease/Detail/PressRelease/1365171514928

5 *SEC v. Bank of America, et al., Press Rel. 2013-148 (August 6, 2013)*
   www.sec.gov/News/PressRelease/Detail/PressRelease/1370539751924

mortgages presented vastly greater risks of severe delinquencies, early defaults, underwriting defects, and prepayment, such that the bank's then-CEO referred to the mortgages as "toxic waste." The SEC further alleged that Bank of America misrepresented that the mortgage loans backing BOAMS 2008-A were underwritten in conformity with the bank's own guidelines, when in fact the loans were riddled with ineligible appraisals, unsupported statements of income, misrepresentations regarding owner occupancy, and evidence of mortgage fraud. The SEC's action in this matter is continuing.

The same day, the SEC charged UBS Securities with illegally structuring and marketing a CDO by failing to disclose that it had retained millions of dollars in upfront cash it received in the course of acquiring collateral for the CDO.[6] UBS received $23.6 million in upfront payments in the process of acquiring credit default swaps as collateral, but did not transfer that money to the CDO despite releasing marketing materials that inaccurately represented otherwise. To settle the charges against it, UBS agreed to pay $50 million, which includes the $23.6 million in upfront payments (plus interest) as well as a $5.7 million penalty.

Actions Related to Exchanges, Broker-Dealers, and Market Structure Issues

In FY 2013, the Commission continued its commitment to bringing actions for compliance failures and rules violations relating to stock exchanges, alternative trading platforms, and other market structure participants. In October, the SEC charged Boston-based dark pool operator eBX LLC with failing to protect the confidential trading information of its subscribers and failing to disclose to all subscribers that it allowed an outside firm to use their confidential trading information.[7] Alternative trading systems (ATS) like eBX's LeveL, called dark pools, do not display quotations to the public, meaning that investors who subscribe to a dark pool have access to potential trade opportunities that other investors using public markets do not. eBX inaccurately informed its subscribers that their flow of orders to buy or sell securities would be kept confidential and not shared outside of LeveL. eBX instead allowed an outside technology firm to use information about LeveL subscribers' unexecuted orders for its own business purposes. The outside firm's separate order routing business therefore received an information advantage over other LeveL subscribers because it was able to use its knowledge of their orders to make routing decisions for its own customers' orders and increase its execution rate. eBX had insufficient safeguards and procedures to protect subscribers' confidential trading information. To settle the charges, eBX agreed to pay an $800,000 penalty.

In April, the SEC charged a former employee at a Connecticut-based brokerage firm with scheming to personally profit from placing unauthorized orders to buy Apple stock.[8] When the scheme backfired, it ultimately caused the firm to cease operations. David Miller, an institutional sales trader, misrepresented to Rochdale Securities LLC that a customer had authorized the Apple orders and assumed the risk of loss on any resulting trades. The customer order was to purchase just 1,625 shares of Apple stock, but Miller instead entered a series of orders totaling 1.625 million shares at a cost of almost $1 billion. Miller planned to share in the customer's profit if Apple's stock profited, and if the stock decreased he would claim that he erred on the size of the order. The stock wound up decreasing after an earnings announcement later that day, and Rochdale was forced to cease operations in the wake of covering the approximately $5.3 million loss suffered from the rogue trades. In a partial settlement, Miller has agreed to be enjoined from future violations of the antifraud provisions of the Federal securities laws. A financial penalty will be determined at a later date by the court upon the SEC's motion.

The following month, the SEC charged NASDAQ with securities laws violations resulting from its poor systems and decision-making during the initial public offering (IPO) and secondary market trading of Facebook shares.[9] Exchanges have an obligation to ensure that their systems, processes,

---

[6] *In the Matter of UBS Securities LLC, Press Rel. 2013-146 (August 6, 2013)*
www.sec.gov/News/PressRelease/Detail/PressRelease/1370539751175

[7] *In the Matter of eBX, LLC, Press Rel. 2012-204 (October 3, 2012)*
www.sec.gov/News/PressRelease/Detail/PressRelease/1365171485204

[8] *SEC v. David Miller, Press Rel. 2013-60 (April 15, 2013) www.sec.gov/News/PressRelease/Detail/PressRelease/1365171514650*

[9] *In the Matter of the NASDAQ Stock Market, LLC, et al., Press Rel. 2013-95 (May 29, 2013)*
www.sec.gov/News/PressRelease/Detail/PressRelease/1365171575032

and contingency planning are robust and adequate to manage an IPO without disruption to the market. Despite widespread anticipation that the Facebook IPO would be among the largest in history with huge numbers of investors participating, a design limitation in NASDAQ's system to match IPO buy and sell orders caused disruptions to the Facebook IPO. NASDAQ's decision to initiate trading in the IPO before fully understanding the problem caused violations of several rules, including NASDAQ's fundamental rule governing the price/time priority for executing trade orders. The problem caused more than 30,000 Facebook orders to remain stuck in NASDAQ's system for more than two hours when they should have been promptly executed or cancelled. NASDAQ agreed to settle the SEC's charges by paying a $10 million penalty – the largest ever against an exchange.

In June, the SEC brought the first action seeking a financial penalty against an exchange for violations related to its regulatory oversight when it charged the Chicago Board Options Exchange (CBOE) and its affiliate C2 Options Exchange for various systemic breakdowns in their regulatory and compliance functions as a self-regulatory organization (SRO), including a failure to enforce or even fully comprehend rules to prevent abusive short selling.[10] SROs must enforce the Federal securities laws as well as their own rules to regulate trading on their exchanges by their member firms. In doing so, they must sufficiently manage an inherent conflict that exists between self-regulatory obligations and the business interests of an SRO and its members. CBOE put the interests of the firm ahead of its regulatory obligations by failing to properly investigate the firm's compliance with Regulation SHO (short selling practices) and then interfering with the SEC investigation of the firm. CBOE agreed to pay a $6 million penalty and implement major remedial measures to settle the SEC's charges.

That same month, the SEC charged five individuals, including the head of the Miami office at brokerage firm Direct Access Partners (DAP), with violations related to a massive kickback scheme to secure the bond trading business of a state-owned Venezuelan bank.[11] The SEC alleged that the scheme enabled the global markets group at DAP to generate more than $66 million in revenue from transaction fees related to fraudulent trades they executed for Banco de Desarrollo Económico y Social de Venezuela (BANDES), with a portion of this revenue illicitly paid to the Vice President of Finance at BANDES, who authorized the fraudulent trades. The defendants were charged with deceiving DAP's clearing brokers, executing internal wash trades, interpositioning another broker-dealer in the traders to conceal their role in the transactions, and engaging in massive roundtrip trades to pad their revenue. The SEC's action in the matter is continuing.

Actions Relating to the Foreign Corrupt Practices Act

It is important that investors have faith that the economic performance of public companies reflects lawful considerations of markets, price, and product rather than a mirage resulting from bribery and corruption. In FY 2013, the Division of Enforcement was very active in this area. In addition to releasing a 120-page joint guidance with the Department of Justice designed to assist enterprises of all sizes in analyzing issues related to Foreign Corrupt Practices Act (FCPA), the Division of Enforcement continued to file enforcement actions for violation of the FCPA.

In December, the SEC charged Germany-based insurance and asset management company Allianz SE with violating the books and records and internal controls provisions of the FCPA for improper payments to government officials in Indonesia during a seven-year period.[12] The SEC's investigation uncovered 295 insurance contracts on large government projects that were obtained or retained through improper payments by Allianz's subsidiary in Indonesia to employees of state-owned entities. An audit of accounting records at the Indonesian subsidiary showed that managers were using "special purpose accounts" to make illegal payments to government officials, but the misconduct continued in spite of the audit's findings. Further, Allianz's external auditor found that

---

[10] *In the Matter of Chicago Board Options Exchange Inc., et al., Press Rel. 2013-107 (June 11, 2013)*
  www.sec.gov/News/PressRelease/Detail/PressRelease/1365171575348

[11] *SEC v. Tomas Alberto Clarke Bethancourt et al., Press Rel. 2013-109 (June 12, 2013)*
  www.sec.gov/News/PressRelease/Detail/PressRelease/1365171574826

[12] *In the Matter of Allianz SE, Press Rel. 2012-266 (December 17, 2012)*
  www.sec.gov/News/PressRelease/Detail/PressRelease/1365171486902

the company failed to properly account for improper payments that were disguised in invoices as "overriding commissions" for government agents or were structured as overpayments by government insurance contract holders. Allianz lacked sufficient internal controls to detect and prevent the wrongful payments and accounting practices. Allianz agreed to pay more than $12.3 million to settle the SEC's charges.

Also in December, the SEC charged Eli Lilly and Company with violations of the FCPA for improper payments its subsidiaries made to foreign government officials to win millions of dollars of business in Russia, Brazil, China, and Poland.[13] The SEC alleged that pharmaceutical company's subsidiary in Russia used offshore "marketing agreements" to pay millions of dollars to third parties chosen by government customers or distributors, despite knowing little or nothing about the third parties beyond their offshore address and bank account information. These offshore entities rarely provided any services and in some instances were used to funnel money to government officials in order to obtain business for the subsidiary. Transactions with offshore or government-affiliated entities did not receive specialized or closer review for possible FCPA violations. The SEC further alleged that when the company became aware of possible FCPA violations in Russia, Eli Lilly did not curtail the subsidiary's use of the marketing agreements for more than five years. The SEC charged that Eli Lilly subsidiaries in Brazil, China, and Poland also made improper payments to government officials or third-party entities associated with government officials. Eli Lilly agreed to pay more than $29 million to settle the SEC's charges.

In April, the SEC obtained a final judgment in its ongoing civil action against former officer and board member of Siemens Aktiengesellschaft (Siemens) for his role in Siemens' decade-long scheme to retain a $1 billion contract with the government of Argentina.[14] The SEC first filed a civil action against Sharef and six other defendants in December 2011, claiming that Sharef and other Siemens executives had paid more than $27 million in bribes to senior government officials in Argentina in connection with a contract to provide identity

cards to all Argentine citizens. Sharef was the most senior officer charged in relation to the scheme, and the SEC alleged that his role involved coordinating with payment intermediaries in the United States to facilitate the bribes and enlisting subordinates to conceal the payments by circumventing Siemens' internal accounting controls. The final judgment, to which Sharef consented, enjoins him from further violations of the FCPA and orders him to pay a $275,000 civil penalty, the second-highest penalty ever assessed against an individual in an FCPA case.

Also in April, the SEC announced a non-prosecution agreement (NPA) with Ralph Lauren Corporation, in which the company agreed to disgorge more than $700,000 in illicit profits and interest obtained in connection with bribes paid by a subsidiary to government officials in Argentina.[15] The improper payments were made to secure the importation of Ralph Lauren products into Argentina without the necessary paperwork, to avoid inspection of prohibited products, and to avoid inspections by customs officials. The payments, bribes, and gifts, totaling more than $593,000, were discovered by Ralph Lauren during the implementation of an FCPA compliance training program in Argentina. The SEC determined not to charge Ralph Lauren with violations of the FCPA due to the company's prompt reporting of the violations on its own initiative, the completeness of the information it provided, and its extensive, thorough, and real-time cooperation with the SEC's investigation. Ralph Lauren Corporation's cooperation saved the agency substantial time and resources ordinarily consumed in investigations of comparable conduct. The NPA is the first that the SEC has entered involving FCPA misconduct.

In May, the SEC charged France-based oil and gas company Total S.A. (Total) with violating the FCPA by paying $60 million in bribes to intermediaries of an Iranian government official who then exercised his influence to help the company obtain valuable contracts with the National Iranian Oil Company for the country's Sirri A and E oil and gas fields.[16] The SEC alleged that Total made more than $150 million in profits

---

[13] *SEC v. Eli Lilly and Company, Press Rel. 2012-273 (December 20, 2012)*
www.sec.gov/News/PressRelease/Detail/PressRelease/1365171487116

[14] *SEC v. Uriel Sharef, et al., Lit. Rel. No. 22676 (April 16, 2013) www.sec.gov/litigation/litreleases/2013/lr22676.htm*

[15] *Ralph Lauren Non-Prosecution Agreement, Press Rel. 2013-65 (April 22, 2013)*
www.sec.gov/News/PressRelease/Detail/PressRelease/1365171514780

[16] *In the Matter of Total, S.A., Press Rel. 2013-94 (May 29, 2013)*
www.sec.gov/News/PressRelease/Detail/PressRelease/1365171575006

through the bribery scheme. Total attempted to cover up the true nature of the illegal payments by entering into sham consulting agreements with intermediaries of the Iranian official and mischaracterizing the bribes in its books and records as legitimate "business development expenses" related to the consulting agreements. Total had inadequate systems to properly review the consulting agreements and lacked sufficient internal controls to comply with Federal laws prohibiting bribery. Total agreed to pay disgorgement of more than $153 million in illicit profits and retain an independent compliance consultant to review and consult on Total's compliance with the FCPA.

Actions Involving Financial Fraud, Issuer Disclosure, and Gatekeepers

Accounting and financial fraud, issuer disclosure, reporting violations at public companies, and violations by "gatekeepers" (including attorneys, accountants, and compliance professionals) remained a priority for the Commission in FY 2013. In November, the SEC charged global oil and gas company BP p.l.c. with misleading investors by making fraudulent public statements that significantly understated the flow rate of the oil that was spilling into the Gulf of Mexico from the damaged Deepwater Horizon oil rig.[17] BP reported to the SEC that its estimates indicated a flow rate of 5,000 barrels of oil per day, and its executives continued to make public statements reiterating the 5,000 barrels per day estimate despite BP's own internal data that showed potential flow rates could be as high as 146,000 barrels of oil per day. To settle the SEC's charges, BP agreed to pay a $525 million penalty, the third highest in SEC history, with which the SEC plans to establish a Fair Fund to compensate BP investors for losses they sustained as a result of the fraud.

In December, the SEC charged the China affiliates of the "Big Four" accounting firms and another large U.S. accounting firm for refusing to produce audit work papers and other documents related to China-based companies under investigation by the SEC for potential accounting fraud against U.S. investors.[18] The SEC brought charges against affiliates of BDO, Deloitte, Ernst & Young, KPMG, and PricewaterhouseCoopers for failing to provide the SEC with audit materials sought as part of SEC investigations into potential wrongdoing by nine China-based companies whose securities are traded on U.S. markets despite being legally required to do so by the Securities Exchange Act and the Sarbanes-Oxley Act. The SEC's action in this matter is ongoing.

In another case tied to the financial crisis, the SEC brought charges against three former executives at Virginia-based Bank of the Commonwealth for understating millions of dollars in losses and hiding from investors the deterioration of the bank's loan portfolio.[19] The SEC charged Edward J. Woodard, Jr., the former CEO, President, and Chairman of the Board, along with CFO and Secretary Cynthia Sabol, and Executive Vice President and Commercial Loan Officer Stephen Fields with making false statements to the public and in SEC filings that its portfolio of loans was conservatively managed to avoid losses during the height of the economic crisis. The SEC's action in this matter is ongoing.

In May, the SEC charged the gatekeepers of a pair of mutual fund trusts with causing untrue or misleading disclosures about the factors they considered when approving or renewing investment advisory contracts on behalf of shareholders.[20] The SEC's investigation that arose from an examination of the Northern Lights Fund Trust and the Northern Lights Variable Trust found that some of the trusts' shareholder reports either misrepresented material information considered by the trustees or omitted material information about how they evaluated certain factors in reaching their decisions on behalf of the funds and their shareholders. The trustees and the trusts' chief compliance officer Northern Lights Compliance Services (NLCS) were responsible for causing violations of the SEC's compliance rule, and the trusts' fund administrator Gemini Fund Services (GFS) caused violations of the Investment Company Act recordkeeping and reporting

---

[17] *SEC v. BP p.l.c., Press Rel. 2012-231 (November 15, 2012) www.sec.gov/News/PressRelease/Detail/PressRelease/1365171485962*

[18] *In the Matter of BDO China Dahua CPA Co., Ltd., et al., Press Rel. 2012-249 (December 3, 2012) www.sec.gov/News/PressRelease/Detail/PressRelease/1365171486452*

[19] *SEC v. Edward J. Woodard, Jr., et al., Lit. Rel. No. 22587 (January 9, 2013) www.sec.gov/litigation/litreleases/2013/lr22587.htm*

[20] *In the Matter of Northern Lights Compliance Services, LLC, et al., Press Rel. 2013-78 (May 2, 2013) www.sec.gov/News/PressRelease/Detail/PressRelease/1365171514096*

provisions. In settling the proceedings, GFS and NLCS each agreed to pay $50,000 penalties, and the firms and trustees agreed to engage an independent compliance consultant to address the violations found in the SEC's order. They also agreed to cease and desist from committing or causing any violations and any future violations of those provisions.

In June, the SEC charged cosmetics manufacturer Revlon with violating Federal securities laws by misleading shareholders during a "going private transaction" wherein Revlon agreed to allow shareholders to exchange common stock for preferred stock as part of a deal to pay off a debt.[21] The trustee administering Revlon's 401(k) plan decided that 401(k) members could participate in the exchange only if a third-party financial advisor determined that the preferred stock was at least as valuable as the common stock they would be exchanging. In its settled order, the Commission found that when the third-party adviser found that the proposed transaction was inadequate for 401(k) members, Revlon engaged in a "ring-fencing" scheme to avoid disclosing the results of the adviser's determination. In order to avoid any obligation that would cause it to disclose the results of the third-party determination, Revlon amended its trust agreement with its trustee to ensure that the trustee would not share the determination with Revlon and directed the trustee to inform Revlon of the trustee's decision about the 401(k) members without making any reference to the determination. Revlon agreed to settle the SEC's charges and to pay an $850,000 penalty.

In July, the SEC filed fraud and related charges against China-based jewelry company Fuqi International, Inc., and its Chairman of the Board of Directors and former CFO and President, Yu Kwai Chong.[22] Fuqi and Chong were charged with violations stemming from cash transfers of approximately $134 million to three purportedly unknown entities. The Commission alleged that Chong, who directed and authorized the transfers, fraudulently certified that Fuqi's quarterly financial reports contained no material omissions or misstatements, while Fuqi lacked adequate internal accounting controls and incorrectly recorded the undisclosed transfers in its books and records. Both Fuqi and Chong agreed to settle the SEC's charges, with both consenting to being permanently enjoined from future violations of the Federal securities laws, to pay civil penalties of $1 million and $150,000, respectively, and a five-year bar on serving as an officer or director for Chong.

The SEC filed two actions charging violations in connection with a fraudulent scheme to conceal the extent of massive trading losses, totaling more than $500 billion, at J.P. Morgan Chase & Co.'s Chief Investment Office.[23] In August, the SEC brought charges against Javier Martin-Artajo and Julien Grout, who were formerly traders at J.P. Morgan, for deliberately mismarking hundreds of positions held by a Chief Investment Office portfolio known as the "Synthetic Credit Portfolio." The Commission alleged that the two former traders mismarked the positions by recording their maximum value, rather than mid-market values as required by generally accepted accounting principles and by J.P. Morgan internal accounting policy. Their scheme caused J.P. Morgan's reported first quarter income to be overstated by more than $660 million. In September, the SEC charged J.P. Morgan with misstating its financial results and lacking effective internal controls to detect and prevent the scheme. J.P. Morgan settled the SEC's charges by publicly acknowledging that it had violated Federal securities laws and by paying a $200 million penalty. The SEC's action against Martin-Artajo and Grout is continuing.

In September, as part of the agency's ongoing effort to hold gatekeepers accountable for the important roles they play in the securities industry, the SEC charged three auditors for violating federal securities laws or failing to comply with U.S. auditing standards during their audits and reviews of financial statements for publicly traded companies.[24] Internally designated "Operation Broken Gate," the

[21] In the Matter of Revlon, Inc., Press Rel. 2013-110 (June 13, 2013)
www.sec.gov/News/PressRelease/Detail/PressRelease/1365171574852

[22] SEC v. Fuqi International, Inc. and Yu Kwai Chong, Lit. Rel. No. 22739 (July 1, 2013) www.sec.gov/litigation/litreleases/2013/lr22739.htm

[23] SEC v. Javier Martin-Artajo and Julien G. Grout, Press Rel. 2013-154 (August 14, 2013)
www.sec.gov/News/PressRelease/Detail/PressRelease/1370539776091#.Uj_K0lYjLmg

In the Matter of J.P. Morgan Chase & Co., Press Rel. 2013-187 (September 19, 2013)
www.sec.gov/News/PressRelease/Detail/PressRelease/1370539819965#.Uj_Ky4YjLmg

[24] SEC Crackdown on Violations or Failures By Gatekeepers, Press Rel. 2013-207 (September 30, 2013)
www.sec.gov/News/PressRelease/Detail/PressRelease/1370539850572

Enforcement Division's efforts seek to identify auditors who fail to carry out their duties and responsibilities consistent with professional standards. Gatekeepers that fail to comply with professional standards put investors at risk due to the possibility of undetected fraud or other financial misstatements. The actions were against certified public accountants Malcolm L. Pollard, who practices in Erie, Pennsylvania, and Wilfred W. Hanson and John Kinross-Kennedy, who live in the Irvine, California area. The SEC's order instituting a settled administrative proceeding against Pollard and his firm alleged they engaged in improper professional conduct while auditing three companies that are empty shells or in the developmental stages. The companies' public stock is quoted on the Over-the-Counter Bulletin Board. Pollard and his firm's audits of the issuers were seriously deficient. They failed to include evidence of procedures performed or conclusions reached, and they failed to retain required documentation, perform the required engagement quality reviews, and consider fraud risks and obtain written management representations. Despite these audit failures, Pollard and his firm represented in each of their audit reports that they had conducted the audits in accordance with the standards of the Public Company Accounting Oversight Board (PCAOB). The SEC's order instituting a litigated administrative proceeding against Kinross-Kennedy alleged that there were significant deficiencies in six of Kinross-Kennedy's audit engagements, that he failed to obtain engagement quality reviews (EQRs) for more than 30 other audit engagements, and that he falsely represented that he conducted his audits in accordance with PCAOB standards. As to Hanson, the Commission's order found that he conducted EQRs for five of Kinross-Kennedy's audits, but was not competent to serve as the engagement quality reviewer and failed to exercise due professional care. Accordingly, he failed to conduct multiple EQRs in accordance with PCAOB standards. Pollard and Hanson agreed to settle the respective actions against them and will be prohibited from practicing as an accountant on behalf of any publicly traded company or other entity

regulated by the SEC. Kinross-Kennedy is litigating his action in a proceeding before an administrative law judge.

Actions Related to Insider Trading

Insider trading remained a high priority in FY 2013, with the Commission filing 58 insider trading actions. Many of these cases involved financial professionals, hedge funds managers, corporate insiders, and others who unlawfully traded on material, nonpublic information, undermining the level playing field that is fundamental to the integrity and fairness of the securities markets.

In December, the SEC charged hedge fund manager Sung Kook "Bill" Hwang with conducting a pair of insider trading schemes that reaped $16.7 million dollars in illicit profits.[25] Hwang, the founder and manager of hedge fund's Tiger Asia Management and Tiger Asia Partners LLC, schemed with Raymond Y. H. Park, the head trader at both firms, to misuse confidential information that Hwang and his advisory firms had obtained while working on private placements for stock in Bank of China and in China Construction Bank. One scheme involved making short sales in the banks' stock in the days prior to the private placement, and in the second scheme, Hwang ordered Park to place losing trades in order to depress the stock prices while inflating the fees collected by Tiger Asia Management. Hwang, Park, and both firms agreed to settle the SEC's charges by paying $44 million in penalties, disgorgement, and prejudgment interest.

The SEC continued to bring charges related to the massive insider trading scheme spearheaded by Raj Rajaratnam and hedge fund advisory firm Galleon Management, having charged a total of 34 firms and individuals in its Galleon-related enforcement actions.[26] In March, the SEC charged Rajaratnam's younger brother, Regnan Rajaratnam, with receiving inside information from his brother and trading on that information to reap more than $3 million in illicit profits for himself and hedge funds that he managed at Galleon and

---

[25] *SEC v. Tiger Asia Management, LLC, et al., Lit. Rel. No. 22569 (December 13, 2012) www.sec.gov/litigation/litreleases/2012/lr22569.htm*

[26] *SEC v. Douglas F. Whitman and Whitman Capital, LLC, Lit. Rel. No. 22653 (March 20, 2013)*
www.sec.gov/litigation/litreleases/2013/lr22653.htm

SEC v. Rajarengan (a/k/a/ Rengan) Rajaratnam, Lit. Rel. No. 22658 (March 22, 2013)
www.sec.gov/litigation/litreleases/2013/lr22658.htm

SEC v. Kieran Taylor, Press Rel. 2013-189 (September 20, 2013)
www.sec.gov/News/PressRelease/Detail/PressRelease/1370539824633

Sedna Capital Management, a hedge fund advisory firm that he co-founded. The SEC's action in this matter is ongoing.

In another action, the SEC obtained a final judgment in its case against hedge fund manager Douglas Whitman and his firm Whitman Capital. The SEC alleged that Whitman and Whitman Capital illegally traded based on material nonpublic information that Whitman had received from his friend and neighbor Roomy Khan, a close associate of Raj Rajaratnam. Hedge funds managed by Whitman Capital reaped over $900,000 in ill-gotten gains by trading on Khan's illegal tips about a technology company's earnings reports. The final judgment enjoins Whitman and Whitman Capital from future violations of the Federal securities laws and requires Whitman and Whitman Capital to jointly and severally disgorge $935,306 in illicit profits. The judgment also orders Whitman to pay a civil penalty of $935,306, which will be offset by his obligation to make a criminal forfeiture in the same amount.

Later, in September, the SEC charged Kieran Taylor, a former executive at Massachusetts-based technology firm Akamai Technologies, with insider trading for illegally tipping fund portfolio manager Danielle Chiesi with confidential information about Akamai's plans to lower its revenue guidance. Chiesi then passed the nonpublic information along to Raj Rajaratnam and others so they could trade ahead of the negative news and make millions of dollars in illegal profits. Taylor settled the SEC's charges by accepting a bar from serving as an officer or director of a public company for five years and agreeing to pay more than $145,000 in disgorgement, interest, and penalties.

In March, the SEC charged California hedge fund analyst Matthew Teeple with insider trading in advance of an announcement that technology firm Foundry Networks, Inc. had acquired Brocade Communication Systems, Inc. for approximately $3 billion.[27] The SEC alleged that Foundry's Chief Information Officer, David Riley, tipped Teeple about the impending announcement. According to the complaint, Teeple caused the San Francisco-based hedge fund advisory

firm where he works to buy Foundry shares in large quantities in the days leading up to the public announcement, and he then tipped Denver-based investment professional John Johnson about the deal. The SEC's complaint alleged that Riley continued to provide tips to Teeple throughout the acquisition process, which allowed Teeple and his firm to continue trading profitably. The SEC alleges that the scheme resulted in $29 million in illicit profits and avoided losses. The SEC's action in this matter is ongoing.

The SEC also reached settlements with several parties whose assets were frozen as part of major insider trading case that involved trading in the securities of Nexen Inc.[28] The SEC obtained an emergency court order in July 2012 to freeze multiple accounts that had conducted suspicious trades in the securities of Nexen prior to an announcement that the company was being acquired by China-based CNOOC Ltd. The SEC reached a settlement with lead defendant Well Advantage in October 2012. Hong Kong-based trading firm Well Advantage agreed to pay more than $14.2 million to settle the insider trading charges. In April, the SEC reached a settlement with Chinese businessman Ren Feng and his wife Zeng Huiyu, as well as Ren's private investment company CT Prime Assets Limited and four of Zeng's brokerage customers on whose behalf she traded. That settlement requires the traders to pay more than $3.3 million combined in disgorgement and penalties. In May, Singapore businesswoman Choo Eng Hong agreed to pay more than $500,000 to settle SEC charges that she generated more than $400,000 in illicit profits by trading in Nexen stock in the days leading up to the acquisition announcement.

In April, the SEC charged Scott London, the former partner in charge of KPMG's Pacific Southwest audit practice, and his friend Bryan Shaw with insider trading on nonpublic information about firm clients.[29] The SEC's complaint alleges that London tipped Shaw with confidential details about five KPMG audit clients and enabled Shaw to make more than $1.2 million in illicit profits trading ahead of earnings or

[27] SEC v. Matthew G. Teeple, David T. Riley, and John V. Johnson, Press Release 2013-47 (March 26, 2013) www.sec.gov/News/PressRelease/Detail/PressRelease/1365171513470#.UkER3IYjLmg

[28] SEC v. Well Advantage Limited, et al., Lit. Rel. No. 22693 (May 1, 2013) www.sec.gov/litigation/litreleases/2013/lr22693.htm
SEC v. Well Advantage Limited, et al., Lit. Rel. No. 22663 (April 1, 2013) www.sec.gov/litigation/litreleases/2013/lr22663.htm

[29] SEC v. Scott London and Bryan Shaw, Press Rel. 2013-58 (April 11, 2013) www.sec.gov/News/PressRelease/Detail/PressRelease/1365171514600#.UkER2oYjLmg

merger announcements. London allegedly provided tips to his golfing friend Shaw in exchange for more than $50,000 in cash, a $12,000 Rolex watch and other jewelry, meals, and tickets to entertainment events. London was able to obtain extensive material, nonpublic information as a result of his role as the lead partner on several KPMG audits, including Herbalife and Skechers USA, and was the firm's account executive for Deckers Outdoor Corp. Shaw allegedly traded on this information at least a dozen times, and grossed more than $714,000 in illicit profits. The SEC's action in this matter is ongoing.

In another insider trading case, the SEC charged Bangkok-based trader Badin Rungruangnavarat with trading on inside information in advance of a public announcement about a proposed acquisition of Smithfield Foods by Chinese firm Shuanghui International Holdings.[30] The SEC obtained an emergency asset freeze on June 5 after filing a complaint that Rungruangnavarat reaped more than $3 million in illicit profits just days earlier by trading in Smithfield securities. The complaint alleged that Rungruangnavarat could have obtained the material, nonpublic information about the impending deal from a friend who was an associate director at an investment bank for a company that had also considered a Smithfield acquisition. Rungruangnavarat settled the SEC's charges by agreeing to pay $3.2 million in disgorgement and a $2 million penalty, and consented to a permanent injunction barring him from future violations of the securities laws.

The SEC also brought a series of related insider trading cases beginning in late November 2012. In the first of three actions the SEC filed its largest insider trading case to date when it charged hedge fund advisory firm CR Intrinsic Investors LLC and its former portfolio manager, along with a medical consultant for an expert network firm, for their roles in an insider trading scheme that reaped $276 million in illicit gains.[31] The SEC alleged that portfolio manager Matthew Martoma illegally obtained confidential details about clinical trials of a potential Alzheimer's drug from Dr. Sidney Gillman, who was selected by the drug's developers to present the

final drug trial results to the public. The complaint charged that Dr. Gilman tipped Martoma about negative clinical trial results about two weeks before they were made public, and Martoma directed several hedge funds managed by CR Intrinsic to liquidate their holdings in the drug's producers and to take short positions in the securities. These positions allowed CR Intrinsic and its affiliates, including S.A.C. Capital Advisors, to earn approximately $82 million in profits and avoid losses of $194 million. Martoma allegedly received a $9.3 million bonus at the end of 2008 which was largely attributable to the illegal profits reaped by CR Intrinsic and its affiliates, while Dr. Gilman received more than $100,000 for his consultations with Martoma and others. Gilman settled the SEC's charges by agreeing to pay more than $234,000 in disgorgement and interest, and the court will determine at a later date whether any additional financial penalty is appropriate. In March, CR Intrinsic agreed to the largest insider trading settlement in SEC history to settle charges over the scheme. The terms of the historic settlement required CR Intrinsic to pay more than $600 million to settle the charges, including $274.9 million in disgorgement, $51.8 million in prejudgment interest, and a $274.9 million penalty.

Also in March, the SEC charged hedge fund advisory firm Sigma Capital Management and Michael Steinberg, a portfolio manager employed by Sigma, with trading on insider information ahead of quarterly earnings announcements by Dell and Nvidia Corporation.[32] The SEC alleged that Steinberg's illegal conduct allowed Sigma Capital and its affiliate S.A.C. Capital to generate more than $6 million in illicit profits and avoid losses. Steinberg allegedly received tips from a former analyst at Sigma, Jon Horvath, who was himself the target of an SEC action in January 2012 that targeted hedge fund managers and analysts associated with expert networks firms. Sigma agreed to settle the SEC's charges by paying nearly $14 million in disgorgement, interest, and penalties.

Relatedly, in July, the SEC charged hedge fund manager Steven A. Cohen for failing to supervise Matthew Martoma and Michael Steinberg and prevent them from insider trading under

---

[30] *SEC v. Badin Rungruangnavarat, Press Rel. 2013-173 (September 5, 2013)*
   www.sec.gov/News/PressRelease/Detail/PressRelease/1370539798614#.Uj-NxoYjLmg

[31] *SEC v. CR Intrinsic Investors, LLC, et al., Press Rel. 2012-237 (November 20, 2012)*
   www.sec.gov/News/PressRelease/Detail/PressRelease/1365171486118

[32] *SEC v. Michael S. Steinberg, Press Rel. 2013-49 (March 29, 2013)*
   www.sec.gov/News/PressRelease/Detail/PressRelease/1365171513522

his watch.[33] The SEC alleged that Cohen, who managed S.A.C. Capital, received highly suspicious information that should have caused any reasonable hedge fund manager to investigate the basis for the trades, but ignored the red flags and allowed Martoma and Steinberg to execute the trades, and praised Steinberg for his work and rewarded Martoma with a $9 million bonus. Cohen's hedge funds earned profits and avoided losses of more than $275 million as a result of the illegal trades.

In August, the SEC charged Chad McGinnis, a former systems administrator at Vermont-based Green Mountain Coffee Roasters, alleging that he repeatedly obtained quarterly earnings data and traded in advance of its public release.[34] The SEC also charged his friend, Sergey Pugach, with insider trading. According to the complaint, McGinnis and Pugach together garnered $7 million in illegal profits by using inside information to correctly predict the reaction of Green Mountain Coffee's stock price to 12 quarterly earnings announcements since 2010. The complaint alleged that McGinnis and Pugach violated Section 17(a) of the Securities Act of 1933 and Section 10(b) of the Securities Exchange Act of 1934 and Rule 10b-5. Pugach's mother, Bella Pugach, was named as a relief defendant in the SEC's complaint for the purpose of recovering ill-gotten gains in her trading account.

Actions Related to Market Manipulation

In December, the SEC charged securities industry professionals Danny Garber, Michael Manis, Kenneth Yellin and Jordan Feinstein with conducting a fraudulent penny stock scheme in which they illegally acquired more than one billion unregistered shares in microcap companies at deep discounts and then dumped them on the market for approximately $17 million in illicit profits.[35] The Commission alleged that the defendants acquired the shares at deep discounts off the market price by misrepresenting to the penny stock companies that they intended to hold the shares for investment purposes rather than immediately re-selling them. Instead, the defendants immediately sold the shares without registering them,

purporting to rely on an inapplicable state law exemption. The SEC also charged 12 entities that the defendants established to create corporate presences in an attempt to claim the exemption was valid.

In June, the SEC continued its crackdown against the manipulation of microcap shell companies by suspending trading in the securities of 61 empty shell companies, the second-largest trading suspension in agency history and a follow-up to its 2012 "Operation Shell Expel." Because microcap companies are thinly traded, once they become dormant they have great potential to be hijacked by fraudsters who hope to falsely hype the stock to trick investors into "pump-and-dump" schemes. Fraudsters purchase shares in the shell company at a low price, use false and misleading statements to increase investor activity in the stock, and then dump the stock for significant profit once other investors have been tricked into buying shares. In this latest nationwide review of microcap stocks, the SEC used enhanced intelligence technology in the Division of Enforcement's Office of Market Intelligence and identified clearly dormant shell companies in at least 17 states and one foreign country. By suspending trading in these companies, the SEC obligated the companies to provide updated financial information to prove that they are still operational, essentially rendering them useless to scam artists as the companies are no longer allowed to fly under the radar.

In September, the SEC announced enforcement actions against 23 firms for short selling violations as part of an agency-wide sweep focused on preventing firms from improperly participating in public stock offerings after selling short those same stocks.[36] SEC Rule 105 of Regulation M prohibits the short sale of any equity security during a restricted period – generally five business days before a public offering – and the purchase of the same security through the offering. The firms charged in these cases allegedly bought offered shares from an underwriter, broker, or dealer participating in a follow-on public offering after having sold short the same security during the restricted period. Of the 23 firms charged, 22 agreed to

---

[33] *SEC v. Steven A. Cohen, Press Rel. 2013-129 (July 19, 2013) www.sec.gov/News/PressRelease/Detail/PressRelease/1370539726923*

[34] *SEC v. Chad C. McGinnis, et al., Press Rel. 2013-144 (August 2, 2013)*
   www.sec.gov/News/PressRelease/Detail/PressRelease/1370539747390

[35] *SEC v. Danny Garber, et al., Press Rel. 2012-278 (December 21, 2012)*
   www.sec.gov/News/PressRelease/Detail/PressRelease/1365171487234

[36] *"SEC Charges 23 Firms With Short Selling Violations in Crackdown on Potential Manipulation in Advance of Stock Offerings," Press Rel.*
   2013-182 (September 17, 2013) www.sec.gov/News/PressRelease/Detail/PressRelease/1370539804376

settle the SEC's charges, resulting in more than $14.4 million in monetary sanctions.

Actions Related to Municipal Securities

In FY 2013, the SEC remained committed to the prior year's focus on the municipal securities markets, bringing high profile and many "first-of-its-kind" enforcement actions. In March, the SEC charged the State of Illinois with securities fraud for misleading municipal bond investors by failing to inform them about the impact of problems with a pension funding schedule before the state offered and sold more than $2.2 billion worth of municipal bonds between 2005 and 2009.[37] Illinois failed to disclose to investors that its statutory plan significantly under-funded the state's pension obligations and increased the risk to its overall financial conditions. The State of Illinois, which began taking steps in 2009 to improve its pension disclosures and other remedial actions, settled the charges. This marks the second time the SEC has charged a state with violating Federal securities laws in public pension disclosures, following a charge against New Jersey for securities fraud in 2010.

In April, the SEC brought securities fraud charges against the City of Victorville, California, the city's Assistant City Manager Keith Metzler, the Southern California Logistics Airport Authority, and the underwriter of the Airport Authority's bonds Kinsell, Newcomb & DeDios (KND).[38] The SEC charged that Metzler, along with KND owner J. Jeffrey Kinsell and KND Vice President Janees L. Williams were responsible for false and misleading statements made in relation to an Airport Authority bond offering that was intended to raise funds for a construc-tion project that included building four aircraft hangars on a former Air Force base. According to the SEC's complaint, the principal amount of the bond offering was partially based on Metzler, Kinsell, and Williams using a $65 million valuation for the hangars despite the fact that they knew a county assessor had valued the hangars at less than half that amount. The SEC's investigation also found that Kinsell, KND, and another of his companies had misappropriated more than $2.7 million in bond proceeds by taking unauthorized fees to oversee the

construction and management of the hangars. The SEC's action in this case is ongoing.

In early May, the Securities and Exchange Commission charged the City of Harrisburg, Pa., with securities fraud for failing to provide municipal bond investors with accurate financial information and for the misleading public state-ments the city made in its annual and mid-year financial statements, budget report, and State of the City address.[39] In each instance, the SEC found that the City of Harrisburg either misstated or failed to disclose critical information about Harrisburg's financial condition. For example, according to the SEC's order, Harrisburg had not submitted annual financial information or audited financial statements since submitting its 2007 Comprehensive Annual Financial Report (CAFR) to a Nationally Recognized Municipal Securities Information Repository (NRMSIR) in January 2009. Also, Harrisburg's budget did not disclose that the city was unlikely to have sufficient revenues to pay its 2009 debt service obliga-tions and misstated Harrisburg's credit as being rated "Aaa" even though Moody's had downgraded Harrisburg's general obligation credit rating to Baa1 in December 2008. Further, Harrisburg's 2009 mid-year fiscal report did not refer-ence any of the guarantee payments the city had made on the municipal resource recovery facility debt, which at this mid-year point totaled $2.3 million (7 percent of its general fund expenditures). Additionally, the April 9, 2009 State of the City address failed to mention that Harrisburg had already made $1.8 million in guarantee payments on the resource recovery facility bond debt, that the total amount of the debt that the city would likely have to repay from its general fund, and would likely have to repay $260 million of the debt as guarantor. This marked the first time that the SEC has charged a municipality for misleading statements made outside of its securities disclosure documents. The Commission also sent a message to municipal issuers by issuing a report of its investigation pursuant to Section 21(a) of the Exchange Act.

---

[37] *In the Matter of State of Illinois, Press Rel. 2013-37 (March 11, 2013)*
www.sec.gov/News/PressRelease/Detail/PressRelease/1365171513202

[38] *SEC v. City of Victorville, et al., Press Rel. 2013-75 (April 29, 2013)*
www.sec.gov/News/PressRelease/Detail/PressRelease/1365171514980

[39] *In the Matter of The City of Harrisburg, Pennsylvania, Press Rel. 2013-82 (May 6, 2013)*
www.sec.gov/News/PressRelease/Detail/PressRelease/1365171514194

Later in May, the SEC charged the City of South Miami, Florida, with defrauding bond investors about the tax-exempt financing eligibility of a mixed-use retail and parking structure being built in its downtown commercial district.[40] An SEC investigation found that the city of 11,000 residents located in Miami-Dade County borrowed approximately $12 million in two pooled, conduit bond offerings through the Florida Municipal Loan Council (FMLC). South Miami's participation in those offerings enabled it to borrow funds at advantageous tax-exempt rates. The city represented that the project was eligible for tax-exempt financing in various documents for the second offering that were relied upon by bond counsel in rendering its tax opinion. However, South Miami failed to disclose that it had actually jeopardized the tax-exempt status of both bond offerings by impermissibly loaning proceeds from the first offering to a private developer and restructuring a lease agreement prior to the second offering. According to the SEC's order, annual certifications made by the city to the FMLC from 2003 to 2009 incorrectly stated that South Miami was in compliance with the terms of the loan agreements, which included representations that no event had occurred affecting the tax-exempt status of the bonds. South Miami agreed to settle the SEC's charges and retain an independent third-party consultant to review and make recommendations concerning the adequacy of its policies, procedures, and internal controls for bond disclosures.

That same month the SEC settled charges related to a "pay-to-play" scheme with Neil M.M. Morrison, a former vice president in the banking division of Goldman, Sachs & Co. (Goldman). Morrison and Goldman were charged in September 2012 with providing prohibited contributions to the political campaign of then-Massachusetts State Treasurer Timothy Cahill while he was a candidate in a gubernatorial race.[41] The SEC alleged that Morrison conducted campaign activities for Cahill from his Goldman Sachs office, using the firm's phones and email. The SEC further alleged that these non-cash campaign contributions were attributable to Goldman, and disqualified the firm from participating in municipal underwriting business with certain Massachusetts municipal advisors for two years after the contributions. Nevertheless, Goldman

subsequently participated in multiple prohibited underwritings with Massachusetts issuers and earned more than $7.5 million in underwriting fees. To settle the SEC's charges, Morrison consented to being barred from the securities industry for five years, and agreed to pay a penalty in the amount of $100,000.

In July, the SEC brought charges against the City of Miami and its former budget director, Michael Boudreaux, for securities fraud in connection with several municipal bond offerings and misrepresentations made to investors.[42] An SEC investigation found that Miami and Michael Boudreaux made materially false and misleading statements and omissions about certain interfund transfers that were orchestrated by Boudreaux to mask increasing deficits in the City's General Fund, viewed by investors and bond rating agencies as a key indicator of financial health. According to the SEC's complaint, Miami was forced to reverse most of the transfers following a report by its Office of Independent Auditor General, after which the City declared a state of fiscal emergency and had its debt ratings downgraded by ratings agencies. The complaint also charges the City of Miami with violating an SEC cease-and-desist order that was entered against it in 2003 based on similar misconduct, the first time that the SEC has alleged further wrongdoing by a municipality subject to an existing cease-and-desist order.

Later that same month, the SEC charged West Clark Community Schools of the Indiana school district, its municipal bond underwriter, City Securities Corporation, and the underwriter's head of public finance and municipal bond department, Randy G. Ruhl, for making materially false and misleading statements to bond investors.[43] Following the issuance of a $31 million bond offering in 2007, West Clark Schools released an official statement, supported by a signed certificate and affidavit that the school district "never failed to comply, in all material respects, with any previous undertakings." The SEC alleged that West Clark had in fact failed to submit the required financial information for five years as they had undertaken to do so, and City Securities and Ruhl had failed to conduct adequate due diligence regarding West Clark's compliance.

---

[40] *In the Matter of City of South Miami, Florida, Press Rel. 2013-91 (May 22, 2013)* www.sec.gov/News/PressRelease/Detail/PressRelease/1365171514424

[41] *In the Matter of Neil M.M. Morrison (May 23, 2013)* www.sec.gov/litigation/admin/2013/34-69627.pdf

[42] *SEC v. City of Miami, Florida and Michael Boudreaux, Press Rel. 2013-130 (July 19, 2013)* www.sec.gov/News/PressRelease/Detail/PressRelease/1370539727618

[43] *In the Matter of West Clark Community Schools; In the Matter of City Securities Corporation and Randy G. Ruhl, Press Rel. 2013-136 (July 19, 2013)* www.sec.gov/News/PressRelease/Detail/PressRelease/1370539734122

The SEC also alleged that City Securities and Ruhl violated Municipal Securities Rulemaking Board rules by providing representatives of municipal securities issuers with valuable gifts, and then fraudulently charging these and other expenses back to the issuers as "printing, preparation and distribution of official statements." The parties adopted a number of remedial measures and settled the matter for approximately $620,000. As part of the settlement, Ruhl was permanently barred from association in a supervisory capacity with any broker, dealer, investment adviser, municipal securities dealer, municipal advisor, transfer agent, or credit rating agency. This action marked the first time that the SEC charged a municipal issuer for falsely claiming in a bond offering's official statement that it was fully compliant with the annual disclosure obligations it agreed to in prior offerings, and also charged the underwriter and its principal for not doing the necessary research to attest to the truthfulness of that claim.

In September, the SEC charged the Public Health Trust (PHT), the operator of the largest hospital in Miami-Dade County, with misleading investors about the extent of its deteriorating financial condition prior to an $83 million bond offering.[44] An SEC investigation found that the official statement accompanying the bond offering represented that PHT projected a $56 million non-operating loss for its fiscal year ending September 30, 2009. Several months after the bonds were sold, external auditors discovered problems with the PHT's patient accounts receivable valuation. This discovery required a large accounting adjustment to the reported net income, and the PHT ultimately reported a non-operating loss of $244 million for FY 2009 – more than four times the projection made to bond investors. The SEC found that PHT made material misstatements to investors because it lacked a reasonable basis for its original loss projection and failed to properly account for a multi-million dollar arbitration award as required under the relevant accounting standards. PHT agreed to settle the SEC's charges, and the SEC declined to issue a monetary penalty due to PHT's financial condition, its cooperation during the SEC's investigation, and remedial measures undertaken.

Actions Related to Mutual Funds and Investment Advisers

The Commission brought numerous actions against mutual funds, investment advisers, and investment companies in FY 2013. In October 2012, the SEC charged former $1 billion hedge fund advisory firm Yorkville Advisors LLC, its founder and President Mark Angelo, and CFO Edward Schinik with scheming to overvalue assets under management and exaggerate the reported returns of hedge funds they managed in order to hide losses and increase the fees collected from investors.[45] The defendants were charged with enticing pension funds and other investors to invest in their hedge funds by falsely portraying Yorkville as a firm with a highly-collateralized investment portfolio and a robust valuation procedure. The defendants also allegedly misrepresented the safety and liquidity of the investments made by the hedge funds, and charged at least $10 million in excessive fees to the funds based on fraudulently inflated values of Yorkville's assets under management. The SEC's action in this case is ongoing.

In March, the SEC obtained a final judgment against former investment adviser Timothy Roth for misappropriating millions of dollars from the accounts of his advisory clients. The SEC filed an emergency action in March 2011 that froze Roth's assets and the assets of several companies he controlled for stealing more than $16 million worth of mutual funds shares from several deferred compensation plans for whom he provided investment advice.[46] The United States District Court for the Central District of Illinois also granted the SEC's motion to dismiss its monetary claims against Roth in light of a parallel criminal proceeding in which Roth was sentenced to 151 months of incarceration and was ordered to pay more than $16 million dollars in restitution to his victims.

In another action, the SEC charged Houston-based hedge fund manager and radio talk show host George R. Jarkesy Jr. and his firm with defrauding investors in two hedge funds and with steering bloated management fees to Thomas Belesis, CEO of brokerage firm John Thomas Financial.[47] Jarkesy and Belesis

---

[44] *In the Matter of Public Health Trust of Miami-Dade County, Florida, Press Rel. 2013-181 (September 13, 2013)*
www.sec.gov/News/PressRelease/Detail/PressRelease/1370539807423

[45] *SEC v. Yorkville Advisors, LLC, Mark Angelo, and Edward Schinik, Press Rel. 2012-209 (October 17, 2012)*
www.sec.gov/News/PressRelease/Detail/PressRelease/1365171485332

[46] *SEC v. Timothy J. Roth, et al., Lit. Rel. No. 22656 (March 22, 2013) www.sec.gov/litigation/litreleases/2013/lr22656.htm*

[47] *In the Matter of John Thomas Capital Management Group LLC, d/b/a Patriot28 LLC, et al. Press Rel. 2013-46 (March 22, 2013)*
www.sec.gov/News/PressRelease/Detail/PressRelease/1365171513444

were charged with multiple offenses related to two hedge funds they launched together that raised $30 million from investors. The SEC alleged that Jarkesy and his firm, John Thomas Capital Management (since renamed to Patriot 28 LLC), inflated valuations of the fund's assets, causing investors' shares to be overstated and his management and incentive fees to be increased. Jarkesy also allegedly lied to investors about the identity of the funds' auditor and prime broker, and falsely portrayed John Thomas Capital Management as an independent entity while Belesis sometimes supplanted Jarkesy as the decision maker and directed the hedge funds' investments into a company in which John Thomas Financial was heavily invested. The SEC's action in this matter is ongoing.

In April, the SEC charged Umesh Tandon, the CEO of Chicago-based investment advisory firm Simran Capital Management, with lying to the California Public Employees' Retirement System (CalPERS) and other current and potential clients about the amount of money managed by the firm.[48] The SEC's complaint alleged that Tandon falsely certified to CalPERS that his firm satisfied CalPERS's minimum assets under management (AUM) requirements, fraudulently reported inflated AUM in communications with other potential clients and in filings with the SEC, and later attempted to mislead SEC examiners during a routine exam of Simran. To settle the SEC's charges, Tandon agreed to be barred from the securities industry and to pay more than $120,000 in disgorgement, interest, and penalties.

In May, the SEC charged Charles Dushek, Sr., and his son, Charles Dushek, Jr., and their Illinois-based investment advisory firm, Capital Management Associates, Inc. (CMA), with violations of the Federal securities laws for defrauding CMA clients in a cherry picking scheme that garnered the Dusheks nearly $2 million in illicit profits.[49] The SEC alleged that the Dusheks placed millions of dollars in securities trades without designating in advance whether they were trading their personal funds or the funds of CMA clients, and delayed allocating the trades until they knew whether the trades would be profitable. The Dusheks then allegedly cherry picked the winning trades for their personal accounts and dumped losing trades on CMA's unwitting clients. The SEC's claims against CMA alleged that the firm violated the antifraud provisions of the Federal securities laws by misrepresenting its trading activity to investors. The SEC's action in this matter is ongoing.

In another action, the SEC charged Chauncey Mayfield, the leader of Detroit-based investment adviser, MayfieldGentry Realty Advisors, for stealing nearly $3.1 million from the Police and Fire Retirement System of the City of Detroit so he could buy two strip malls in California.[50] The SEC further alleged that when other MayfieldGentry executives became aware of the theft, they covered up the theft by making material misrepresentations to fund trustees and devised a plan to secretly repay the pension fund by cutting costs and selling the strip malls. This plan ultimately failed when MayfieldGentry could not raise enough capital to return the stolen money to the fund. The SEC's action in this matter is ongoing.

The SEC brought charges against two investment advisers and a portfolio manager at Oppenheimer & Co. for misleading investors by releasing quarterly reports and marketing materials that misrepresented the valuation policies and performance of a private equity fund they managed.[51] The Commission's order found that the two advisers, Oppenheimer Asset Management and Oppenheimer Alternative Investment Management, disseminated materials that characterized the fund's holdings of other private equity funds as being valued "based on the underlying managers' estimated values," when, in reality, the portfolio manager of the Oppenheimer fund actually valued the fund's largest investment at a significant markup, making the fund's performance appear significantly better. Oppenheimer agreed to pay more than $2.8 million to settle the SEC's charges. The SEC's action against former Oppenheimer portfolio manager Brian Williamson, who was responsible for improperly valuing the fund, is ongoing.

---

[48] *In the Matter of Umesh Tandon, Press Rel. 2013-64 (April 18, 2013)*
www.sec.gov/News/PressRelease/Detail/PressRelease/1365171514754

[49] *SEC v. Charles J. Dushek, et al., Lit. Rel. No. 22703 (May 17, 2013) www.sec.gov/litigation/litreleases/2013/lr22703.htm*

[50] *SEC v. MayfieldGentry Realty Advisors, LLC, et al., Lit. Rel. No. 22720 (June 10, 2013)*
www.sec.gov/litigation/litreleases/2013/lr22720.htm

[51] *SEC v. Oppenheimer Asset Management Inc., et al., Press Rel. 2013-38 (March 11, 2013)*
www.sec.gov/News/PressRelease/Detail/PressRelease/1365171513228#.Uj_TroYjLmg

In the Matter of Brian Williamson, Press Rel. 2013-160 (August 20, 2013)
www.sec.gov/News/PressRelease/Detail/PressRelease/1370539783859#.Uj_TnIYjLmg

In August, the SEC filed charges against North Carolina-based investment adviser Chariot Advisors LLC and its former owner, Elliot Shifman, alleging that he misled an investment fund board of directors about the firm's ability to conduct algorithmic trading so they would approve the firm's contract to manage the fund.[52] The Commission's order alleged that despite telling the directors of the Chariot Absolute Return Portfolio that his firm would use 20 percent of the fund assets to engage in algorithmic currency trading, Chariot Advisors did not have an algorithm capable of conducting such currency trading, and Shifman instead hired an individual trader who was allowed to use discretion on trade selection and execution. The SEC's action in this matter is ongoing.

Actions Related to Offering Frauds/Ponzi Schemes

In January, the SEC charged former real estate executives of Cay Club Resorts and Marinas, Fred Davis Clark, Jr. (president and CEO), Cristal R. Coleman (manager and sales agent), Barry J. Graham (sales director) Ricky Lynn Stokes (sales director), and David W. Schwarz (chief accounting officer), for defrauding $300 million from nearly 1,400 investors in a nationwide Ponzi scheme.[53] According to the SEC's complaint, the fraud began in 2004 where the executives used an insider flipping scheme to prop up false investor's profitability reports in order to lure investors. The executives allegedly continued to defraud investors after Cay Clubs abandoned its operations and investors' properties went into foreclosure. Meanwhile, the executives paid themselves more than $30 million in salary and commissions, misappropriated investor money to purchase airplanes and boats, and funneled millions of dollars into offshore accounts. The SEC action remains ongoing.

The following month, the Commission charged Richard K. Olive and Susan L. Olive of We The People Inc. with defrauding over 400 investors from over 30 states of $75 million.[54] The SEC alleged that the husband and wife team sold the investments as Charitable Gift Annuities (CGAs) and particularly targeted senior citizens, but only a small percentage of the money was directed to charitable services, while the Olives siphoned away investor funds for their personal use, and received more than $1.1 million in salary and commissions. The SEC's complaint also charges We The People and the company's in-house counsel, William G. Reeves. Among the settlement conditions, We The People consented to a final judgment that will enable the appointment of a receiver to protect more than $60 million of investor assets still held by the company. The SEC preceding remains ongoing.

Later in February, the SEC obtained an emergency court order to freeze investor assets that were at risk of being misappropriated in a scheme that purported to offer foreign investors a path to citizenship.[55] The SEC charged Anshoo R. Sethi and two companies that he created in Chicago to sell more than $147 million in securities to purportedly finance the construction of a hotel and conference center near O'Hare Airport. The SEC alleged that Sethi misled Chinese investors about both the purported investment opportunity and the prospect of gaining legal U.S. residency through the EB-5 Immigrant Investor Pilot Program. A U.S. District Court judge modified the asset freeze order on April 19 and directed the return of more than $147 million in escrowed funds to investors. The litigation continues as the SEC seeks further monetary relief and permanent injunctions against Sethi and his companies.

In March, the SEC charged Craig Berkman, a former Oregon gubernatorial candidate living in Florida, for masquerading as a sophisticated fund manager and defrauding investors seeking to acquire highly coveted pre-IPO shares of Facebook and other social media companies.[56] According to the SEC's order instituting administrative proceedings, Berkman raised at least $13.2 million from 120 investors by selling membership interests in limited liability companies that he controlled. Instead of

---

[52] *In the Matter of Chariot Advisors, LLC and Elliot L. Shifman, Press Rel. 2013-162 (August 21, 2013)*
www.sec.gov/News/PressRelease/Detail/PressRelease/1370539785773#.Uj_ZQYYjLmg

[53] *SEC v. Barry J. Graham, et al., Press Rel. 2013-15 (January 30, 2013)*
www.sec.gov/News/PressRelease/Detail/PressRelease/1365171513950

[54] *SEC v. Richard Olive and Susan Olive; SEC v. We The People, Inc. of the United States; SEC v. William G. Reeves, Esq., Press Rel. 2013-19*
(February 4, 2013) www.sec.gov/News/PressRelease/Detail/PressRelease/1365171512714

[55] *SEC v. A Chicago Convention Center, LLC, et al., Press Rel. 2013-20 (February 8, 2013)*
www.sec.gov/News/PressRelease/Detail/PressRelease/1365171512748

[56] *In the Matter of Craig Berkman, d/b/a Ventures Trust LLC, et al., Press Rel. 2013-44 (March 19,2013)*
www.sec.gov/News/PressRelease/Detail/PressRelease/1365171513392

purchasing shares on investors' behalf as promised, Berkman misused their investments to make Ponzi-like payments to earlier investors, fund personal expenses, and pay off claims against him stemming from an earlier bankruptcy case. The SEC's Enforcement Division also charged John B. Kern of Charleston, South Carolina, for his participation in the fraud as legal counsel to some of Berkman's companies.

In June, the SEC charged Duncan MacDonald and Gloria Solomon, both executives at a Dallas-based medical insurance company, with operating a $10 million Ponzi scheme that victimized at least 80 investors.[57] The SEC alleged that MacDonald and Solomon solicited investments for Global Corporate Alliance (GCA) by creating fake monthly statements to falsely portray GCA as a thriving health insurance company successfully enrolling 100,000 premium-paying policyholders each month, where, in reality, the company never had more than 40 policyholders. The SEC alleged that by the time the scheme collapsed, GCA had raised nearly $10 million from investors and returned about $2 million to investors in the form of Ponzi payments. MacDonald and Solomon each took around $1 million of investor funds, and spent the remaining investor funds on various business-related expenses until GCA's accounts were left with a negative balance. The SEC's complaint sought various relief for investors including disgorgement of ill-gotten gains with prejudgment interest, financial penalties, and permanent injunctions.

In July, the SEC charged Trendon T. Shavers and his company, Bitcoin Savings and Trust (BTCST), with defrauding investors in a Ponzi scheme involving Bitcoin, a virtual currency traded on online exchanges for conventional currencies like the U.S. dollar or used to purchase goods or services online.[58] The SEC alleged that between 2011 and 2012, Shavers used BTCST to fraudulently raise at least 700,000 Bitcoin in BTCST investments, which at that time was worth over $4.5 million and would be worth over $60 million today. According to the SEC's complaint filed in U.S. District Court for the Eastern District of Texas, Shavers sold BTCST investments over the Internet to investors in such states as Connecticut, Hawaii, Illinois,

Louisiana, Massachusetts, North Carolina, and Pennsylvania. The SEC sought a court order to freeze the assets of Shavers and BTCST in addition to other relief, including permanent injunctions, disgorgement of ill-gotten gains with prejudgment interest, and financial penalties. Additionally, the SEC issued an investor alert, prepared by the Office of Investor Education and Advocacy, warning investors about the dangers of potential investment scams involving virtual currencies promoted through the Internet. This was the first enforcement action involving virtual currencies.

In September, the SEC charged TD Bank and its former regional vice president Frank A. Spinosa with violating securities laws in connection with a massive Florida-based Ponzi scheme conducted by Scott Rothstein.[59] Rothstein, who is now serving a 50-year prison sentence, fraudulently sold fabricated legal settlements that were purported to be payable over time to actual investors in exchange for a substantial lump sum. The SEC alleged that TD Bank and Spinosa defrauded investors by producing a series of misleading documents and making false statements. According to the SEC's complaint, Spinosa falsely represented to several investors that TD Bank restricted the movement of the funds in the investment accounts via so called "lock letters" that in reality did nothing to restrict Rothstein's ability to transfer the investors' money, and also Spinosa orally assured investors that the accounts held the tens of millions of dollars that Rothstein had fraudulently claimed there to be. TD Bank agreed to settle the SEC's charges in an administrative proceeding and pay $15 million, and the SEC has filed a complaint against Spinosa in U.S. District Court for the Southern District of Florida.

Also in September, the SEC charged 10 former brokers at McGinn Smith & Co. for making material misrepresentations and omissions to their customers in connection with a $125 million investment scheme involving unregistered investment products. In order to halt the scheme, in 2010, the SEC filed an emergency action to freeze the assets of the firm and its owners, Timothy M. McGinn and David L. Smith, who have since been criminally charged by the U.S. Attorney's Office for the Northern District

---

[57] *SEC v. Duncan J. Macdonald, III and Gloria Solomon, Press Rel. 2013-113 (June 17, 2013)*
  www.sec.gov/News/PressRelease/Detail/PressRelease/1365171574926

[58] *SEC v. Trendon T. Shavers and Bitcoin Savings and Trust, Press Rel. 2013-132 (July 23, 2013)*
  www.sec.gov/News/PressRelease/Detail/PressRelease/1370539730583

[59] *SEC v. TD Bank, N.A.; SEC v. Frank A. Spinosa, Press Rel. 2013-192 (September 23, 2013)*
  www.sec.gov/News/PressRelease/Detail/PressRelease/1370539827946

of New York. This latest SEC action alleges that the 10 brokers also ignored significant red flags that should have led them to conduct more due diligence. According to the SEC's order, the scheme victimized approximately 750 investors and led to $80 million in investor losses. The SEC's civil case continues against the firm as well as McGinn and Smith, who were sentenced to 15 and 10 years imprisonment, respectively, in the criminal case.

Other Significant Matters

In FY 2013, the Division of Enforcement enjoyed several successes at trial. In September 2011, the SEC filed a civil action against Jeffrey Liskov and his advisory firm, EagleEye Asset Management, LLC (EagleEye), for defrauding advisory clients in connection with foreign currency exchange (forex) investments. The SEC's complaint alleged that, between at least November 2008 and August 2010, Liskov made material misrepresentations to several advisory clients to induce them to liquidate investments in securities and instead invest in forex. The forex investments resulted in client losses totaling nearly $4 million, while EagleEye and Liskov came away with over $300,000 in performance fees, in addition to other management fees they collected from clients. In November 2012, after an eight-day trial, a jury found that EagleEye and Liskov violated Section 10(b) of the Exchange Act and Rule 10b-5 thereunder and Section 206(1) of the Advisers Act. After a further hearing, a U.S. District Court judge found violations by EagleEye and Liskov concerning their recordkeeping obligations relating to EagleEye's advisory business. In December of 2012, the court entered a final judgment against EagleEye and Liskov and ordered that they be permanently enjoined from future violations of the foregoing provisions of the securities laws, that they pay disgorgement of $301,502.26, pre-judgment interest of $29,603.59, and that both EagleEye and Liskov pay a civil penalty of $725,000.

In April 2010, the SEC charged Goldman, Sachs & Co. and one of its vice presidents, Fabrice Tourre, for defrauding investors by misstating and omitting key facts about a financial product tied to subprime mortgages as the U.S. housing market was beginning to falter. Later, in July of that same year, Goldman, Sachs & Co. settled the charges against it by paying $550 million and undertaking to reform its business practices. At the time, the penalty was the second largest penalty ever paid to the SEC by a Wall Street firm. Tourre, however, did not settle with the SEC and, in August of this year, a jury found Tourre liable for fraud based on his role in putting together a complicated financial product that was secretly designed to maximize the likelihood of its failure and then marketing and selling it to investors without appropriate disclosure.

FY 2013 also marked a change in the Divison's policy concerning settling certain matters without admissions of the facts giving rise to the alleged violations. In the SEC's first settlement reflecting this shift in policy, in August, New York-based hedge fund adviser Phillip A. Falcone and his advisory firm Harbinger Capital Partners agreed to settle an SEC enforcement action from June 2012 that alleged Falcone had misappropriated $113 million in fund assets to pay his personal taxes, to pay redemption requests to favored customers at the expense of other investors, and to conduct an improper "short squeeze" in bonds issued by a Canadian manufacturing company.[60] In the settlement, Falcone and Harbinger must pay more than $18 million in disgorgement, interest and fines; and Falcone agreed to be barred from the securities industry for five years. The settlement also required Falcone and Harbinger to admit to multiple acts of misconduct that harmed investors and interfered with the normal functioning of the securities markets.

---

[60] *SEC v. Phillip A. Falcone, et al.; SEC v. Harbinger Capital Partners LLC, et al., Press Rel. 2013-159 (August 19, 2013)*
www.sec.gov/News/PressRelease/Detail/PressRelease/1370539780222#.Uj_TnoYjLmg

Appendix C: SEC Divisions and Offices

Headquarters Offices

DIVISION OF CORPORATION FINANCE
Keith F. Higgins, Director
(202) 551-3110

DIVISION OF ENFORCEMENT
George Canellos, Co-Director
Andrew Ceresney, Co-Director
(202) 551-4500

DIVISION OF INVESTMENT MANAGEMENT
Norm Champ, Director
(202) 551-6720

DIVISION OF ECONOMIC AND RISK ANALYSIS
Craig Lewis, Director and Chief Economist
(202) 551-6600

DIVISION OF TRADING AND MARKETS
John Ramsay, Acting Director
(202) 551-5500

OFFICE OF ACQUISITIONS
Vance Cathell, Director
(202) 551-8385

OFFICE OF ADMINISTRATIVE LAW JUDGES
Brenda P. Murray,
Chief Administrative Law Judge
(202) 551-6030

OFFICE OF THE CHIEF ACCOUNTANT
Paul A. Beswick, Chief Accountant
(202) 551-5300

OFFICE OF THE CHIEF OPERATING OFFICER
Jeffery Heslop, Chief Operating Officer
(202) 551-2105

OFFICE OF COMPLIANCE INSPECTIONS AND EXAMINATIONS
Andrew Bowden, Director
(202) 551-6200

OFFICE OF CREDIT RATINGS
Thomas J. Butler, Director
(212) 336-9080

OFFICE OF EQUAL EMPLOYMENT OPPORTUNITY
Alta G. Rodriguez, Director
(202) 551-6040

OFFICE OF ETHICS COUNSEL
Shira Pavis Minton, Director
(202) 551-7938

OFFICE OF FINANCIAL MANAGEMENT
Kenneth A. Johnson,
Chief Financial Officer
(202) 551-4306

OFFICE OF THE GENERAL COUNSEL
Anne K. Small, General Counsel
(202) 551-5100

OFFICE OF HUMAN RESOURCES
Lacey Dingman, Director
(202) 551-7500

OFFICE OF INFORMATION TECHNOLOGY
Thomas A. Bayer, Chief Information Officer
(202) 551-8873

OFFICE OF INSPECTOR GENERAL
Carl W. Hoecker, Inspector General
(202) 551-6061

OFFICE OF INTERNATIONAL AFFAIRS
Robert M. Fisher, Acting Director
(202) 551-6690

OFFICE OF THE INVESTOR ADVOCATE
Vacant

OFFICE OF INVESTOR EDUCATION AND ADVOCACY
Lori Schock, Director
(202) 551-6500

OFFICE OF LEGISLATIVE AND INTERGOVERNMENTAL AFFAIRS
Tim Henseler, Director
(202) 551-2010

OFFICE OF MINORITY AND WOMEN INCLUSION
Pamela A. Gibbs, Director
(202) 551-6046

OFFICE OF MUNICIPAL SECURITIES
John Cross, Director
(202) 551-5680

OFFICE OF PUBLIC AFFAIRS
John Nester, Director
(202) 551-4120

OFFICE OF THE SECRETARY
Elizabeth M. Murphy, Secretary
(202) 551-5400

OFFICE OF SUPPORT OPERATIONS
Barry Walters, Director
(202) 551-8400

Regional Offices

ATLANTA REGIONAL OFFICE

Rhea Kemble Dignam, Regional Director
950 East Paces Ferry Road NE, Suite 900
Atlanta, GA 30326
(404) 842-7600
e-mail: atlanta@sec.gov

BOSTON REGIONAL OFFICE

John T. Dugan, Acting Regional Director
33 Arch Street, Floor 23
Boston, MA 02110
(617) 573-8900
e-mail: boston@sec.gov

CHICAGO REGIONAL OFFICE

Timothy L. Warren, Acting Regional Director
175 W. Jackson Boulevard, Suite 900
Chicago, IL 60604
(312) 353-7390
e-mail: chicago@sec.gov

DENVER REGIONAL OFFICE

Julie K. Lutz, Acting Regional Co-Director
Kevin W. Goodman, Acting Regional Co-Director
1801 California Street, Suite 1500
Denver, CO 80202
(303) 844-1000
e-mail: denver@sec.gov

FORT WORTH REGIONAL OFFICE

David R. Woodcock, Jr., Regional Director
Burnett Plaza, Suite 1900
801 Cherry Street, Unit 18
Fort Worth, TX 76102
(817) 978-3821
e-mail: dfw@sec.gov

LOS ANGELES REGIONAL OFFICE

Michele Wein Layne, Regional Director
5670 Wilshire Boulevard, Floor 11
Los Angeles, CA 90036
(323) 965-3850
e-mail: losangeles@sec.gov

MIAMI REGIONAL OFFICE

Eric Bustillo, Regional Director
801 Brickell Avenue, Suite 1800
Miami, FL 33131
(305) 982-6300
e-mail: miami@sec.gov

NEW YORK REGIONAL OFFICE

Andrew M. Calamari, Regional Director
200 Vesey Street, Suite 400
New York, NY 10281
(212) 336-1100
e-mail: newyork@sec.gov

PHILADELPHIA REGIONAL OFFICE

Daniel M. Hawke, Regional Director
The Mellon Independence Center
701 Market Street, Suite 2000
Philadelphia, PA 19106
(215) 597-3100
e-mail: philadelphia@sec.gov

SALT LAKE REGIONAL OFFICE

Kenneth Israel, Regional Director
15 W. South Temple Street, Suite 1800
Salt Lake City, UT 84101
(801) 524-5796
e-mail: saltlake@sec.gov

SAN FRANCISCO REGIONAL OFFICE

Jina L. Choi, Regional Director
44 Montgomery Street, Suite 2800
San Francisco, CA 94104
(415) 705-2500
e-mail: sanfrancisco@sec.gov

Appendix D: Glossary of Selected Terms

Advisers Act

The Investment Advisers Act of 1940 is a U.S. Federal law that was created to regulate the actions of investment advisers.

Agency Financial Report (AFR)

An annual requirement that provides financial and high-level performance results that enable the President, Congress, and the public to assess an agency's accomplishments each fiscal year (October 1 through September 30). This report includes audited financial statements and provides an overview of an agency's programs, accomplishments, challenges, and management's accountability for entrusted resources. The report is prepared in accordance with the requirements of Office of Management and Budget (OMB) Circular A-136, Financial Reporting Requirements. Under Circular A-136, agencies may prepare an Agency Financial Report and Annual Performance Report, or may combine these two reports into the Performance and Accountability Report.

Annual Performance Report (APR)

A report that outlines goals and intended outcomes of an agency's programs and initiatives. This report provides program performance and financial information that enables the President, Congress, and the public to assess an agency's performance and accountability over entrusted resources.

Asset

An asset is a resource that embodies economic benefits or services that the reporting entity controls.

Statement of Cash Flows

Reports a company's inflows and outflows of cash over time by classification.

Clawback Policies

Under the Dodd-Frank Act, all listed companies will eventually be required to institute a mechanism for reclaiming executive pay that had been granted under misstated earnings.

Collateralized Debt Obligation (CDO)

A type of structured asset-backed security (ABS) with multiple "tranches" that are issued by special purpose entities and collateralized by debt obligations including bonds and loans. Each tranche offers a varying degree of risk and return so as to meet investor demand.

Crowd Funding/Sourcing

In the JOBS Act, a new means of raising capital enabling the raising of small amounts of equity capital without having to register with the SEC.

Deposit Fund

Consists of funds that do not belong to the Federal Government, such as disgorgement, penalties, and interest collected and held on behalf of harmed investors, registrant monies held temporarily until earned by the SEC, and collections awaiting disposition or reclassification.

Derivative

A contract between two parties that specifies conditions (dates, resulting values of the underlying variables, and notional amounts) under which payments are to be made between the parties.

Disgorgement

A repayment of funds received or losses forgone, with interest, as a result of illegal or unethical business transactions. Disgorged funds are normally distributed to those affected by the action, but in certain cases may be deposited in the General Fund of the Treasury.

Dodd-Frank Wall Street Reform and Consumer Protection Act (Dodd-Frank Act)

A Federal law that regulates the U.S. financial industry. The legislation, enacted in July 2010, created new financial regulatory processes that enforce transparency and accountability while implementing rules for consumer protection.

Entity Assets

Assets that an agency is authorized to use in its operations. For example, the SEC is authorized to use all funds in the Investor Protection Fund for its operations.

Entity Accounts Receivable

Monies owed to the SEC generated from securities transaction fees and filing fees paid by registrants.

Exchange Revenue

Exchange revenues are inflows of earned resources to an entity. Exchange revenues arise from exchange transactions, which occur when each party to the transaction sacrifices value and receives value in return. Examples include the sale of goods and services, entrance fees and most interest revenue.

Family Offices

A family office, or single family office (SFO), is a private company that manages investments and trusts for a single wealthy family. The company's financial capital is the family's own wealth, often accumulated over many family generations.

Federal Accounting Standards Advisory Board (FASAB)

A U.S. Federal advisory committee sponsored by the Secretary of the Treasury, the Director of the Office of Management and Budget, and the Comptroller General of the United States, whose mission is to develop generally accepted accounting principles (GAAP) for the United States Government.

Federal Information Security Management Act (FISMA)

A law that requires Federal agencies to conduct annual assessments of their information security and privacy programs, develop and implement remediation efforts for identified weaknesses and vulnerabilities, and report on compliance to OMB.

Financial Industry Regulatory Authority, Inc. (FINRA)

A private corporation that acts as a self-regulatory organization (SRO). FINRA is the successor to the National Association of Securities Dealers, Inc. (NASD) and is a non-governmental organization that performs financial regulation of member brokerage firms and exchange markets. The Government organization which acts as the ultimate regulator of the securities industry, including FINRA, is the SEC.

Fund Balance with Treasury (FBWT)

A Federal entity's fund balance with Treasury (FBWT) is the amount of funds in the entity's accounts with Treasury for which the entity is authorized to make expenditures and pay liabilities and that have not been invested in Federal securities.

Funds from Dedicated Collections

Accounts containing specifically identified revenues, often supplemented by other financing sources, that are required by statute to be used for designated activities, benefits or purposes, and must be accounted for separately from the Government's general revenues. For example, Investor Protection Fund resources are funds from dedicated collections and may only be used for the purposes specified by the Dodd-Frank Act.

General Funds – Salaries and Expenses

Appropriations by Congress that are used to carry out the agency's mission and day to day operations that may be used in accordance with spending limits established by Congress.

Generally Accepted Accounting Principles (GAAP)

Framework of accounting standards, rules, and procedures defined by the professional accounting industry. The Federal Accounting Standards Advisory Board (FASAB) is the body designated by the American Institute of Certified Public Accounting (AICPA) as the source of GAAP for Federal reporting entities.

Imputed Financing

Financing provided to the reporting entity by another Federal entity covering certain costs incurred by the reporting entity. For example, some Federal employee retirement benefits are paid by the Federal Government's central personnel office, the Office of Personnel Management. The SEC recognizes a financing source and corresponding expense to represent its share of the cost of providing pension and post-retirement health and life insurance benefits to all eligible SEC employees.

Insider Trading

The buying or selling of a security by someone who has access to material, nonpublic information about the security.

Intragovernmental Costs

Costs that arise from the purchase of goods and services from other components of the Federal Government.

Investor Protection Fund

A fund established by the Dodd-Frank Act to pay awards to whistle-blowers. The program requires the Commission to pay an award, under regulations prescribed by the Commission and subject to certain limitations, to eligible whistleblowers who voluntarily provide the Commission with original information about a violation of Federal securities laws that leads to the successful enforcement of a covered judicial or administrative action, or a related action.

Liability

A liability is a present obligation of the reporting entity to provide assets or services to another entity at a determinable date, when a specified event occurs, or on demand.

Limit Up-Limit Down Plan

A one-year pilot program to protect equity markets from volatile price swings which would pause trading.

Market Based Treasury Securities

Debt securities that the U.S Treasury issues to Federal entities without statutorily determined interest rates.

Microcap Securities

Low priced stocks issued by the smallest of companies.

Miscellaneous Receipt Account

A fund used to collect non-entity receipts from custodial activities that the SEC cannot deposit into funds under its control or use in its operations. These amounts are forwarded to the General Fund of the Treasury and are considered to be non-entity assets of the SEC.

NASDAQ

The NASDAQ Stock Market, also known as simply NASDAQ, is an American stock exchange. NASDAQ originally stood for National Association of Securities Dealers Automated Quotations. It is the second-largest stock exchange by market capitalization in the world, after the New York Stock Exchange.

Non-Entity Assets

Those assets that are held by an entity but are not available to the entity. Examples of non-entity assets are disgorgement, penalties, and interest collected and held on behalf of harmed investors.

Office of Management and Budget (OMB) Circular A-123

Defines management's responsibilities for internal financial controls in Federal agencies.

Office of Management and Budget (OMB) Circular A-136

Establishes a central point of reference for all Federal financial reporting guidance for Executive Branch departments, agencies, and entities required to submit audited financial statements, interim financial statements, and Performance and Accountability Reports (PAR), and Agency Financial Reports (AFR) under the Chief Financial Officers Act of 1990, the Accountability of Tax Dollars Act of 2002, and Annual Management Reports under the Government Corporations Control Act.

Performance and Accountability Reports (PAR)

An annual report that provides program performance and financial information that enables Congress, the President, and the public to assess an agency's performance and accountability over entrusted resources.

Performance Indicators Results Summary

A summary of performance by outcome within each strategic goal.

Pay to Play Schemes

Payments or gifts made to influence awarding of lucrative contracts for securities underwriting business.

Public Company Accounting Oversight Board (PCAOB)

A nonprofit corporation established by Congress to oversee the audits of public companies in order to protect the interests of investors and further the public interest in the preparation of informative, accurate, and independent audit reports. The PCAOB also oversees the audits of broker-dealers, including compliance reports filed pursuant to Federal securities laws, to promote investor protection.

Pump and Dump Schemes

A form of micro stock fraud involving artificially inflating the price of an owned stock through false and misleading positive statements.

Reserve Fund

A fund established by the Dodd-Frank Act that may be used by the SEC to obligate amounts up to a total of $100 million in one fiscal year as the SEC determines it necessary to carry out its functions.

Resource Extraction Rule

As implemented by Dodd-Frank, the resource extraction rule requires disclosure of payments of $100,000 or more made to governments for the commercial development of oil, natural gas, or minerals. This rule applies to U.S. and foreign companies that are 1) engaged in the commercial development of oil, natural gas, or minerals, and 2) required to file annual reports with the SEC.

Section 31 Fees

Transaction fees paid to the SEC based on the volume of securities that are sold on various markets. Under Section 31 of the Securities Exchange Act of 1934, self-regulatory organizations (SROs) – such as the Financial Industry Regulatory Authority (FINRA) and all of the national securities exchanges (including the New York Stock Exchange) – must pay transaction fees to the SEC based on the volume of securities that are sold on their markets. These fees recover the costs incurred by the Government, including the SEC, for supervising and regulating the securities markets and securities professionals.

Securities Exchange Act of 1934 (Exchange Act)

A law governing the secondary trading of securities (stocks, bonds, and debentures) in the United States. It was this piece of legislation that established the Securities and Exchange Commission. The Exchange Act and related statutes form the basis of regulation of the financial markets and their participants in the United States.

Self-Regulatory Organization (SRO)

An organization that exercises some degree of regulatory authority over an industry or profession. The regulatory authority could be applied in addition to some form of Government regulation, or it could fill the vacuum of an absence of Government oversight and regulation. The ability of an SRO to exercise regulatory authority does not necessarily derive from a grant of authority from the Government.

Strategic Plan

A report initially required by the Government Performance and Results Act (GPRA) that defines the agency mission, long-term goals, strategies planned, and the approaches it will use to monitor its progress in addressing specific national problems, needs, challenges, and opportunities related to its mission. The Plan also presents general and long term goals the agency aims to achieve, what actions the agency will take to realize those goals, and how the agency will deal with challenges and risks that may hinder achieving result. Requirements for the Strategic Plan are presented in OMB Circular A-11, Preparation, Submission and Execution of the Budget.

U.S. Commodity Futures Trading Commission (CFTC)

An independent agency of the U.S. Government that regulates futures and option markets.

U.S. Exchanges

A place (physical or virtual) where stock traders come together to decide on the price of securities.

U.S. Securities and Exchange Commission (SEC)

The SEC is an independent agency of the U.S. Government established pursuant to the Securities Exchange Act of 1934 (Exchange Act), charged with regulating the country's capital markets. It is charged with protecting investors, maintaining fair, orderly and efficient markets; and facilitating capital formation.

Appendix E: Acronyms

ADA	Antideficiency Act	FMFIA	Federal Managers' Financial Integrity Act of 1982
AFR	Agency Financial Report		
AICPA	American Institute of Certified Public Accountants	FMOC	Financial Management Oversight Committee
		FOIA	Freedom of Information Act
APR	Annual Performance Report	FSB	Financial Stability Board
ATS	Alternative Trading Systems	FSIO	Financial Systems Integration Office
CBOE	Chicago Board Options Exchange	FSSP	Federal Shared Services Provider
CDO	Collateralized Debt Obligation	FTC	Federal Trade Commission
CEO	Chief Executive Officer	FTE	Full-Time Equivalents
CFO	Chief Financial Officer	FY	Fiscal Year
CFR	Code of Federal Regulations	GAAP	Generally Accepted Accounting Principles
CFTC	Commodities Futures Trading Commission	GAO	Government Accountability Office
CRQA	Center for Risk and Quality Analysis	GPRA	Government Performance and Results Act
CSRS	Civil Service Retirement System	GSA	U.S. General Services Administration
DERA	Division of Economic and Risk Analysis	GSS	General Support System
Dodd-Frank Act	Dodd-Frank Wall Street Reform and Consumer Protection Act	IAC	Investor Advisory Committee
		ICFR	Internal Control over Financial Reporting
DOL	U.S. Department of Labor	IOSCO	International Organization of Securities Commissions
EDGAR	Electronic Gathering, Analysis and Retrieval		
ESC	Enterprise Service Center	IPERA	Improper Payments Elimination and Recovery Act of 2010
Exchange Act	Securities Exchange Act of 1934		
FASAB	Federal Accounting Standards Advisory Board	IPIA	Improper Payments Information Act of 2002
		IPO	Initial Public Offering
FBWT	Fund Balance with Treasury	JAB	Joint Authorization Board
FCPA	Foreign Corrupt Practices Act	JOBS Act	Jumpstart Our Business Startups Act
FECA	Federal Employees' Compensation Act	MD&A	Management's Discussion and Analysis
FedRAMP	Federal Risk Authorization Management Program	MIDAS	Market Information Data and Analytics System
FERS	Federal Employees Retirement System	NEP	National Examination Program
FFMIA	Federal Financial Management Improvement Act	NIST	National Institute of Standards and Technology
FINRA	Financial Industry Regulatory Authority	NPA	Non-Prosecution Agreement
FISMA	Federal Information Security Management Act	NRSRO	Nationally Recognized Statistical Rating Organization

OA	Office of Acquisitions	REITS	Real Estate Investment Trusts
OCIE	Office of Compliance Inspections and Examinations	Reserve Fund	Securities and Exchange Commission Reserve Fund
OFM	Office of Financial Management	RMBS	Residential Mortgage-Backed Securities
OGC	Office of the General Counsel	S/L	Straight-Line
OIA	Office of International Affairs	SBR	Statement of Budgetary Resources
OIG	Office of Inspector General	SEC	U.S. Securities and Exchange Commission
OIP	Order Instituting Cease-and-Desist Proceedings	SFFAS	Statement of Federal Financial Accounting Standards
OIT	Office of Information Technology	SIPA	Securities Investor Protection Act of 1970
OMB	Office of Management and Budget	SIPC	Securities Investor Protection Corporation
OPM	Office of Personnel Management	SRO	Self-Regulatory Organization
PCAOB	Public Company Accounting Oversight Board	TCR	Tips, Complaints and Referrals
PIA	Privacy Impact Assessment	TSP	Thrift Savings Plan
RAS	Office of Risk Analysis and Surveillance	UDO	Undelivered Order

This Agency Financial Report was produced through the energies and talents of the SEC staff. To these individuals we offer our sincerest thanks and acknowledgement. We would also like to acknowledge the Government Accountability Office and the SEC 's Office of Inspector General for the professional manner in which they conducted the audit of the FY 2013 financial statements. Finally, we offer special thanks to AOC Solutions and The DesignPond for their contributions in the design and production of this report. To comment on this report, please send an e-mail to SECAFR@sec.gov.

U.S. SECURITIES AND EXCHANGE COMMISSION

100 F Street, NE, Washington, DC 20549

GAO's Mission	The Government Accountability Office, the audit, evaluation, and investigative arm of Congress, exists to support Congress in meeting its constitutional responsibilities and to help improve the performance and accountability of the federal government for the American people. GAO examines the use of public funds; evaluates federal programs and policies; and provides analyses, recommendations, and other assistance to help Congress make informed oversight, policy, and funding decisions. GAO's commitment to good government is reflected in its core values of accountability, integrity, and reliability.
Obtaining Copies of GAO Reports and Testimony	The fastest and easiest way to obtain copies of GAO documents at no cost is through GAO's website (www.gao.gov). Each weekday afternoon, GAO posts on its website newly released reports, testimony, and correspondence. To have GAO e-mail you a list of newly posted products, go to www.gao.gov and select "E-mail Updates."
Order by Phone	The price of each GAO publication reflects GAO's actual cost of production and distribution and depends on the number of pages in the publication and whether the publication is printed in color or black and white. Pricing and ordering information is posted on GAO's website, http://www.gao.gov/ordering.htm. Place orders by calling (202) 512-6000, toll free (866) 801-7077, or TDD (202) 512-2537. Orders may be paid for using American Express, Discover Card, MasterCard, Visa, check, or money order. Call for additional information.
Connect with GAO	Connect with GAO on Facebook, Flickr, Twitter, and YouTube. Subscribe to our RSS Feeds or E-mail Updates. Listen to our Podcasts. Visit GAO on the web at www.gao.gov.
To Report Fraud, Waste, and Abuse in Federal Programs	Contact: Website: www.gao.gov/fraudnet/fraudnet.htm E-mail: fraudnet@gao.gov Automated answering system: (800) 424-5454 or (202) 512-7470
Congressional Relations	Katherine Siggerud, Managing Director, siggerudk@gao.gov, (202) 512-4400, U.S. Government Accountability Office, 441 G Street NW, Room 7125, Washington, DC 20548
Public Affairs	Chuck Young, Managing Director, youngc1@gao.gov, (202) 512-4800 U.S. Government Accountability Office, 441 G Street NW, Room 7149 Washington, DC 20548

Please Print on Recycled Paper.

www.ingramcontent.com/pod-product-compliance
Lightning Source LLC
Chambersburg PA
CBHW080251290526
45790CB00005B/1770